The Pubs of Radnorshire

The Pubs of Radnorshire

by

Tony Hobbs

Logaston Press

LOGASTON PRESS
Little Logaston Woonton Almeley
Herefordshire HR3 6QH

First published by Logaston Press 2006
Copyright © Tony Hobbs 2006

ISBN 1 904396 62 3
(978 1 904396 62 8)

Set in Times New Roman by Logaston Press
and printed in Great Britain by
Oaklands Book Services

Contents

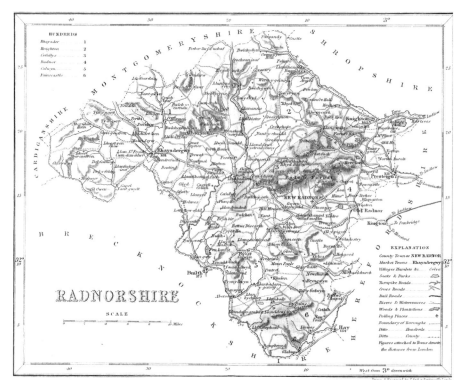

An 1870 map of Radnorshire

When mighty brown beer was the old Briton's taste,
Our wives they were merry and daughters were chaste,
Their lips were like violets whenever embraced.

'Ere coffee and tea and such slipslops were known,
Our granddames by their fires sat merrily down;
Their bread it was white and their ale it was brown.

When the Spanish Armada on our coasts did bear,
Our sailors took each one a jorum of beer,
Then sent them away with a flea in their ear.

O, the brown beer of Old Britain and old British brown beer!

(*The Song of Old British Brown Beer*)

Acknowledgments

First and foremost I must acknowledge the help and support given to me by the landlords of all the presently open pubs and hotels in Radnorshire. They spared the time to answer my questions, dig out old deeds and photographs and introduce me to ex-landlords and old customers with a tale to tell. Unfortunately, I was all too often told: 'Old George would have told you all about this pub and many more besides. Pity you didn't come three or four years ago before he died'. My thanks go, too, to all the owners and inhabitants of former licensed houses who went out of their way to provide historical information, often coming up with their own research details and showing me, a complete stranger, round their homes. Without their assistance, my task would have been a lot harder.

I have lent heavily on research carried out previously by two local historians, firstly, the Revd. D. Stedman Davies, who produced an article on Radnorshire Inns in the 1940s, followed by up-dates by W.H. Howse in the 1950s. Both men were a mine of information, particularly about pubs which have long since ceased trading. In his book on Radnorshsire and on some of the villages, Howse provided further information on the drinking habits in times long gone by.

My main sources of research were the Powys County Archives Office; the Radnorshire Museum (with special thanks to Will Adams, the joint curator); the Llandrindod Wells Library, whose staff were extremely helpful; and the Tourist Information Centre in Llandrindod Wells. For local knowledge my thanks to the Library and Offa's Dyke Centre in Knighton, the Judge's Lodging and Library in Presteigne, the Tourist Information Centre and Library in Rhayader, and the Libraries in Builth Wells and Kington.

Among the many individuals I am beholden to for their invaluable assistance, I must make special mention of Brian Lawrence and Margaret Hughes (Rhayader), Bob Henderson (an old Knightonian now living in Norfolk), Keith Parker (Presteigne), Sid Meredith (Newbridge), Joel Williams (Llandrindod Wells), and Hilary Roe (Crossgates).

Other important contributions were made by Alan Lewis, Richard Hughes, Lloyd Lewis, Mike and Stella Hodgson, Dave Francis, and David

Futcher (Rhayader), John Crowe (Presteigne), Derek Price, Roger Bright, and Ursula Bayer (Knighton), Brenda Davies (Llanfair Waterdine), Clarice Thomas and Geoff Duthie (Felindre), Jim Price and Robert Southcott (Llanellwedd), Joyce Holder (Howey), Joyce Phillips and Marion Griffiths (Glasbury), Lewis Jones (Walton) and Sian Gartery (Aberedw). Also John Eisel and, last but not least, my editor Ron Shoesmith, for all his hard work and forbearance.

Sources of Illustrations

t – top; b – bottom; m – middle; l – left; r – right

Radnorshire Museum
pp. 106, 111(2), 121 (t, l), 129, 133 (t), 134 (b, l), 310 (t), 311 (2)

Cherry Leversedge Estate
pp. 43 (b), 45 (b), 51, 53, 54, 55, 89, 93 94 (b)

Lloyd Lewis
pp. 150, 155, 157 (b), 172 (b), 178 (b), 182 (t), 184 (t)

Ron Shoesmith
pp. 67, 112(b), 118, 121(b), 122(t), 123(t), 131, 133(m & b), 134(t), 135(2), 138(l), 206(3), 327(t)

Roger Bright pp. 22, 24 (b), 25, 28 (t), 50	**Alan Lewis** pp. 163 (t), 193 (t)
Mary Cadwallader pp. 7 (t), 45, 50	**Richard Hughes** pp. 190 (2), 121 (t)
Mrs. L. Lister pp. 48, 49	**County Times & Gazette** p. 203 (t)
John Crowe pp. 22, 41 (t), 43 (t), 47, 83, 94 (b), 98 (t)	**William McKaig** pp. 203 (b), 210 (2), 212 (t), 213 (l), 216
Tony Bird p. 95	**Geoff Duthie** p. 236
Olivia Harris pp. 110(t), 122 (b), 125, 138(t, r)	**Meredith Collection** pp. 326 (2), 330, 331 (b)
Joel Williams pp. 138 (b), 139 (t)	**Joyce Holden** pp. 338 (t), 339 (2)
June Mackintosh p.144 (b)	

And the gentleman whose name I have completely forgotten
who allowed me to copy pp. 321 and 322

Introduction

When you look at a map of Wales, Radnorshire does not seem all that big. However, it does cover 301,164 acres, or 470 square miles, and when you have to travel along every single highway and byway it grows in size, particularly during the winter months and when it is pouring with rain. But the journeys are rendered more enjoyable when the quest in hand is to visit all the existing pubs and hotels in the area and to try and locate all those other hostelries that have welcomed customers over the years but have since closed.

With the population being only 23,630, as recorded in the 1991 census – a figure only some 3,000 higher than a century before – the proportion of pubs to people has been somewhat on the high side, to say the least. But over the years many drinking establishments have closed following changes in trends such as the demise of the drovers who roamed the hillsides as they drove their herds and flocks to meet England's insatiable meat markets, and the end of spa towns which used to attract customers by the trainload. Llandrindod Wells, for instance, was once a major spa resort with a proliferation of hotels which have since either come under the demolition hammer, or now serve other purposes. Today, it is still the county's major town and the seat of local government, although with a population of less than 5,000. There are very few other towns – Knighton, New Radnor, Presteigne,and Rhayader – whilst villages and hamlets are isolated amidst the mainly barren and mountainous terrain. Hill-farming and tourism, although limited, are the main activities.

After being a separate entity for some 438 years, Radnorshire is now part of Powys, following its amalgamation with Brecon and Montgomery as part of the local government re-organisation in 1974. However, it became clearly transparent during my travels that the people of Radnorshire still retain faith in their old county rather than supporting Powys. Also obvious was their friendliness and helpfulness, many going out of their way to help me track down information.

At times I almost felt like a latter-day Sherlock Holmes following up clues and engaging strangers in my attempt to trace a building's connection to the licensed trade. And then it was like trying to put together a giant jigsaw puzzle, often with pieces irretrievably lost or of doubtful origin. While the project has taken me over three years to complete, there are still some parts of the county which, I must confess, I have not researched as well as I might. However, having missed last year's deadline, I was duty bound to meet this year's and I apologise in advance where some of the information is a bit on the sketchy side. But I hope that the finished product gives some idea of the diversity and range of hostelries, backed with anecdotes where possible, that have flourished over the years, together with an insight into some of Radnorshire's fascinating history.

Basically, the book is divided into chapters which deal with the towns, with the rest of the county carved up as best I could. Street maps and photographs, both ancient and modern, should help the reader recognise the various pubs and hotels, present and past. As an appetizer, there is a chapter on the basic history of the inn, how it has changed over the ages, and the changes that have taken place in the licensing laws. A second chapter details the growth of brewing and breweries and of that essential product beer, or ale, particularly real ale.

As with the other volumes in this series, it is suspected that this book may prompt many memories, which you may care to share and which may lead eventually to an up-date of this title. Having drunk at least one pint in just about every public house and hotel in Radnorshire, I can but say 'cheers – and happy reading'.

Tony Hobbs
August 2006

CHAPTER ONE

Alehouses, Taverns and Inns

Say, for what were hop-yards meant,
Or why was Burton built on Trent?
Oh many a peer of England brews
Livelier liquor than the Muse,
and malt does more than Milton can
To justify God's way to man.
Ale, man, ale's the stuff to drink
For fellows whom it hurts to think:
Look into the pewter pot
To see the world as the world's not.
And faith, 'tis pleasant till 'tis past:
The mischief is that 'twill not last.

(*A Shropshire Lad*, A.E. Housman, 1896)

After Julius Agricola had brought the whole of Wales under Roman control in A.D. 78, the Welsh region remained as a Roman military zone for the next 300 years with the local Celtic people enjoying relative peace and tranquillity. Early on the Romans constructed two major roads through the area which came to be known as Radnorshire. One ran from Llandovery to what is now Llandrindod Wells and the other from Brecon via Clyro to Kenchester, near Hereford. Near Llandrindod they built Castell Collen as a major fort, while another lesser fort was constructed at Clyro. Initially meant solely for military purposes, the roads later attracted other travellers and to meet their needs alcoholic drinking places, or inns, were introduced. The Romans imported wine from other parts of the Empire, and would have made mead from honey, cider from locally grown apples, and ale from barley.

The break-up of the Roman Empire in England and Wales took place following the withdrawal of Roman troops shortly after A.D. 410, after which the country was plunged into what has become known as the Dark Ages. In Wales a patchwork of kingdoms gradually emerged to fill the vacuum left by

1

the Romans. Hostilities broke out again against the English which to a certain extent was curbed when Offa, King of Mercia, built his famous Dyke which today still closely follows the border with England, running along the eastern edge of Radnorshire. As well as being a defensive work, the Dyke also helped regulate trade between the two countries.

At the time of the Norman Conquest the Radnorshire area was split into three units – the commote of Gwrthrynion in the west and the cantrefs of Elfael and Maelienydd in the south and east respectively. Into these lands now came Norman conquerors bent on conquest and soon Elfael fell to the de Braose family and Maelienydd and Gwrthrynion came under the rule of the Mortimers. Castles were built at Radnor, Cefnllys, Knucklas and Painscastle, but the very nature of the land, barren and mountainous, precluded the establishment of firm Norman control. This led to more upheaval with the Anglo-Noman marcher lords, the princes of Gwynedd and the lords of southern Wales all vying for power with their armies marching through the region. But with the defeat and death of Llywelyn ap Gruffudd in 1282, Welsh resistance came to an end.

It was during the 13th century that, with the increase in the sale of wine, a separation came into being between 'taverns', which sold both ale and wine, and 'alehouses' which sold only ale. In addition to these there were the inns or 'hostels' that provided accommodation for travellers as well as food and drink. Outside the towns and villages the principal hospitality for travellers during the medieval period was provided by monasteries. There would have been a steady trickle of monks and other travellers going between the abbey at Strata Florida, in Dyfed, to Rhayader and then on to Abbeycwmhir and from there, via Rhydspence to either Llanthony Abbey or to Hereford Cathedral. During the 14th and 15th centuries, a gradual change occurred as merchants began to travel and the influence of the church started to wane. Wayside inns became features of the countryside and hotels providing accommodation and food began to appear in the market towns. Another aspect of Radnorshire was the centuries old hill routes largely used by drovers and along which appeared alehouses or cider houses, often in a farmer's house or cottage.

A 14th-century inn.

The Rev. D. Stedman Davies in his book *Radnorshire Inns* states:

2

Though the Church may trace its origin to the 6th century and the Manor to the Norman period, the Inn is not probably earlier than the 16th century. When the Inn stands near the Churchgate, as at Aberedw, it strongly suggests it was the successor of the Church house, where the Churchwardens brewed beer and baked bread for the village feast and other local events.

With Henry VIII's Act of Union in 1536, Radnorshire came into being as a county and for the first time was subject to the same laws as England. Two MPs were elected with New Radnor chosen as the shire town. One of these laws demanded that a sign should identify all drinking establishments. The signs were originally suspended from poles which became longer and heavier. In the case of a tavern, there would also be an evergreen bush, which represented the vine and indicated that wine was for sale. This new law for Radnorshire probably explains the Rev. Stedman Davies's

An evergreen bush, representing an inn, from a 14th-century manuscript

observation that most of the inns in the county bear English names, except those which take the name of the village or hamlet, and those named after local landowners. After the Restoration the old ale-stake (the pole projecting from the front of an inn) outside licensed premises was replaced by the painted inn sign.

Although there had been previous attempts at curtailing the number of drinking houses, the first formal licensing law came at the end of the 15th century. It empowered Justices of the Peace to obtain sureties for good behaviour from the landlords and, if necessary, to close alehouses. Some 50 years later the Justices obtained the power to both license and suppress alehouses – hence 'licensed premises'. Legislation continued and 1553 saw an Act of Parliament that curtailed the number of 'taverns', and thus the sale of wine. The Act also prohibited the sale of French wines. The early alehouses were probably little different from the timber-framed and thatched houses that surrounded them. The larger ones would have had sheds at the rear where brewing was carried out, and possibly cellars in which to store their brew at a constant temperature.

By the 1570s there were nine inns and alehouses in the liberties and boroughs of New Radnor and Radnor Foreign, and 105 (with taverns) in the rest of the county. This led in 1575 to the Council in Wales and the Marches charging the Justices of Radnor with responsibility

> inasmuch as divers vagabonds, sturdy beggars, and others having no master or entertainment to live are daily allowed to wander about within the county of Radnor without apprehension, whereby robberies, felonies, and other offences are daily committed to the great disquiet of the inhabitants of that county. ... The Justices suffer too many alehouse keepers in places inconvenient, and so by the resort of idle persons no kind of disorder is left unattempted, and Dice, Cards, Bowls, and other unlawful games are practised. The Justices to meet speedily together, and execute the laws against the offenders mentioned.

A 15th-century tavern and cellar

Radnorshire was on the side of the king in the Civil War of 1642-49. Little fighting took place, but a Royalist garrison was beseiged at Abbeycwmhir, completing the destruction of the abbey, whilst New Radnor castle was totally destroyed by Parliamentary cannon. During the war various attempts were made to levy duty on both the manufacture and sale of beer – attempts which were consolidated after the war and are still in force. At this time beer was brewed in three different qualities – strong, table, and small – and each variety attracted a different rate of duty. It was not until the late 19th century that the duty levied became based on the original gravity of the beer.

Although there was a duty on beer, spirits were exempt and towards the end of the 17th century and well into the 18th there was what Monckton in his *History of the English Public House* described as 'one of the biggest orgies of over-indulgence our island history has ever seen'. Every small

16   **99**

Whereas by the Laws and Statutes of This Realm

NOTICE

IS HEREBY GIVEN TO ALL

INN KEEPERS, ALEHOUSE KEEPERS, SUTLERS, VICTUALLERS

and other Retailers of

ALE and BEER,

AND EVERY OTHER PERSON or PERSONS KEEPING A PUBLIC HOUSE
IN ANY
CITY, TOWN CORPORATE, BOROUGH, MARKET TOWN, VILLAGE, HAMLET, PARISH,
PART or PLACE IN THE *Kingdom of England*

That, as from the **24**th *day of* **JUNE, 1700**

THEY SHALL BE REQUIRED TO RETAIL and SELL THEIR ALE & BEER

by the **FULL ALE QUART** or **PINT**

According to the Laid Standard

IN VESSELS DULY MARKED *with* **W. R** *and* **CROWN**

be they made of

WOOD, GLASS, HORN, LEATHER or PEWTER *etc.*

Any Person Retailing Ale or Beer to a **TRAVELLER** *or* **WAYFARER** *in Vessels not
signed and marked as aforesaid will be liable to a* **PENALTY** *not exceeding*

FORTY SHILLINGS

FOR EVERY SUCH OFFENCE

By Act of Parliament ~ at WESTMINSTER
In the Reign of Our Sovereign ~ **WILLIAM III** by the Grace of God, King,
Defender of the Faith &c

*In 1700 it became a legal requirement that vessels in which ale and beer
were served should be accurate and marked*

alehouse in the country was in a position to sell cheap brandy and in particular gin. The result was that consumption of spirits increased from half a million gallons in 1684 to over eight million gallons in 1743. The various 'Gin Acts' that followed, together with increased duties and a strengthening of the powers of the Justices, rapidly changed this trend and by 1758 excise duty was paid on less than two million gallons per year. The 'gin era' was over. However, according to the Rev. Stedman Davies, the drinking of gin in Radnorshire went its harmful way until the 1860s (among the poor as well as the rich). The depth of the liquor potations of the gentry can be seen from the following example:

> Thomas Jones, of Pencerrig, near Llanelwedd, received a consignment of drink for his house from Kington by wagon in 1795. It consisted of a hogshead of port wine, 20 gallons of rum, 22 gallons of gin, and 11 gallons and three pints of malt spirit.

However, means of regulating the public house continued to attract government interest and from 1729 licence renewal had to be made at annual Brewster Sessions, originally in September then, at a later date, in February.

With an ever-increasing demand for beef in England, the drovers' journeys across Radnorshire became a common feature. The main routes went through Rhayader, Newbridge and near Builth Wells to Kington, and from Erwood and Llyswen via Rhydspence to Hereford. Drovers' inns were available in the towns and villages they passed through providing hospitality for the men and grazing for the animals. Blacksmiths' forges were often an integral part of the inn or close by. And cider houses were strategically situated along many of the routes over the highlands where drovers could graze their herds and flocks on common lands. The arrival of drovers was often celebrated by impromptu entertainment with travelling fiddlers joining in the fun, and sometimes boxing and wrestling matches arranged with local farmers.

As Shirley Toulson mentioned in her book *Drovers' Roads of Wales*,

> only the top drovers and older men slept in the dormitories of the inn. The younger men protected the cattle. The cost of indoor accommodation varied little throughout the centuries, and for years it stood at 4d. in the summer and 6d. in the winter. A halfpenny a night per beast was the standard charge for grazing and any halfpenny fields throughout Wales bear witness to the fact that the drovers once passed that way.

Blacksmiths were often kept very busy providing the cattle with shoes, or cues, to protect their hoofs, while pigs were given boots, little woollen socks with leather soles, and geese's feet were protected by a covering of tar and sand.

Old **C Y D E R** for Ever!

A woodcut celebrating
the repeal of the cider tax

While the introduction of turnpike roads meant better and speedier travel for coaches, it also saw toll gates and charges, with cattle being charged 10d. per score. However, drovers avoided payment by taking alternative routes and many of the toll gates were torn down during the Rebecca Riots in the 1840s. Next came the railways in the 1850s and '60s which, while opening up Radnorshire to the rest of Britain as never before, began to see the demise of the old cattle drives.

It was during the 19th century that most of the legislation that affects the present-day consumption and sale of alcoholic drink was enacted. The Alehouse Act of 1828 meant that the licensee no longer had to find sureties for his behaviour. He also was bound to use the legal, stamped measures, not to adulterate his drinks, and not to permit drunkenness on his premises.

The Beerhouse Acts of 1830, 1834 and 1840 followed – the first allowed premises to open for the sale of beer, but not spirits, on payment of a simple excise licence; the second differentiated between 'on' and 'off' licences and made 'on' more difficult to obtain; whilst the third ensured that licences were issued only to the occupier of the premises. The first Act abolished all duty on beer and enabled any householder to sell beer on the purchase of a two-guinea licence from the Excise. As a consequence, a number of illegal drinking places became legal, and many craftsmen also sold beer as part of their business, naming the beer-house after their craft such as the Three Horseshoes, the Mason's Arms and the Butcher's Arms. 1828 was the last year that alehouse keepers had to provide recognizances.

At about the time of the Beerhouse Acts the temperance movement was also getting under way. Originating in America in 1808, temperance societies started founding temperance hotels and by 1865 there were some 200. The first one to open in Radnorshire was the Chandos in Knighton in 1880.

Until the Wine and Beer House Act of 1869 was passed, the licensing of inns had been, since 1830, in the hands of the Excise, and there was little check on their number. In Radnorshire, the Chief Constable's quarterly reports up to 1870 constantly urged the need for the reduction of licences.

DRUNKARD'S CATECHISM

1. Q. What is your name?
   A. Drunken sot.
2. Q. Who gave you that name?
   A. As drink is my idol, Landlords and their wives get all my money; they gave me that name in one of my drunken sprees, wherein I was made a member of strife, a child of want, and an inheritor of a bundle of rage.
3. Q. What did your Landlords and Landladies promise for you?
   A. They did promise and vow three things in my name; first, that I should renounce the comforts of my own fireside; second, starve my wife and hunger my children; third, walk in rags and tatters, with my shoe soles going flip flap, all the days of my life.
4. Q. Rehearse the articles of the belief.
   A. I believe in the existence of one Mr. Alcohol, the great head and chief of all manner of vice, the source of nine-tenths of all diseases; lastly, I not only believe, but am sure when my money is all gone and spent, the Landlord will stop the tap and turn me out.
5. Q. How many commandments have ye sots to keep?
   A. Ten.
6. Q. Which be they?
   A. The same which the Landlord and Landlady spoke in the bar, saying, We are thy master and mistress, who brought thee out of the paths of virtue, placed thee in the ways of vice, and set thy feet in the road which leadeth to New South Wales.

   I. Thou shalt use no other house but mine.
   II. Thou shalt not make for thyself any substitute for intoxicating drinks, such as tea, coffee, ginger pop, or lemonade; for I am a jealous man, wearing a coat that should be on thy back, eating thy children's bread, and pocketing the money which should make thee and the wife comfortable all the days of thy life.
   III. Thou shalt not use my house in vain.
   IV. Remember that thou eat but one meal on the Sabbath day, for six days hast thou been drinking, and nought else wouldst thou do; but the seventh is the sabbath day, and thou canst have no trust; therefore thou skulketh on the seventh day and abominates it.
   V. Thou shalt honour the Landlords and Landladies and Gin-shops with thy presence, that thy days may be few and miserable in the land wherein thou dwellest.
   VI. Thou shalt commit murder, by starving, and hungering, and beating thy wife and family.
   VII. Thou shalt commit self-destruction.
   VIII. Thou shalt sell thy wife and children's bread and rob thyself of all thy comforts.
   IX. Thou shalt bear false witness when thou speakest of the horrors, saying thou art in good health when thou art labouring under the barrel fever.
   X. Thou shalt covet all thy neighbour is possessed of, thou shalt covet his house, his land, his purse, his health, his wealth, and all that he has got, that thou mayest indulge in drinking, help the brewer to buy a new coach, a pair of fine horses, a new dray and a fine building, that he may live in idleness all his days: likewise to enable the Landlord to purchase a new sign to put over his door, with 'Licensed to be drunk on the premises', written thereon.

An 1850s Temperance Society Tract based on the Ten Commandments

By far the most common charges at that time were for drunkenness or for being drunk and disorderly. In October 1870 the Chief Constable reported to the Radnor General Sessions that in the preceding quarter there had been 96 cases of drunkenness and 130 of drunkenness with 'notorious behaviour'. He urged that the granting of licences should be vested in the magistrates and not in the Excise, a reform which was put into operation by the Licensing Act of 1872. He also urged that there should be earlier closing hours, anticipating another reform which was carried out later. His plea for fewer licensed houses, however, went unheeded as in 1904 Knighton had 16 inns for its population of 2,100, whilst Presteigne had 14 and Rhayader 13 inns, each with populations barely over 1,200.

As W.H. Howse pointed out in his book *Radnorshire* practically all the inns brewed their own ale or beer up to the 1870s and some later than that. Some had cockpits which were in use up to the 1820s or '30s. Skittle alleys were a familiar feature of many inns until the opening years of the 20th century. Fair and market days saw the town inns at their busiest, when the demand for the accommodation of the people and their carts and horses filled house, yard, and stables to overflowing. The auction sales of houses, property and lands invariably took place at inns, and added considerably to their custom. Up to the 1850s and '60s, the sellers provided wine and spirits for all comers. For some reason the Radnorshire inn sales got a particularly bad name, and a writer of the 1860 period said that the scenes were sometimes 'positively disgraceful'.

At the time of the Beerhouse Acts there were few restrictions on licensing hours. As a whole, the only non-permitted hours were during Divine Services on Sundays, Christmas Day and Good Friday. However, beer houses could only open between 4 a.m. and 10 p.m. The 1872 Licensing Act tidied up and tightened the complex legislation, but at the beginning of the

The APPRENTICE's MONITOR.

o r,

INDENTURES

IN VERSE

Shewing what they are bound to do.

Proper to be hung up in all Shops.

EACH young Apprentice, when he's bound to Trade,
This folemn vow to God and Man has made,
To do with joy his Mafter's juft commands,
Nor truft his fecrets into other hands.
He muft no damage to his fubftance do,
And fee that others do not wrong him too.
His Mafter's goods he fhall not wafte nor lend,
But all his property with care defend.
He fhall not buy nor fell without his leave,
Nor lie, nor injure, nor at all deceive,
Taverns and ALE-Houfes he fhall not haunt,
Thofe fnares to Youth, thofe fcenes of vice and want,
At CARDS and DICE he fhall not dare to play,
But fly from fuch temptations far away.

O Youth ! remember thou to this art BOUND.
See that no breach of this in thee be found.

Apprentices were not allowed to visit taverns and ale-houses

20th century public houses were, in general, still allowed to open for some 20 hours each day.

However, in Radnorshire and the whole of Wales an Act to prohibit the sale of intoxicating liquors on Sunday was passed on 27th August 1881.

An Act to prohibit the Sale of Intoxicating Liquors on Sunday in Wales.
[27th August 1881.]

WHEREAS the provisions in force against the sale of fermented and distilled liquors during certain hours of Sunday have been found to be attended with great public benefits, and it is expedient and the people of Wales are desirous that in the principality of Wales those provisions be extended to the other hours of Sunday :

Be it therefore enacted by the Queen's most Excellent Majesty, by and with the advice and consent of the Lords Spiritual and Temporal, and Commons, in this present Parliament assembled, and by the authority of the same, as follows :

1. In the principality of Wales all premises in which intoxicating liquors are sold or exposed for sale by retail shall be closed during the whole of Sunday. *Premises where intoxicating liquors sold to be closedonSundays in Wales.*

2. The Licensing Acts, 1872–1874, shall apply in the case of any premises closed under this Act as if they had been closed under those Acts. *Application of Licensing Acts. 35 & 36 Vict. c. 94. 37 & 38 Vict. c. 40.*

3. This Act shall commence and come into operation with respect to each division or place in Wales on the day next appointed for the holding of the general annual licensing meeting for that division or place. *Commencement of Act.*

4. Nothing in this Act contained shall preclude the sale at any time at a railway station of intoxicating liquors to persons arriving at or departing from such station by railway. *Sale of intoxicating liquors at railway stations.*

5. This Act may be cited as the Sunday Closing (Wales) Act, 1881. *Short title.*

The 1881 Welsh Sunday Closing Act

Towards the end of the 19th century and in the early years of the following one, considerable efforts were made to close down inns and public houses by refusing to renew licences for a large variety of reasons. This resulted in the payment to the owners of compensation, of which about 10 per cent went to the landlord; the remainder to the owner. As a result many inns in Radnorshire ceased trading with a further reduction following the Licensing (Consolidation) Act of 1910.

It is not often realised nowadays that the regulations concerning licensed houses, alcohol and children are mainly of 20th century origin. Although the 1872 Act made it an offence to sell spirits to those using licensed premises under the age of 16, it was not until the Children's Act of 1908 that children under the age of 14 were prohibited from being in licensed premises. It was only in 1923 that it became, in general, an offence to serve alcoholic drinks to those under 18.

Regulations brought in at a time when the country is at war often have a habit of staying long after hostilities have ceased. Thus it was during the First World War that limited opening hours were instigated. The Licensing Act of 1921 regularised the regulations concerning opening hours by defining 'permitted hours'. These were stipulated as being eight hours

10

Published for Bettering the Condition and Increasing the
Comforts of the POOR.

C*A*UTION

To Alehouse Keepers, & their Guests.

*It is better that Offences against the Laws should be Prevented, than that Offenders
should be Punished.*

THE PROPER USE OF INNS, &c.

THE proper use of Inns and Alehouses, is to furnish Refreshment and Lodging to Travellers, upon a reasonable profit; to accommodate persons meeting on *necessary* business; Soldiers in his Majesty's service; and some whose occupations require a frequent change of residence, or who cannot provide themselves with meat and drink in a more convenient manner.

The neighbouring Justices of the Peace have the Power of granting a License for keeping a Publick House, and they have the like Power of refusing to grant a License, without giving any reason whatever for such refusal, which is entirely at their discretion; it is therefore the Interest as well as the Duty of an Alehouse keeper to take care, that he conduct himself and his House in a becoming manner, lest he forfeit the good opinion of the Justices and be deprived of his License.

A principal duty of an Alehouse keeper is to prevent Artificers and Labourers from drinking more than for their necessary Refreshment; and not to allow them to lose their time and spend their money to the injury of themselves and their families: therefore, almost all debts (commonly called Ale Scores) are incurred in an improper manner; and are such, as the lawful means (if any) of recovering such debts would often discover bad conduct in the Alehouse keeper, and hazard the loss of his License.

The Law protects the Alehouse keeper from losses, by giving him the power of detaining the Person of any Guest who refuses to pay the reasonable charges for the meat and drink which have been furnished him: Debts are seldom incurred by Travellers, who are generally Strangers, and when they are incurred by Artificers and Labourers, great blame will attach to the Alehouse keeper from the manner in which such Ale Scores must have been contracted.

An Alehouse keeper is liable to heavy penalties for allowing Tippling, Drunkenness, or disorderly behaviour in his House, extending to the Forfeiture of his Recognizance, and that of his Surety or Bondsman, and the loss of his License.

The Guests who are guilty of Tippling, Drunkenness, and disorderly Behaviour are also liable to heavy penalties; and Artificers and Labourers who waste their time and their money at Publick Houses, ought to consider that although they may avoid punishment from the forbearance with which the Laws are executed, yet their Wives and their Families cannot escape from the miseries of Poverty, the certain consequence of their Husband's misconduct; and that the wholesome restraint which the Law lays upon a man in this respect, gives the best assurance of protection to his Family and to Himself, when it forbids him to waste his time and his money in a Publick House, and disturb the peace of others by his intemperance and bad example.

To   *Alehouse keeper.*

*You are desired to have this Paper pasted up in your Kitchen, or some other usual place where
your Guests take their Refreshment.*

SIGNED

T. DAVIES, BRITANNIA PRINTING-OFFICE, HEREFORD.

Should this notice still be posted in landlords' kitchens?

between 11 a.m. and 10 p.m except for Sunday, which was limited to five hours. In 1934, there was a slight improvement – an extension could be granted to 10.30 p.m. during the summer months, especially in rural areas where it was appreciated that evening work was necessary.

After the Second World War there were several minor Acts, including the 1953 Licensing Act which directed that Sunday closing in Radnorshire and Wales would only apply in administrative districts where the electors so decided. Following this, Wales gradually became 'wet' on a Sunday, starting with districts closest to England, including Radnorshire. Sunday closing could return and the Licensing Act of 1964 made provision for a poll on this issue to take place on request every seven years. For instance, a referendum on Sunday drinking in 1975 led to six districts remaining 'dry' while the rest decided to go 'wet', including Radnorshire.

The seat of government within the county had already moved in 1889 from New Radnor to Presteigne, and when Powys came into being, with the amalgamation of Radnorshire, Brecon and Montgomery, a new county council was set up in Llandrindod Wells in 1974.

Licensing restrictions continued to be simplified and the 1961 Act provided for 'restaurant' and 'residential' licences and also gave the customers' grace – the ten minutes of 'drinking-up time'. A late 20th century Act restored the situation to more or less what it was at the beginning of the century by allowing inns to stay open throughout the day if they so wished, most commonly any times between 11 a.m. and 11 p.m., with a somewhat shorter 'window of opportunity' on Sundays. A new millennium has brought new thought and the 2003 Licensing Act has led to the possibility of 24-hour opening once again. However, there seems to be little local need or take-up of this opportunity. The same act also removed the provision for polls on Sunday opening – Wales will now remain permanently 'wet' on Sundays.

CHAPTER TWO

Brewing and Breweries

That Ale's the true liquor of life
(Praise of Ale, a 17th century ballad)

Ale, or beer, has been the staple drink in England and Wales since the introduction of grain. It was central to life, on an equal footing to bread, if not higher. The Romans found the Welsh drinking fermented liquor made from barley and also mead made from honey. The Normans built castles and monasteries and every monastery had a brewery for the refreshment of monk and traveller. According to Dr. William Rees in his *South Wales and the March, 1284-1415*, there was also 'a close connection between the Mill and the Brewing people, especially in Wales.' The Mill contributed to the Lord's income, and he derived from each brewing within his domain 'A Prise' or its equivalent. In some cases he encouraged the making of ale, by hiring out his cauldron for that purpose.

As well as monasteries, churches began brewing with the nearby church house often the precursor of the village inn. In an article in *Yr Haul*, the Church in Wales magazine of July 1932, it is asserted that the churches brewed their own beer in order to keep the people sober! The logic behind this was that Welsh people at that time used to brew home-made mead, and this particular drink was apparently extremly intoxicating. And according to Myrddin ap Dafydd, in his book of *Welsh Pub Names*, the old church houses, or inns, more often than not were opposite the graveyard entrance. They were convenient meeting places to discuss parish matters, fulfilling the function that was later met by church halls. They were also places where travellers could rest and take refreshment, and it was there also that the courts of law, rent settling meetings, tithe paying and social meetings were held. Again, Mr. J. Charles Cox in his book on *Churchwardens' Accounts,* said:

> The Church Ale was, by the end of the fifteenth century, the Church Wardens most universal resort for eliciting the bounty of the Parish. The Ale was held in the Church House, a building close to the Church.

As is also explained in *Welsh Pub Names*, most of the rural Welsh inns were originally ordinary houses and cottages – houses which opened their doors to the public so that they could have something to eat and drink. The man of the house would often have another job and his wife would be the innkeeper. The family would live in the house, usually setting aside one room for the drinkers. Nearly every farm would make their own home-brew. If a farmhouse happened to be in a convenient position, they would open their doors to visitors or travellers and sell the beer that remained once the farm's own requirements had been fulfilled.

By the late Middle Ages ale was the only safe liquid to drink and people drank it all day. For breakfast it was 'small beer', a weaker beer made from a second boiling of the barley mash, and at other times strong ale. There was no alternative until tea was introduced in the country as a whole at the end of the 18th century, but in Radnorshire it was more likely to have been much later, probably not until the early 19th century.

For perhaps 1,000 years ale had been the basic drink but a fundamental change occurred during the early 15th century. This was due to the introduc-

tion of hops, described by the authorities in Shrewsbury at the time as that 'wicked and pernicious weed', and the resultant manufacture of 'beer'. The hop not only gave the new drink a more bitter flavour, it was also of considerable importance for its preservative properties enabling the beverage to be kept much longer than ale before 'going-off'. For well over 100 years brewers produced both ale and beer, but the popularity of the former gradually declined and beer eventually became the accepted drink, although cider was still popular.

A 16th-century brewer

14

A mid-18th-century brewhouse

The Protestant Reformation and early Nonconformism had very little influence on the old links that had been forged between beer and religion. The early peripatetic preachers were given a 'beer allowance' and the 'beer of the cause' was always drunk at monthly meetings. The earliest prayer meetings and services in some areas were held in pubs.

Until the beginning of the 19th century nearly all the landlords in Radnorshire made their own ale in small brewhouses behind their inns. However, many of the small inns and beer-houses that opened during the first half of the 19th century had no brewing facilities and were dependent on other inns or on the growing number of breweries for their supply. This change accelerated as breweries bought public houses whenever they came onto the market, a process that resulted in a substantial decrease in the number of 'free-houses' and of independent breweries.

Surprisingly, however, there were no breweries actually in Radnorshire, although they were to be found across the borders in towns such as Builth Wells, Newtown, Brecon, Tredegar and Hereford. Perhaps the most influential brewer was David Williams, of Builth, later David Williams (Builth) Ltd., who in the early 20th century bought a number of inns in the county, putting tenants in on the understanding that they only sold his beer and spirits. Other brewers who not only sold beer in Radnorshire but also bought pubs when they came on the market were Evans Bevan, of the Vale of Neath Brewery, in Swansea, later taken over by Whitbreads, and the Wrekin Brewery, of Wellington, Shropshire.

The order form image contains the following text:

BEWELL STREET, HEREFORD.

ORDER CARD

HEREFORD BREWERY BEER FOR FAMILIES

Telephone No: 26. Tel. Address "MALT, HEREFORD."

THE HEREFORD & TREDEGAR BREWERY, Ltd.

HEREFORD PALE ALE 1/6
*** ALE 2/-
HEREFORD EXTRA STOUT 1/6 PER Doz

_____ Doz. PALE ALE
_____ Doz. *** ALE _____ Doz. EXTRA STOUT

BOTTLES & STOPPERS TO [NETT PRICES] BE PAID FOR ON DELIVERY

IN CASK.	PINS.	FIRKS.	KILS.
MILD ALE	4/6	9/-	18/-
LIGHT BITTER	5/3	10/6	21/-
BEST BITTER	6/-	12/-	24/-
LUNCHEON STOUT	5/3	10/6	21/-
EXTRA STOUT	6/-	12/-	24/-

PLEASE FORWARD ONE @

FULL NAME
ADDRESS

HARVEST ALE from 6d. per Gallon.

*A Hereford and Tredegar Brewery
order form printed on a postcard*

At the beginning of the 20th century, the Tredegar Brewery Company owned breweries in Tredegar and Brecon. The company then acquired the Hereford Imperial Brewery and changed its name to the Hereford and Tredegar Brewery Company. In 1906, when they closed their Brecon and Tredegar breweries, the Hereford base became their main production centre. By 1950 another merger saw the name changed to the Hereford, Tredegar and Cheltenham Breweries Ltd.

With the advent of the railways, delivery of beer to inns in Radnorshire became a practical proposition. For instance, Ind Coope and Allsop from Burton upon Trent, Staffordshire, home to some of the country's finest brewers, was able to send beer to the Elan Valley Hotel in Rhayader which arrived the day after it had been ordered. National breweries who also came to own pubs in the area, as well as supplying beer, included Allied Breweries and Ansells.

One of the basic ingredients of beer, both pale ale and stouts, is barley grains which have passed through the malting process to become maltose sugars. Malting as a trade was of some importance in Knighton, for instance, where there were four malt houses, but by 1928 the local pubs were supplied from breweries outside the county.

Breweries throughout the country were closing at an alarming rate. In 1900 there were some 6,390, a number which steadily fell until 70 years later there were fewer than 200. Pasteurised, sterile beer, known as keg, and lager were taking over, which together accounted for the majority of beer sales. As far as real ale was concerned, the national brewing industry had come to a virtual halt following a series of mergers and takeovers – the industry now being concentrated in the hands of a few global giants. However, into this vacuum has sprung a number of small independent breweries. In Shropshire, for instance, there are nine of these small breweries including two in Bishop's Castle, Hobsons at Cleobury Mortimer, and Woods at Wistanstow. Hereford breweries include Wye Valley at Stoke Lacy; Dunn Plowman in Kington; and the Spinning Dog in Hereford. In Wales itself, the closest to Radnorshire is the Breconshire Brewery in Brecon, while beers from Felinfoel, Llanelli and Brains, Cardiff are all to be found in Radnorshire pubs.

KNIGHTON

1 Swan
2 Talbot
3 Bridge
4 Knighton *
5 Globe
6 George & Dragon *
7 Crown
8 Red Lion *
9 Red Lion
10 Duke's Arms
11 Joiners
12 Chandos
13 Bear
14 Salutation

15 Lamb
16 Golden Lion *
17 Fleece
18 Seven Stars
19 King's Head
20 Feathers
21 Plough
22 Harp
23 Old Wine Vaults
24 Conjurer's
25 Horse & Jockey *
26 Kinsley
27 Round House

– Open in 2006

18

CHAPTER THREE

Knighton

We still had sorrows to lighten,
One could not be always glad,
And lads knew trouble at Knighton
When I was a Knighton lad.

(A Shropshire Lad, A.E. Housman, 1896)

Knighton has been likened to an Alpine town, being built on the slopes of a steep hill rising from the River Teme, marking the border with England, beyond which stretches Kinsley Wood. It is the second largest and the main market town of Radnorshire. The name originates from either *Cnwc-din*, meaning fort on the spur, or *Chenistetune*, recorded in the *Domesday Book* and meaning knight's town. Its Welsh name, *Tref-y-Clawdd* – town on the dyke – refers to Offa's Dyke built in the 8th century, about which time the Saxon town of Knighton came into being. This was over-run by the Welsh in 1052 and by the Normans shortly afterwards. William de Braose built a wooden castle, *Bryn-y-Castell*, near the Teme, and later another castle was erected, this time in stone, at the top end of the town, around which medieval Knighton developed. In 1230 the town became a borough with a charter from Henry III granting the townspeople the right to hold weekly markets and an annual fair. In 1402 Owain Glyndwr sacked the castle, then the property of the Mortimers of Wigmore, and much of the town. But within a few decades Knighton had recovered and by the 17th century, when many of its buildings were constructed, was a flourishing market town. Several drovers' roads passed through the town and after corralling their cattle for the night, the herdsmen doubtless sought the hospitality of local inns. In the late 18th century there were five toll gates leading into Knighton, with coaches to Ludlow by 1810 and to Llandrindod Wells by 1836. In 1860 the railway reached Knighton from the east, eventually going to Swansea, enabling the town to become a busy depot. Tanning, cloth production and malting all thrived.

A public health report on Knighton in 1849, a year after the introduction of a Public Health Act, highlighted some of the health hazards people faced in those days. Markets for cattle, sheep and pigs were held in the streets, slaughterhouses were open, household privies were placed in exposed positions, while stone cisterns used for storing refuse for swine gave off an offensive stench.

> Knighton is in the most deplorable state of destitution, as to any means for the removal of decomposing animal and vegetable matter ... the refuse is allowed to accumulate until a shower of rain, ... only removes the obnoxious excreta ... to a lower level.

According to historian W.H. Howse, Knighton has had 37 inns and public houses since the mid-18th century with 22 in 1879. Licensed premises brewed their own beer, using malt from one of four malt houses situated in Broad Street, Station Road, Bridge Street and Church Street, but by 1928 they were supplied from breweries in other towns. The inns would all have done a roaring trade on market days and at the eight annual fairs, when 'the demand for accommodation of people and their carts and horses filled house, yard and stables to overflowing'. A boyhood memory of a May Fair in the 1880s recorded: 'Knighton seemed all pubs in those days, and they were filled to capacity from the faces I saw at every window upstairs and down'. Other events which drew the crowds were the Knighton races, dating back to Queen Anne and held first on Bailey Hill and then by the river; prize fighting with stakes of about £50; cock-fighting and bull-baiting. At public dinners numerous toasts and speeches were given. At one dinner in 1845 the reporter, after detailing 34 toasts, added that the health of several other gentlemen were drunk.

One of the last cases of the illegal form of divorce known as wife selling took place in Knighton as late as 1854. The *Hereford Times* of 6 May under the heading 'Scandalous Proceeding' reported:

> On Saturday last the town crier announced through the streets the public sale of the young wife of William Jones, which was to come off at the market-place on that evening. The sale did not however, take place, the fair dame, as it was understood, having been disposed of privately. All parties concerned in these outrages on public decency ought to know that the sale of a wife is a misdemeanour.

An early form of benefit society, known as clubs, held their meetings at various inns including the **Crown, Fleece, Globe** and **George**. Each club would hold its annual walk – going to church and a good dinner followed by sports events. All the inns were packed on 19th August 1858 when the ceremony of cutting the first sod for the new railway line from Knighton to

Craven Arms was celebrated. Even the police joined in the fun resulting in two constables suffering fines for being absent from duty while drunk.

Today, Knighton is still a bustling market town with visitors attracted to the Offa's Dyke Centre and the start and finish of the Owen Glyndwr's Way, opened in 2002. Another attraction is the Spaceguard Centre, a working astronomical observatory collecting information on the threat posed to life on earth by asteroids and comets.

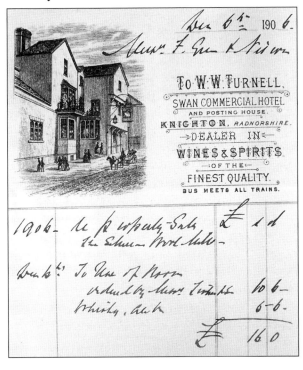

A 1906 account from the Swan Inn

As one approaches Knighton from either the B4355 Presteigne road or the A4113 from Ludlow, one enters Bridge Street, which once boasted at least three pubs. First to be encountered was the **Swan Inn** on the right which, although still licensed, now trades as an Indian restaurant under the name of Saffron. The three-storey building with basement was originally of the Elizabethan period, part half-timbered with a 17th-century timber-framed cross-wing on the right, possibly part of a larger house of the same period. The three-bay front was covered in stucco in the 19th century. In the late 18th and early 19th centuries the **Swan** was an important coaching house. The earliest recorded coach service was in 1794, running to London once a week. In 1841 the publican was Sarah Mead, aged 60, whose son, Thomas, was a cabinet maker. She had two servants. The inn was renowned, or notorious, for its cockpit. Birds carefully bred, fed and trained fought there in matches organised by the local gentry, who wagered heavily on the results. Cockfighting was made illegal in 1849. In 1858 Ann Chandler was in charge.

At the turn of the 20th century the proprietor was William Watkin Turnell, when the **Swan** was described as a commercial hotel and posting house, with

an omnibus meeting all trains. A bill dated 6 December, 1906 shows that Mr. Turnell charged 10s. 6d. for the use of a room, together with a further 6s. 6d. for whisky, when the Silurian Mill, on Mill Street, was sold to George Holroyd. Mr. Turnell was still proprietor in 1928 when the hotel was one of the town's two principal hotels, being described as

The former Swan Inn is now an Indian resturant

a family and commercial hotel and posting house. Swing doors opened onto a splendid staircase leading up to 14 bedrooms, while a semi-circular bar served a piano room and two snugs. The Outrams ran the **Swan** in the 1940s until the Wightmans became the owners in the 1940s and continued into the 1960s, when the **Swan** was a place for business and meetings. In the 1970s extensive modernisation was carried out, the upstairs converted into flats and the stables demolished at the rear, four houses being built on the site. When the **Swan** ceased trading as an inn at the turn of the 21st century, it became an Indian restaurant, but has changed hands two or three times. An altered bar and servery is in the same position, but the lounge bar to the left of the entrance is no longer used, while the main dining room was once a snooker room.

Three former pubs – the Bridge Inn, the Talbot and the Swan Hotel

Next door to the Swan was the **Talbot Inn**, which is now a private house. Described as a beerhouse, it offered little accommodation, the rooms being small and low; not surprisingly it was the last pub in Knighton to brew its own beer. The inn was bought in 1917 for £410 by Edward Hall, who had addresses in Knighton and the United

States. But three years later its licence renewal was refused because it did little trade and the licence was not required to meet the wants of the neighbourhood. Knighton then had 12 other licensed houses. Mr. Hall received £157 compensation and the licensee, William Turner, received £18 – the same amount as his annual rent. It was then run as a confectioners shop by Mrs. Palfrey, continuing in that role during the Second World War and into the 1960s before becoming a private residence. The last shop-keeper was Mrs. Turner who had a little pet dog which, it is claimed, used to smoke a pipe.

The one-time Bridge Inn

At the end of the road next to the Edwardian red-and-yellow brick property is an empty house which used to be the **Bridge Inn**. Near the old bridge over the Cwm Brook, the inn had a lawn in front enclosed with wooden railings. In the 1860s it was run by John Jones, who previously had been the last gate-keeper at a toll-gate where the railway station now stands. By 1908, when John Galliers was the landlord, it became surplus to requirements and renewal of its licence was refused. In that year there were still 16 licensed houses in Knighton for a population of 2,139, or one to every 133 inhabitants, including women and children! A police report stated that in 34 visits to the inn during nine days, 12 persons only were found there and 'the house appears to be very little used'. Compensation of £160 was awarded the owner, John Dover. The inn became a shop and dwelling house.

In Broad Street at the corner with Brookside is the **Knighton Hotel**, previously known as the **Norton Arms Hotel**, built by Sir Richard Green-Price, M.P. for Radnorshire, with large stables at the rear. A stone-built square block, it is a handsome three-storey and basement building with splayed bays to left and right, with iron-railed balconies to the first floor and has a hipped slate roof. It was opened in 1867 when, by agreement, the **Chandos**, Knighton's other hotel, closed down. The adjacent building was formerly a 16th-century coaching inn, on the site of which the **Farmers' Clubhouse and Commercial Hotel** was built in 1852. It was run in 1858 by Jane Tudge, who was also landlady of the nearby **Globe Inn**. Its spacious upper area, later

*An early 20th-century photograph of the Norton Arms Hotel
and Assembly Rooms*

A party outside the Norton Arms Hotel

24

Broad Street with the Norton Arms, the George and Dragon
and the Crown (opposite)

known as the Assembly Rooms, was used as the venue for local meetings, balls and other functions.

Exclusive card and dancing events were held there, usually starting at 9 p.m. and lasting until daybreak, with supper served half-way through the proceedings. Tickets were 5s. or 7s. 6d. A supper for 120 people at a function in 1864 included the following:

> 7 turkeys, 3 chines, 4 spare-ribs, 12 couple fowl, 3 brace pheasants, 2 brace partridge, 6 lobsters, 7 tongues, 3 pieces beef, 2 collared heads, Boar's head, 12 dishes hares, 2 galenies, 10 dishes of mince-pieces, 10 dishes cheese cakes, tartlets, 4 dishes Dutch Flummery, 2 tipsy cakes, 2 dishes trifle, custards with exceptionally fine grapes, oranges, apples and other desert

not to mention the usual 'liberal supply' of champagne, wines, etc'. Another popular event was the New Year Ball, when the **Norton Arms** was open for cloaks and powder-room and people sat out on the grand staircase during the intervals.

Impressive beams in the Knighton Hotel ballroom

Mrs. M.A. Hale was the manageress in 1906 and was still there in 1926 when the **Norton Arms** was described as a 'family and commercial hotel and posting house with good trout fishing, shooting and golfing'. Two years later a market holding up to 6,000 sheep was constructed to the rear of the hotel, which must have boosted trade with well-attended markets held every Thursday and a Fair every month. The Assembly Room, by then owned by the hotel, was still used for socials and dances. It was later run as a picture house, while the ground floor became a garage. Jimmy Outram ran the hotel for about 30 years up until the Second World War, when it was taken over and used as a hostel for ladies.

The Knighton Hotel showing, to the right, the former Assembly Rooms

In 1960 the proprietor was Mr. W. Yeomans and the resident manageress was Mrs. M. Cole. After celebrating their 50th anniversary as motor engineers in Knighton at the **Norton Arms** in 1970, S.W. Brisbane and Son Ltd. bought the hotel in that same year. They modernised it throughout and it became a three-star hotel, but a few years later it was sold to Mr. and Mrs. Fernie. The sheep market was made into the town's car park.

In 1990 the name was changed to the **Knighton Hotel**, being taken over by three partners who instigated major internal alterations including the ballroom where the low ceiling was removed exposing the original beams. Unfortunately the business went into receivership for four years until it was bought in 1998 by Jan Harris. Later landlady of the Bateman Arms in Shobdon, she recalls her tenure there being punctuated with ghostly experiences. On two separate occasions customers reported having seen a maid in a black dress and pinafore falling off the top balcony; on another a fire inspector said he saw the ghost of a man following behind him. Other incidents included Mrs. Harris being flung against the wall near the cellar and lights going off and on; a terrible smell near the reception area possibly linked to a man who drowned in a sewer running under the hotel in Victorian times, and a room which spooked her Labrador and also became freezing. However, as Mrs. Harris said, these experiences 'didn't do me any harm'. The hotel was closed for a nine-month period before the present owners, John Rafferty and Jane Findlar, took over in May 2005. The hotel has 15 en-suite bedrooms, the King Offa's restaurant, and conference rooms off the old ballroom.

According to local historian William Hatfield, writing in 1947: 'Where the new part of the Norton Arms is now built, was a wine vaults kept by Mrs. Mason, who moved up to another in the Narrows, where Mr. Powis's shop now is'.

Two properties further along Broad Street, probably where the Red Cross shop now stands, used to be the **Globe Tavern**, which was of some importance in the late 18th and early 19th centuries. A Benefit Society was held there in the mid-19th century, called the Globe Club. In 1841 the landlord was John Jones, aged 40, who in 1845 bought the **George**. In 1858 it was run by Jane Tudge. However, the tavern closed before the end of the century and was later demolished to make way for a shop with accommodation above. Among the many different trades represented were butchers, shoe makers and chemists.

A large malthouse, owned by John Davies, was conveniently situated between the **Globe** and the **George and Dragon**. He sold it in about 1896 to the North and South Wales Bank and later new premises were erected for the Midlands Bank, now part of HSBC.

Above: The George and Dragon in about 1865.
Below: The carved date

On the corner with George Lane stands the **George & Dragon Inn**, formerly known as the **George**, one of Knighton's oldest buildings, bearing the date 1637 on the side wall. Documents still in the inn's possession date back to 1780 when it was owned by James Donovan, a local baker, and was still in the Donovan family in 1807 when David Donovan, a private in His Majesty's Regiment of Royal Artillery, leased it to James Davies, innkeeper, for 5s. By 1822 the inn was owned by James Morris, who in 1842 sold it to Thomas Bore for £930. Ann Duggan was the innkeeper at the time and in 1845 there was a conveyance of the **George** to John Jones, of the **Globe Inn**. In 1853, the landlord, Mr. G. Eyre, put up a notice reading: 'To avoid disturbing our customers, would coachmen and dealers kindly refrain from saddling and harnessing before sunrise'. It then came into the possession of Lewis Turner, who in 1868 left £100 to the innkeeper William James and directed that James should occupy the inn during the term of his natural life.

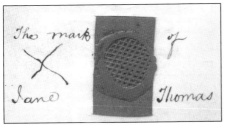

In 1870 the **George** was bought for £680 by Jane Thomas, spinster, of the Three Fishes Inn, Shrewsbury who, two years later, sold it, subject to a £450 mortgage, to Richard Turner, of Bowdlen, Knighton with outbuildings, yard, stables and

KNIGHTON,

RADNORSHIRE.

VALUABLE LICENSED PREMISES.

MR. PHILIP DAVIES

Will offer by Public Auction,

At "The George & Dragon" Hotel, Knighton,

— on —

THURSDAY, 28th NOVEMBER, at 3-30 p.m.

and subject to Conditions,

All that FREEHOLD and FULLY-LICENSED

Family and Commercial Hotel,

— Known as —

'The George & Dragon,'

With the Garden thereto belonging.

Situate in Broad Street and George Lane, Knighton, in the County of Radnor, in the occupation of Mr. Charles Price as yearly Tenant.

The Premises are situated in the principal street and in the centre of the town, and are absolutely free for all trade purposes, and contain well-fitted Bar, Sitting Room, Tap Room, large Kitchen fitted with cooking range, and 2 Pantrys, on the second floor 5 commodious Bedrooms for 8 beds, and on the Third floor large Bedroom and Landing.

Underneath there is a capital Beer and Wine Cellar with inside and outside entrance thereto.

The Outside Premises comprise Brew house, Coal-house, Trap-house, 2 loose Boxes, Stabling for about 20 loose horses with loft over, and hackney stable to hold about 12 loose horses; together with the excellent Kitchen Garden and other appurtenances thereto belonging.

The whole premises are very compact and the house does one of the best trades in the District.

For further particulars to the Auctioneer, Presteign; or

Messrs. F. L. GREEN & NIXSON,

Solicitors, Knighton.

Top: The mark of Jane Thomas when she sold the inn in 1872.
Main: Sale notice for the George and Dragon in 1908

garden in the occupation of William James as tenant. Also included was a cottage or tenement with garden and brewhouse adjoining and a stable and yard on the opposite side of the lane and near the cottage. It then came into the hands of John Davies, of the White Hart Inn, Builth, who in 1876 bequeathed the inn, now called the **George & Dragon**, to his son John and heirs. It was still occupied by William James. John was also left the **Castle Inn**, Kington and a cottage, while the White Hart Inn went to his father's brother-in-law Henry Powell. About this time, one whole wall of the rear bar, or tap room, was cloaked in oak panelling, originally pew ends in the parish church before it was demolished in 1877.

John died intestate in 1886 and the **George & Dragon** was granted to his widow, Ann, along with his daughters, Mary, Adeliza (born after her father's death) and Sarah (who died as an infant in 1890). Mary and Adeliza agreed to sell in 1908 to George Apperley, of the **Crown Inn**, Knighton, for £890 – £150 going to their mother and the remainder divided between both daughters. The 'For Sale' notice stated that the inn:

> contains a well-fitted bar, sitting room, tap room, large kitchen fitted with cooking range, and two pantries. On the second floor are five commodious bedrooms for eight beds and on third floor a large bedroom and landing. Underneath there is a capital beer and wine cellar. The outside premises comprise Brew-house, coal-house, trap-house, 2 loose boxes, stabling for about 20 loose horses with loft over, a hackney stable to hold about 12 loose horses; together with excellent kitchen garden and other appurtenances. ... The whole premises are very compact and the house does one of the best trades in Knighton.

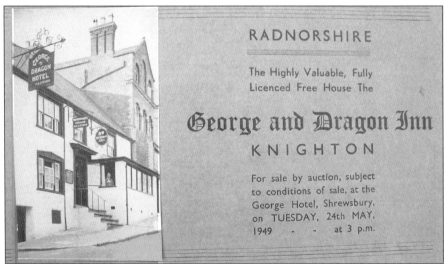

RADNORSHIRE

The Highly Valuable, Fully Licenced Free House The

George and Dragon Inn

KNIGHTON

For sale by auction, subject to conditions of sale, at the George Hotel, Shrewsbury, on TUESDAY, 24th MAY, 1949 - - at 3 p.m.

The George and Dragon for sale by auction in 1949

The George and Dragon in 2005

Apperley undertook to purchase all his beer from Alton Court Brewery, of Stroud, Gloucestershire, for their allowing a £400 mortgage on cottages he owned.

In 1906 the landlord was George Price and in 1926 it was Charles Price. In 1930 Apperley sold the building for £900 to Harold Angelo Steiner, who owned the **Oxford Arms** and the **Bull Hotel** in Presteigne, together with the yard, brewhouse, stables, coachhouse and garden, which he sold off in 1934. Because of ill health, Steiner sold the **George & Dragon** in 1949. In addition to the front and back bars there was a smoke room, while the first floor now consisted of a large lounge, sitting room and three bedrooms with two further rooms on the second floor. Outbuildings included a brew house or store, two stables, and garaging for four cars. In 1962 the inn's owner, Alton Court Brewery, went into voluntary liquidation and was taken over by West Country Breweries Ltd., of Cheltenham. In the 1990s, the inn was bought by Peter Vrettos, who converted the stables into bedrooms and made other internal changes. The present owner, Justin Rees, also works as a dairy bull semen salesman for a New Zealand genetic company. The smoking/piano room is now a dining area, the old coach house at the rear has been converted into a restaurant and the beer storage area has been turned into bedrooms.

On the other side of Broad Street, directly opposite the **George & Dragon**, is No. 11, a building now containing three shops with flats above, which used to be the **Crown Inn** or **Hotel**. In 1771 Radnorshire's first ever Friendly Society was formed there, continuing until the late 1880s. Aaron Whistow became landlord in 1826, taking out a mortgage with the Alton Court Brewery, which was to remain for nearly a hundred years. On his death at the age of 69 in 1845, the inn was taken over by Martha Gayther, then by John Anthony, followed in 1875 by Walter Haines who ran it with his wife, Martha. The following year the Crown Friendly Society held its 105th anniversary with a report of the time stating:

> After meeting at the Crown Hotel and calling over the roll, the members walked in procession to the National School, headed by their beautiful new silk banner and the Knighton brass band under the leadership of Mr. Charles Lloyd. The Rev. J.B. Brown officated at the schoolroom. At the close of the service the procession re-formed and paraded the town until 2 o'clock, when all adjourned to the Crown Inn, where an excellent dinner was provided by Mr. and Mrs. Haines. ... Upwards of 100 sat down to dinner. After the repast, the usual toasts were given and duly responded to.

According to Kelly's *Directory*, Mrs. Jane Haines, presumably the daughter, was at the helm in 1895.

Behind the brick-and-stone built inn was a large stable with a timber-framed club room above, covered by a corrugated iron roof. Known as the Iron Room, it was used for dancing classes, socials, band practice and later for scout meetings and other functions. The **Crown** also had another attraction – a minah bird, which called 'Whoa there' to passing traffic. Horses halted and the bird ordered a quarter of ale before the wagoner could move on. In 1901 the inn and four nearby cottages were bought by George Apperley, who shortly afterwards installed Mrs. Mary Jones as landlady. In 1908 Mr. Apperley bought the **George and Dragon** opposite and later relinquished the **Crown**, where Mary Jones remained as tenant until at least 1926. Soon afterwards the **Crown** ceased trading and was used as the local Conservative Club until the beginning of the Second World War. It later became a clothes shop and was then converted into a grocers and a hairdressers with the upstairs part turned into flats. Three shops now occupy the premises – the Kitchen Shop, Shades Hair Salon and Significant Insurance Brokers.

At the corner of Church Street and West Street is the **Red Lion Inn**, a building erected about 160 years ago on the site of a former blacksmith's shop. It replaced an older inn of the same name almost next door in Church Street. According to local historian Roy Palmer, when Hiring Fairs were held in the 19th century and at the beginning of the 20th century, deals would often be struck over a pint in the **Red Lion**. 'Some men might agree to work for several farmers, and spend several lots of earnest money on beer, with no intention of honouring any of the bargains', he stated.

The former Crown Inn is now divided into three shops

From at least 1895 it was run by Elijah and Emma Gough and in 1926, when it was described as a hotel with 'every accommodation for cyclists', Elijah also advertised himself as 'a monumental mason with free designs on application'. During the Second World War it was run by Mrs. Brokenshaw, who was related to the

At the back of the Red Lion

33

Brokenshaws who ran the **Fleece Inn**, until her death. The owners, Alton Court Brewery, went into voluntary liquidation in 1962, when it was taken over by West Country Breweries Ltd of Cheltenham. It was run for some years by Mr. and Mrs. A. Phillips.

The recently refurbished Red Lion is near the old Red Lion

The **Red Lion** is now owned by Havana Taverns, of Pontesbury, Shropshire, who took it over in mid-2004 and closed it from October to February, 2005 for a major refit. A staircase near the main entrance has been removed and a passageway integrated into an open-plan bar, while a new front door and windows have been fitted. A window at the back has been turned into a door to access new outside decking. Upstairs, some of the bedrooms have been converted into a new restaurant; no letting rooms are available now. The former stables at the rear have long since gone.

Next to the pub's side entrance in Church Street is a three-storey stone building with a brick façade, now comprising the Filmshop and flats, built on the site of the original **Red Lion**, which was still trading in 1851 but had closed down by 1858.

On the other side of the road on the corner with Broad Street is the imposing former Barclay's Bank, now providing flat accommodation, which was built on the site of an even earlier inn, the **Duke's Arms**, or **Old Duke**. It probably derived its name from the Duke of Chandos and was Knighton's leading post and coaching inn in the late 18th and early 19th centuries. It closed in 1831. The inn was later demolished, together with a drapers' shop, and the bank premises built on the site in 1893. There are supposed to be some remains of the inn in the house next door.

Further down Church Street, where an archway leads to new houses in Victoria Close, once stood an alehouse called the **Joiners** or **Builders Arms**. In the late 19th century it was occupied by a blind man, Richard Langford, also called Friday. According to one local inhabitant, the **Joiners** may have been known as **Dirty Dick's**, 'with high back benches, chickens flying around and muck everywhere. People were frightened to go in'. It closed sometime in the 1930s.

Opposite the Red Lion at the corner of West Street and High Street was the **Chandos Arms Hotel**, an old coaching inn named after the Duke of Chandos, wealthy land-owner and Lord Lieutenant of Radnorshire in 1721. The three-storey building started life as a private house occupied by the Brydges, a branch of the Chandos family, and then by Richard Price, M.P. for Radnor Boroughs, until 1824 when it was converted into a coaching house and hotel. The main functions of the town were held there and on the closure of the **Duke's Arms** in 1831 it became the town's leading post and coaching inn. The post office was at the **Chandos** with letters arriving by mail carts or on foot; post carriers were Jolly's Wagons from Ludlow.

In his *History of Radnorshire*, the Rev. Jonathan Williams described the wedding in 1840 of the Rev. J.R. Cooper and Miss F. Cresswell:

> Tradesmen subscribed for the purchase of 6 sheep, which were carried round the town, preceded by a band, and followed by a procession of the subscribers. Arrived at the halting point the sheep were cut up and distributed among 70 poor families, with bread and beer, while 150 children were regaled with plum cake and wine. There was dancing on the green in the evening, and the tradesmen dined at the Chandos. The day ended with a large bonfire and a display of fireworks.

In 1842 two barristers, appointed to revise the list of voters in the election of a Knight of the Shire, met at the inn for the Hundred of Knighton. About this time the hotel was run by William Weyman and his wife Hannah. A letter written by a lady, Charlotte, to her sister Lucy, in Manchester, describes her stay at the **Chandos** while visiting her cousin:

> This time we were met at the station by Hannah and William with the pony and trap, a man following later with our valises and were soon at home. Over tea and wafers at 9.30 in the evenings we have discussed at

length the problems of the many changes taking place - What will happen to the roads and the coaching inns we visited, where will all the people, hostlers, maid servants, cooks and scullions go to find work? And what of the coachmen and guards.

On William's death the hotel continued to be run by Hannah Weyman and in the 1851 census she was described as a 48-year-old widow with a 21-year-old daughter, post-mistress, and four other children. She employed an 18-year-old waitress, a 19-year-old kitchen maid, a hostler, and a horse-keeper. Also staying there were a commercial traveller and a bailiff. In 1858 the **Chandos**, which now included an Inland Revenue Office, was run by John Roberts who provided lunch – a cold collation and wine for 5s. – for 500 in a marquee near the hotel to celebrate the cutting of the first sod for the new railway line from Knighton to Craven Arms. In 1863 it was taken over by his daughter, Lucy, and her husband Charles Rocke – the last proprietors, for the **Chandos Arms Hotel** closed four years later. It soon re-opened, however, this time as a Temperance Hotel, the first of its kind in Radnorshire. Extensive changes were made including the removal of the building's pillared portico and iron railings and a butcher's shop front installed and a double-fronted café with separate entrance constructed.

From 1900 it was owned and run by David Davies, who also held the part-time position of sanitary inspector with the Radnor District Council. He was still there in 1926, but soon afterwards the hotel closed and in 1931–32 half the property was demolished on the West Street side for road widening. However, Mr. Davies' daughter, Marion Machin, continued

A local hunt outside the Chandos Temperance Hotel

running the remaining half as the Chandos Private Hotel and Café. In 1932 two petrol pumps were installed in the adjoining West Street yard, selling petrol until the late 1950s. In 1935 the butcher's shop was transferred to its present position in West Street, the vacant shop becoming a restaurant and café. The hotel's former stables on the

Partial demolition of the Chandos Hotel for road widening

The former Chandos Hotel

opposite side of the yard became farm buildings and were demolished in 1950. Having worked through the war years, when the hotel was busy catering and housing refugees, factory workers, and members of the armed forces from different nations, Mrs. Machin retired in 1966 and the **Chandos** ceased to operate as a hotel. A Kebab House and Evans Windows now operate on the ground floor of the building.

Just off Broad Street on the left is High Street where facing the Clock Tower stands the Old House, and a butcher's shop run since 1988 by Carl Evans which was once the **Bear Inn**. The sign of the Bear comes from the coat of arms of the dukes of Worcester. It is said that in the mid-19th century it was run by the Price family, who were given the nick-name of the bears. After closing, the main front portion became a butcher's shop in the 1890s.

The Old House and Carl Evans butcher's shop was the Bear Inn in the 19th century

Four shop-fronts in a building which once held the Salutation Inn

The extensive accommodation above the shop belongs to the Old House, which has a narrow entrance set back from the road.

Further up High Street, also known as the Narrows, on the same side is a large, terraced building, with four shop-fronts, which was formerly the **Salutation Inn**. The sign was an early religious one referring to the Annunciation with the greeting and proclamation of the Archangel Gabriel to the Virgin Mary. The Puritans objected so strongly to such signs that they were changed to represent a gallant kneeling before his lady love. The inn has 17th-century origins hidden by late 18th-century or early 19th-century extensions at the front. The jettied frontage has since been replaced with shop fronts, but the great steps up to the original front entrance still remain. The owner was Lord Chandos who probably housed some of his retainers there. Local tradition has it, however, that the inn was also a house of ill repute at a time when Knighton was renowned for 'its bad butter, poor sanitation and loose women'. Another intriguing story is that the attic, which then ran the whole length of the building, was used for archery practice. The

Salutation is believed to have closed in the 1770s, when it was split into four units, with No. 22 being sold for about £90 of 'good money'. The new occupants were given 'Ingress, egress and regress for legal carriages' to the yard at the rear, which housed a bakehouse and stables 'with or without manure'. Over the years the shops, ancient beams still visible, continued to trade under different guises until the present day. The Salutation name is remembered only by the yard at the rear.

In the 19th century one of the shops, No. 21, was converted into the **Wine Vaults**, with a full licence to sell beer and spirits after Mrs. Mason transferred the name and business from the **Norton Arms** complex. Mrs. Lilian Thomas was landlady for some years, followed by Geoffrey Edwards. But in 1908 its licence was not renewed due to poor trade and the fact that it was no longer required, there being five other licensed houses within a radius of 100 yards. The owner, William Jones, of the Aldersey Arms, near Chester, was granted compensation of £333 with £25 going to Mr. Edwards. It has since been run as a shop, although it was a licensed restaurant for a while in the 1980s.

Still on the left-hand side of High Street, going up the hill, there is a small house two doors down from the **Golden Lion** which used to be a beerhouse called the **Lamb Inn**. In between the two pubs at the beginning of the 20th century was a bicycle shop run by Bill Hughes, who was known as the 'Peacemaker,' as he stood between the **Lamb** and the **Lion**. Trading in the 19th century and possibly earlier as a drovers' inn, the **Lamb** comprised a front bar and smoking room with a

The Lamb Inn (centre left), which closed in 1914

kitchen at the back, while upstairs was a sitting room and three bedrooms. It could accommodate nine lodgers. The premises were bought in 1896 for £400 by Lieutenant-Colonel William Southam, of Shrewsbury, who installed William Clark and his wife, Elizabeth, as tenants. While the water pipeline from Elan Valley to Birmingham was being installed near the town, the Clarks took in some of the workers as lodgers. They worked in shifts and while one shift breakfasted off bread and ale before going to work, the next shift came in to sleep on the straw mattresses while still warm.

In 1911 the inn was threatened with closure by the County Licensing Committee because it seemed to be very little used and was not required as there was still an excessive number of licensed houses in Knighton, with only a slight improvement on 1908, there now being 15 to a population of 2,139, or one to every 140 inhabitants. Mr. Clark, who paid a £16 annual rent, told the hearing he had 'always made a respectable living at the house' and had no other source of income. The former Chief Constable said the **Lamb**, which had increased trade by a third in the last year, was 'very useful for taking men of a certain class to'. The licence was renewed.

On the death of Mr. Clark, the inn was run by his widow, Elizabeth, who appears to have been something of an eccentric. Her skin was burnt the colour of soot from her habit of always sitting in a Welsh settle in front of the open fire, even during the night. Some people would never step inside the **Lamb** as Mrs. Clark gave the impression of being a witch. Then in 1914 the inn's licence came up for renewal again and this time failed after its owner, Lt.-Col. Southam, now engaged on military duty, did a deal with the licensing authority. They agreed to withdraw an objection to the **Fleece Inn**, which he also owned, on the understanding that the **Lamb** was submitted for compensation. This was duly done with Southam receiving £170 and Mrs. Clark £30. In the 1930s, the property became a tailor's shop and then a private residence, being bought in 'a shocking condition' in 1954 by local man Ted Steel, who soon made some interesting discoveries. The flagstones were found to be old grave headstones from the parish church which had been pulled down in the late 19th century. Then, under one of the bedroom floors, some Napoleon coins were discovered together with a hand-made rat-trap and a curry comb for horses.

Standing at the top of High Street is the **Golden Lion**, which has been trading since it first opened in the early 19th century. In those days the road, originally known as the Narrows, used to be busy with nearby markets and being on the main route from Aberystwyth. It was only closed to traffic in 1981, de-cobbled and pedestrianised. The landlord in the mid-19th century may have been a Mr. Wild, for the present owner received a letter from a man in Canada called Wild saying that his great-grandfather used to be the licensee then and that his grandfather was born in the pub and later killed in action during the First World War. In 1858, however, the landlord was Edward Williams. At any rate the **Golden Lion** was owned by Ind Coope, brewers, who extended the inn at the rear. At some point the roof was raised, but the original timbers were retained. In 1890 Ind Coope was fined £2 for allowing a wall to be built at the back which blocked a passage from the house next door – the wall had to be knocked down. In 1895 the landlord was John Griffiths with George Griffiths, possibly the son, taking over in 1906.

Above : The Golden Lion
Left: The inn sign

He owned land by the river where he kept bullocks which were regarded as being among the best in the area. The inn was taken over in the late 1930s by Sid Farmer, who ran it until the early 1960s, when Mrs. Cornes became landlady. It was during her 24-year tenure that internal alterations were made, turning two small rooms into one bar and a second front door converted into a window. An advertisement in the *Knighton Official Guide* of 1981 stated: 'Harold and Iris welcome you to the Golden Lion'.

In 1986 the **Golden Lion** was bought from Allied Breweries (Ind Coope having joined forces with Ansells and Taylor Walker) by the present owners, Brian and Linda Nash. Today, the pub is a popular venue for football players and supporters with Mr. Nash sponsoring Knighton Town Football Club.

The be-decked Fleece Inn for the coronation of Elizabeth II in 1953

Almost opposite the **Golden Lion** on the other side of the road, at the beginning of Market Street is the **Fleece** guest house, which was an 18th-century inn, built on much older foundations. Wide stairs lead down to a capacious cellar where a now-disused spiral staircase finishes at ground floor level. It is conjectured that the staircase may have led up to a watch tower belonging to the nearby castle, the outer wall of which is at the rear of the inn. When being run as a public house, the **Fleece** had a front entrance opposite the **Golden Lion** and another one by the existing mounting block. It had five rooms on the ground floor, three of which were used for drinking. On the first floor was a clubroom, built over the yard, a spirit room and three bedrooms. Another two bedrooms were on the second floor. Outside was a stable for four horses. In 1858 the landlord was Richard Hatfield, about whom an interesting reference is made by William Hatfield in his book *Knighton & District*. After the demolition in 1869 of the old Butter Cross in Market Square, a Market Hall Company was set up. Among the company's trustees was 'Richard Hatfield, The Fleece Inn, a builder and contractor and who is believed to have built it' (the Market Hall, also called the Town Hall).

In 1901 the landlord was Henry Ashley, who was also described as a butcher, but by 1906 Thomas Cooper was in place. In 1914 the **Fleece**, then run by Edward Ford, was in danger of being closed down when objections to the renewal of its licence were raised by the licensing authority, the main one being that there were still too many pubs – a total of 12. However, the owner, Lt.-Col. William Southam, had decided to sacrifice the **Lamb**, the other Knighton pub he owned, and the **Fleece** was allowed to continue.

Now the Fleece guest house

In 1926 the landlord was again Thomas Cooper, followed by Gordon Tudge who, according to two old inhabitants, killed himself with a shotgun in the pub in 1938. In the same year, the *Brecon and Radnor Express* of 24 February reported that Michael Neary was charged with being drunk and disorderly at the **Fleece**, and for assaulting two police officers who came to arrest him. He was sentenced to three months hard labour. During the war years it was run by the Brokenshaw family, who came from the **Kinsley Hotel**, with Mrs. Brokenshaw entertaining customers on the piano. Bob Evans then took it over in the 1950s and after his death it was run for a short time by his widow, Laura, before closing in 1969. The **Fleece** was turned into a guest house 15 years ago by the present owners. A new entrance is now positioned in Market Street.

An empty space on the other side of the road opposite the **Fleece** is where once stood the **Seven Stars** or **Stars**, an ancient hostelry operating in the 18th and 19th centuries. This pub name dates from the 15th century and was popular because of its easily recognisable shape. The landlord in 1851 was John James, aged 72, and then later Thomas White, who remained there until 1869 when the inn was knocked down, together with the Butter Cross. They made way for a new Market Hall, the ground floor being the market and the upstairs used for Quarter Sessions and early assemblies, concerts and entertainments. Later the market area housed the fire engine and during the Second World War it became an egg-packing station, while the upper floor became a canteen used by evacuees and primary school children until the school closed in 1970. The local council then held social functions there before the building was demolished in 1987. Clearance work on the site in

1994 revealed arched cellars, no doubt those of the **Seven Stars**. Nearby Norton Street was once called Stars Close when it belonged to the inn.

Almost next door to the empty Market Hall site on the corner of a lane is a detached property divided into two, Nos. 3 and 4 Market Street, formerly the **King's Head**. Which king's head was illustrated on the sign is not known, but the most popular one is that of Henry VIII. The inn is believed to have started trading in the early 18th century and, built in an L-shape, appears to have consisted of one long room on the ground floor with another above, probably used for dining and functions. At the rear was a yard with a stable. According to a map of 1851, the **King's Head** also had stables in West Street. In that year, Ann James, a 46 year-old widow, was the licensee at about the time when complaints were made that 'the impurities from a Privy at the King's Head Inn washed through the town'. In 1858 the inn was run by Richard Thomas.

The former King's Head, now an art studio and a private house

In 1906 William Davies was the landlord and in 1910 William Savigar was licensee at an annual rent of £24, when it was owned by Mrs. Thomas of Shrewsbury. The inn seems to have occupied only part of the building then, because it was described as 'being a small alehouse with a tap room and bar parlour, both small rooms, and a back kitchen outside'. In 1911 its licence was reviewed by the County Licensing Committee, when takings for the year from March 1910 amounted to £170 3s. 5d., exclusive of food. Sales in 1910 were 36 barrels of beer, 114 dozen bottles of beer, 52 gallons of spirits and 4½ gallons of wine. The average for the years 1908 and 1909 would have been the same. The police reported, however, that in 1911 'very little business is done there' and that there were five other licensed houses within a radius of about 100 yards. The inn's licence was not renewed and compensation of £200 was awarded to the owner and £20 to the licensee. However, it seems to have re-opened at a later date because according to details that went with a 1926 map of Knighton, the **King's Head** was listed with William Davies back as landlord. It must shortly afterwards have finally closed, with the ground floor being converted into two shops. In the 1970s the property was divided into two with a garage built in the back yard. Today, the garage has been integrated into No.4 and forms the studio for its owner, artist Ursula Bayer, who uses the front part as a gallery for her work.

On the other side of the road is a blocked alley, which used to be called Childs Alley, on one side of which is a garage somewhat incongruously called Pooh Corner. This is believed to be the site of the **Feathers** or **Plume of Feathers**, a name usually referring to the plume of three ostrich feathers, first adopted as a crest by the Black Prince, although in Ludlow the sign is for Arthur, Prince of Wales. It could also allude to the expression 'a feather in your cap'. The inn was first mentioned in 1797 and was still in existence in 1851, but probably closed soon afterwards. It later became a lodging house before being demolished in the late 1950s.

The deeds of the **Plough Inn**, at 40 Market Street, date back to 1716 when the square was known as Nelson Square and when it appeared to own the nearby Harp. In the 19th century the area was called the Pig Market with 33 houses and several shops, and described as a virtual 'hive of industry'. The market was held in an orchard between the Plough and the Harp, with sheep also being bought and sold. The **Plough** was also popular for broom weddings, a custom at the time not uncommon in Wales nor confined to gypsies. A broom was placed across the inn's porch over which a couple jumped, who then considered themselves to be married. This may relate to a custom whereby newlyweds leaving church had their path barred by a rope and had to pay dues to be let through. Although the **Plough** is not mentioned by name, the 1841 census reveals that John Jones, aged 45, was a publican in the Pig Market and 10 years later William Jones was victualler, with a 17-

A 1919 celebration outside the Plough Inn

45

year-old son as a corn buyer, who was still there in 1859. By 1895 Kelly's *Directory* lists the **Plough** by name with Mrs. Mary Jones, possibly the daughter, as the landlady. In the early 20th century the inn was owned by Herman Strauss, who also owned the Wine Vaults in the Narrows and the Bull Hotel in Presteigne. In 1926 James Savager was at the helm.

In 1930 the licensee was John Thomas, but five years later the inn, now owned by the Wrekin Brewery, of Wellington, Shropshire, was closed down. This followed a review by the county licensing committee when the **Plough** was described as:

> built of stone, rough cast in front, with slate roof and contains the following accommodation: tap room, bar, bar parlour, smoke room, kitchen, store room, pantry, six bedrooms, box room, passages and cellar. The house is clean and the rooms are in good condition. Years ago, the kitchen was a brewhouse and is not under the same roof as the remainder of the house, and adjoins one of the stables and is connected to the main house by a porch. The outbuildings comprise - two stables, hay loft, trap house, coal and wood shed, back yard, in which there is a lean-to wash house, and a garden. The outbuildings, with the exception of one of the stables, are in a bad state of repair.' The report added that the house was not equipped with a bathroom and that there was one W.C. and one urinal, in fair condition and clean. However, 'The W.C. is used both by the public and the occupants of the house, which is most unsatisfactory.

It was noted that the inn was situated in a quiet part of the town with little or no through traffic and that during 40 visits made by police in the last three years the average number of customers per visit was only three. In refusing renewal of the licence, it was said that the inn was unnecessary, with the comment 'Nearly all the people attending the Auctions now travelled by motor bus and cars, and the call for accommodation and stabling was now very small.' The tenant, John Thomas, claimed all the bar fixtures except the beer engine and fixed seating, adding he was about £150 worse off than when he had first come to the inn. Compensation of £600 was agreed, including £60 to Mr. Thomas.

After ceasing to trade, the hand plough by the front entrance was removed and the **Plough** became a private dwelling lived in by three families. It was owned by Mrs. Parkes, who on her death left it to her daughter, Mary Evans, who in turn left it to her four daughters, one of whom, Sarah Scotford, acquired it. In 1957 Mrs. Scotford lived in part of the property for 18 months before getting married and moving to Leamington Spa to run a pub. Then in the mid-1970s, she returned to Knighton with her husband, Raymond, and two children and lived in the Plough as a private house before deciding to re-open it as a licensed house. Although the whole place needed modernising,

The Plough in 2005

the interior was kept mainly as it used to be but enlarged at the rear with the building of a functions room. Now the focal point of Nelson Square, the **Plough** played a major role in the 200th anniversary celebrations of the death of Nelson at the Battle of Trafalgar in October 2005. On sale at the **Plough** was a specially brewed Victory ale. Today, the inn comprises a public bar, lounge bar and dining area with five letting rooms.

Higher up Market Street on the left-hand side is Harp Cottage, a stone building, which is thought to have been the **Harp Inn** in the 18th century. It became the town's police station before a new one was built in Broad Street and was then converted into a private residence. Also in this area was the **Royal Oak Inn**, which closed sometime in the early 19th century and became a shop and dwelling house.

In Russell Street on the corner of Back Lane is a private dwelling called the Wine Vaults, which used to trade under the name of the **Old Wine Vaults** and previously as the **Horse Shoes** or **Three Horse Shoes**. Originally built of stone with a slate roof, the house became licensed in the early 19th century, and offered a bar, smoke room, jug-and-bottle and parlour. Accommodation included a kitchen, back kitchen, pantry and six bedrooms together with an attic and cellar. There was also a shoemaker's shop and various outbuildings,

47

The Old Wine Vaults in the 1920s with Walter James and daughter Nora

but there was no accommodation for traps and horses and later cars. In the 1858/59 Slater's *Directory* the inn was listed as the **Three Horse Shoes** with Stephen Reynolds as landlord. For over 50 years the licence was held either by William James or his son Walter during which period the name was changed to the **Old Wine Vaults**. One regular customer in the 1910s was Meg the Gypsy (Mrs. Lloyd) who, after walking around with a basket on her head selling everything from cake tins to bits of elastic, ended up in the **Wine Vaults**. In 1926 it was described as selling 'Wines & spirits of the finest quality at reasonable prices', and 'bottles of Burton ales and Coombe's invalid stout'.

In 1929 it was bought by George Oakley and Richard Parkes, of Shrewsbury, for £600 including a cottage let separately at 4s. a week. They retained the services of Walter, who had taken over the licence from his father in 1922, and paid him £1 a week as manager with free coal and light. Walter was by trade a painter and plumber. But in 1932 when the licence came up for renewal it was refused although the 'house is well furnished and clean and in good repair'. Again the licensing authorities were of the opinion there were too many pubs in Knighton. Trade had in fact improved with 94 gallons of spirits and 50 gallons of wine sold in 1931 as against 58 and 44 gallons in 1929. Beer and cider sales had also increased. Average weekly takings were £18 in 1930 – higher in 1931 – while average annual profit was £91. The Compensation Authority recommended that the owners should deal generously with the licensee, who made no claim for

Walter James behind the bar in the Old Wine Vaults

compensation, on his giving up possession of the premises. In the event compensation of £475 was awarded including £50 to Mr. James. Since then the **Old Wine Vaults** has reverted to domestic use, with the name recently revived.

Another pub described as being near the old Market Hall was the **Barley Mow**, which was trading in the 19th century. This may have been on the site of a small house opposite the **Old Wine Vaults** which still has a cellar with a trap door open to the road.

To the north of the town, at the junction of Offa's Road and the B4355 Knucklas road, is Conjuror's Drive, where once stood the **Conjuror's Inn**. Probably trading in the 18th and early 19th centuries, it has since been demolished. The inn was sited

A reminder of the old Conjuror's Pitch where once stood the Conjuror's Inn

near Offa's Dyke in an area known as Conjuror's Pitch, where conjurors, sometimes called wizards or white witches, practised their healing powers for a fee. They knew both good and evil spells and were consulted by people from a wide area regarding their own health and also that of their animals. The conjurors, who often inspired fear, also offered other services including astrology, fortune-telling, the detection of lost or stolen property, and protection against witchcraft.

Back along Broad Street and opposite the **Knighton Hotel** is Station Road, down which stands the **Horse and Jockey Inn**, one of the oldest buildings in the town. Of late medieval origins, it occupies a U-shape around a courtyard at the junction between Wylcwm Street and Wylcwm Place. It is a two-storey stone building with an attic, the roof to which has been heightened, and a chimney stack added in the 17th century. To one side of the courtyard is a separate cottage while at the rear were large stables with hayloft above and gardens behind. The area was originally known as the Bull Ring until at least 1841 when bulls were sold at the Fairs and bull- and bear-baiting was probably held. This was a popular spectacle in Tudor and Stewart times when the beasts were usually tethered and set upon by dogs. The landlord, who probably hired the bear-keeper, would have enjoyed increased trade from the large crowd of all classes that the baiting, on which bets were placed, attracted. It was made illegal in 1835. The inn, which originally traded under another name, possibly even the **Bull Ring**, was probably called the **Horse and Jockey** as the earliest location, of a regular race meeting dating back to Queen Anne was on Bailey Hill. A race-course was later built by the river in 1867.

According to the 1841 census, the publican was William Rogers, aged 35, then in 1858 it was William Cooper to be succeeded by his widow, Mrs. Ann Cooper, in the 1860s. The inn was owned by Lewis Turner who in his will of 1868 directed that Mrs. Cooper, the present tenant, 'shall occupy the same during the term of her natural life'. In 1906 William

The Frothballs at the Horse and Jockey

Edwards had taken over the licence, and was still there in 1926 when the inn was described as having 'every accommodation for cyclists' and provided 'wines & spirits of the finest quality'. Edwards' sister, Topsy, took it over in the 1930s. A popular visitor, especially with the farmer customers, was Tim Bywater – a bonesetter and healer, who held surgeries in the **Horse and Jockey** up until the late 1950s. His mother was a Lloyd and he was possibly related to Silver John Lloyd, the legendary bonesetter of the 19th century (see chapter 11). According to Roy Palmer:

> Bywater boasted that he could pull a bull's hip back in – a tremendous feat of skill and strength. He took no payment for his ministrations but would accept a gift, preferably a whisky. One farmer, invited to choose between a doctor of 40 years' experience and the bonesetter, said 'Bywater every bloody time'.

Bywater died in about 1970.

In the late 1960s and '70s the **Horse and Jockey** was run by Percy and Christine Branford, when it was owned by Ansells Brewery. After being closed and boarded up for a while, it re-opened and then in the 1980s was bought by Keven Unsworth, who turned the old stables into a restaurant. In 1989 it was bought by the present owners, Gary and Jackie Salt. Stairs lead up from the front door to private accommodation, where once was a large room used for dining and functions. The lounge bar is to the left and the public bar on the right with a relatively new counter area serving both bars. Stairs used to be above the counter with a passage way running through into the public bar. Still a feature there, although no longer used, is an inglenook fireplace with a large cross beam scarred with burn marks. These were

caused, or so the story goes, by mugs hung there from nails by wick which some-times caught fire and charred the wood.

To one side is a games room with a false roof which used to be a yard and now leading into the kitchen which has been extended. Ancient timbers are in evidence in the attic which has been

In the Horse and Jockey the old chimney cross-beam shows charred marks

converted into bedrooms. The restaurant now seats 80, but the garden behind was sold off by Ansells and is now a lorry park. On display in the lounge bar is a walker's hat which was auctioned for £98 ten years ago to raise money for Children in Need. To date £1,100 has been collected for the charity. Continuing the connection with local farmers who attend the weekly cattle markets held nearby, Gary and Jackie provide lunch and dinner for them on Christmas Fatstock Day.

General view of the Horse and Jockey with the cottage on the right

By the bridge over the River Teme, before reaching the railway station, is the Kinsley guest house, formerly the **Kinsley Hotel**, the **Central Wales Hotel**, and also known as the **Railway Inn**. Erected about 1865 after the construction of the railway, this three-storey stone building took its name from the Central Wales line. It was owned for many years by the Lichfield Bewery and later by Ansells. As well as providing accommodation for the new rail travellers, the hotel also catered for the railway workers. There were three bars, in one of which was a piano where sing-songs were a popular feature; upstairs was a dining room and six bedrooms. Stables were situated at the rear with an archway leading to open fields. Flooding of the Teme and Cwm brook was often a problem, with the hotel's cellars filling with water and barrels floating about. According to Kelly's *Directory* of 1895, when it was called the **Railway Inn**, the landlady was Mrs Martha Parton. In 1906 the landlord was Edward Roberts, who was still in charge in 1926. One old inhabitant recalls under-age youngsters going round the back past the cellars

The Kinsley, former Central Wales Hotel (centre) with adjoining stables and round house (extreme right) in 1904

and drinking glasses of cider in a back room. Mr. Brokenshaw was landlord in the 1930s when the hotel was re-named the **Kinsley** after the Kinsley Wood across the river, before he moved to the **Fleece** in 1939. Marge and Lance Edwards took over in the late 1950s and ran it for about 30 years before it was bought from Ansells in the late 1980s by Alan and Sarah Screens. Then in 1995 the *County Times* reported:

> A Knighton pub is being saved from extinction by one of its former regulars. The Kinsley, just a few yards inside Wales, changed owners, and even its name, before shutting down 18 months ago. Now it is set to enjoy a new lease of life thanks to local man John Owen. John, who presently works for a firm of builders' merchants, used to play cribbage in the Kinsley after work. His favourite pub changed its name [back] to the Central Wales Hotel to stress its links with the scenic railway but all to no avail. When it closed, most of the regulars shrugged their shoulders and chose another drinking place, but John was determined to see pints being filled in his local again. Even if he had to buy it himself. Now his dream has come true.

Hounds at the Central Wales Hotel

53

The Kinsey before it stopped trading in 2005

John, who was born in Station Road, changed the name back to the **Kinsley**, and ran it with his wife Helen. No longer operating as a hotel, the Owen family lived upstairs, having turned the dining area into a sitting room. There were two bars and a pool room on the ground floor. The stables were demolished a long time ago. It stopped trading as an inn at the end of 2005, and re-opened after refurbishment as a bed-and-breakfast establishment in May 2006

Across the bridge round the corner is a building divided into flats with a circular front known as the **Round House**. It was built as a public house, which could open on Sundays, by Mr. Powis in the late 19th century but was never granted a licence. There was controversy over whether or not the building was in Shropshire because the river, marking the boundary, had been diverted when the railway line was constructed. But if it was in England then the pub would be able to stay open on a Sunday to which there was strong local objection. As it came under the Knighton justices, the licence was refused and it never opened.

About a mile-and-a-half to the east of Knighton on the A4113 road to Ludlow is **Milebrook House Hotel**, in the Teme Valley, a stone building constructed in 1760 as a dower house for the nearby Stanage Castle. It was appropriate, therefore, that in 1922 it should be leased from Charles Rogers, owner of Stanage Park and Lord Lieutenant of Radnorshire, by Mrs. Kathleen Thesiger, whose husband had just died. It was home, too, for the next 20 years for her two sons, Brian and Wilfred, the latter eventually to become famous as an explorer and writer, including *Arabian Sands*. In 1937 Mrs. Thesiger received a visit at Milebrook from an old family friend – the Emperor Haile Selassie. They had first met when Mr. Thesiger was British Minister in Abyssinia, but at that time the Emperor was a refugee in England after his country had been invaded by Mussolini. Dorothy Tantrum, who used to work at Milebrook, recalls: 'The Emperor wore a black cloak and only spoke French and I distinctly remember his lovely long hands and nails'.

Milebrook in those days consisted of an entrance hall, four rooms, a kitchen and a servants' hall with six bedrooms and an attic. 'For years we had no telephone', Wilfred wrote in his auobiography, 'and the house was lit in our time by acetylene gas which we made each evening in the pigsty'.

The house was bought in 1986 by Rodney and Beryl Marsden who converted it into a hotel. After restoring and adapting the building to the needs of a country hotel, they built a new wing, providing space for a restaurant and extra bedrooms. The wing was fittingly opened, in 1996, by Thesiger, now Sir Wilfred, who died seven years later. Four acres of grounds surround the hotel including a kitchen garden, a croquet lawn and a paddock planted with over 600 native trees surrounding a wildlife pond and bog garden.

Other inns or beer houses which are believed to have existed, but whose location is unknown, include the **Angel**, mentioned in 1777; the **New Inn**, mentioned in 1785; the **Queen's Head**, mentioned in 1860; the **Sun**, mentioned between 1823 and 1829; the **Black Swan**; the **New Inn**, possibly in Bridge Street; the **Steer**; and the **White Horse**. It is possible that some of the inns already listed may have traded under these names at an earlier date.

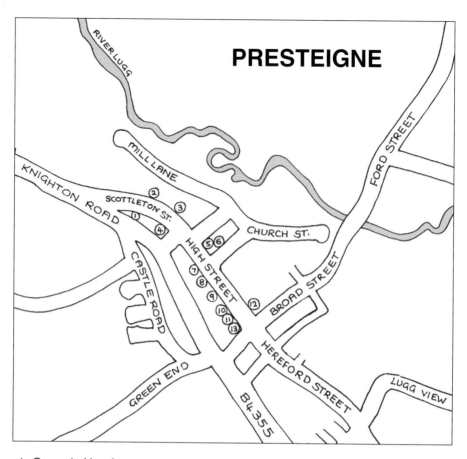

1 Queen's Head
2 Bell
3 Royal Oak *
4 George
5 Globe
6 Bull *
7 Radnorshire Arms *

8 New
9 Castle
10 Lion
11 King's Head
12 White Hart
13 Red Lion

*_– Open in 2006_
See also page 82

CHAPTER FOUR

Presteigne

SCOTTLETON ST., ST. DAVID'S ST. & HIGH ST.

Yes, where I spent my childhood days
I long again to be,
The wide world holds no sweeter place
Than old Presteign for me.

(Corporal W.G. Millichamp, 7th King's Shropshire Light Infantry. Killed at Bapame 2 September 1918.)

Lying on the south bank of the river Lugg with Offa's Dyke close to the west, Presteigne is a border town which has come under the influence of both England and Wales. For centuries it was the county town of Radnorshire with courts and a thriving market.

Originally known as Presthemede, it was a small community of priests which later came under St. Andrew's church and the centre of the Lordship of Presteigne. The Lordship passed to the Mortimer family of Wigmore and the town expanded with a castle built on the Warden, later destroyed by Llewelyn ap Gruffydd in 1262. With the accession by Edward, Duke of York and heir of the Mortimers, to the throne as Edward IV, the Mortimer estates passed into royal hands.

Later, in the 16th century, the union of England and Wales saw the formation of five new counties including Radnorshire. At first Presteigne shared the role of county town with New Radnor, but by 1660 it gained sole control. The town also became the venue for Great and Quarter Sessions, where lesser crimes were tried and county administration included regulations concerning baking bread and brewing. Both courts were held at the Shire Hall which stood at the junction of High Street and Broad Street. The goal, previously at New Radnor castle, was relocated in Presteigne.

Presteigne suffered plague epidemics with the worst in 1636 when 44 people died. During the Civil War, the town was loyal to the Royalists having personal links with Charles I who went hunting in the nearby 240 acre Northwood. It was the scene of one of the earliest skirmishes in Wales, being raided in 1642 to block a possible Royalist advance. Three Royalist soldiers were killed and six of the leaders captured. In 1643 it was again raided by Parliamentarian forces when two troops of cavalry occupied the town briefly. Some 3,000 Royalist troops were quartered in the town when Charles made two journeys through Radnorshire in 1645. In December of that year Colonel John Birch, the parliamentarian governor of Hereford, established a garrison at Presteigne to try and control the largely Royalist borderland. The town was compelled to maintain the garrison on free quarter for 12 months.

Attempts by Cromwell to try and improve the nation's morals and drinking habits did not go down well, or at any rate not in Presteigne. The Great Sessions of 1652 presented 45 people as 'common tipplers, common drunkards and alehouse haunters'.

By now the population of Presteigne had grown to about 750 with 128 houses, but tragedy was to strike with the great fire of 12 September 1681 when the town was 'almost burned to the ground'. The fire destroyed between 55 and 65 timber-framed buildings, mainly with walls of wattle and daub and thatched roofs, including commercial properties and the school. The fire, which principally affected High Street and St. David's Street, which then included Church Street, caused damage that was estimated at £6,150.

However, Presteigne recovered and was soon thriving as a market town. Cattle were of some considerable importance with a weekly 'Beaste Markett' and the holding of livestock fairs. And local beasts joined the flow of Welsh cattle heading for London on the minor drovers' road that passed through the town together with two 'feeder' roads.

Another staple industry in the 18th century was malting, with barley being grown locally. Several of the town's inns including the **Duke's Arms**, the **Castle**, the **George** and the **Barley Mow** produced malt for their own brewing needs, and there were at least five commercial malthouses. One malthouse alone produced between 4,000 and 6,000 bushels of malt per season. But this industry was ruined by the Malt Tun Act of 1880 which provided more favourable taxation for large-scale businesses and the last malthouse closed in 1892. As a result a large cooperage at Green End saw business decline. Other specialised crops such as flax and hops were processed in the town and there was a Hop Yard near Gallows Lane.

The Great Sessions and Quarter Sessions were also good for trade with dinners and assemblies being held at local inns. Similar events happened following Parliamentary elections when the successful candidates provided dinners for the gentry and meals and beer for the other supporters. Even prisoners in the gaol sometimes received free meals and beer!

Dinners were sumptuous in comparison to today's standards. The menu for an Agricultural Society dinner in 1878 comprised: soup, turbot and lobster sauce, cod and oyster sauce; roast beef, sucking pig, boiled turkey and celery sauce, roast turkey and bread sauce, boiled fowls, roast fowls, tongues, roast goose and apple sauce, roast duck and onion sauce, haunch of mutton and caper sauce, roast veal, pheasant, hares. The 'pastry' course was apricot tartlets, apple pie, custards, damson tarts, plum pudding, jelly, followed by cheese, butter and dessert. The wines were of the choicest brands. These dinners, which were for men only, usually began at 3.30 or 4 p.m. and might continue until midnight. There were rarely fewer than 20 toasts, each preceded by a speech. County, Hunt and Race balls were equally popular with substantial suppers served at 1 a.m. and dancing continuing until 6 a.m.

Two annual days — the May Fair, and the Warden's Wake held in June – attracted large crowds. The Warden's Wake boasted wrestling, drinking booths and various competitions including skittling for a pig, but the event caused so many fights and drunkenness that it was stopped soon after 1900.

With the London to Aberystwyth road, known as the Great Road, passing through Presteigne, the town soon saw an increase in traffic. Carrier's carts and stagewagons rumbled through the town, with changes of horse and postchaises for hire being available at the **Rose and Crown**, the **White Hart** and the **New Inn**. By 1794 a weekly stagecoach service was operating between Knighton and London, via Presteigne and Wigmore alternately. The coach left Knighton at noon on Friday but did not reach London until Sunday morning. By the turn of the century the Aberystwyth to Worcester coach was running via Presteigne on a regular basis. Coaching facilities were then available at the **Oxford, Castle, Radnorshire Arms**, and **Duke's Arms**, the last two inns being the most popular.

The increased prosperity of the town in the late 18th and early 19th centuries saw a steady increase in the number of inns. From about 1750 onwards records show that at least 32 inns, beer and cider houses have operated in the town, with the maximum number in any year being 16 in 1822. However, some of them were simply a room in someone's home that provided food and drink on market and fair days. In Pigot's *Directory* of 1830 12 innkeepers and three malsters were listed.

According to W.H. Howse, an old man recalling the 1870s, commented that

> the numerous houses in Presteigne were open from 6 a.m. until 11 p.m. without a break; brawls were frequent, especially on Saturday nights, when it was seldom that there was not a free fight in one part of the town or another.

But things were beginning to change. In the 1820s the London to Aberystwyth road was re-routed through Kington and by 1889 Presteigne's primary role in local government came to an abrupt end when the newly formed County Council went to Llandrindod Wells, followed the next year by the police authority.

Today, Presteigne has lapsed into somewhat of a backwater although it comes to life during the holding of three annual festivals. The recently refurbished and award-winning Judge's Lodging in Broad Street is one visual reminder of the town's past history.

The **Queen's Head** used to be at 1 Castle Dyche, at the top end of Scottleton Street. Probably named after Elizabeth I, it was a beer house in the 18th and 19th centuries and may have operated as an inn for a time. It is now a private house.

A beer house called the **Bell** (of which it has been said 'it speaks all languages') at No. 2/3 opened in the 18th century. It was originally known

The one-time Queen's Head

as the **Bluebell Inn**, and a garden gate at the rear of the property perpetuates the name with bluebells depicted in wrought iron. The pub probably closed in the late 19th century. Now a private house, the building retains its original external shape apart from a new front door.

Opened in 1823, the **Royal Oak** was known as the 'Top Oak' to distinguish it from its Broad

Once the Bell Inn, the garden gate still preserves the memory

Street rival. But while the latter closed in the early 20th century, the **Royal Oak** continues to flourish. The name, of course, is associated with King Charles II, who hid from noon to dusk in the Boscobel Oak near Shifnal in Shropshire while trying to evade pursuing Roundhead soldiers. In 1830 the

The Royal Oak in the late 1950s

The Royal Oak in 2004

landlord was John Bywater and between at least 1857 and 1859 William Watkin was in charge. By 1890 the landlord was George Harper who also described himself as a butcher, and in 1914 Mrs. Margaret Harper had taken over. There used to be two bars, one on each side of the front entrance, with probably an off-licence outlet in between. The pub was closed for a while in the 1990s with all the windows boarded up, but new landlords eventually came along who turned the two bars into one and established a small restaurant at the back. A case of silverware on display in the inn demonstrates the expertise of some of the regulars when taking part in Presteigne Golfing Society events.

Another beerhouse called the **George,** referring either to the patron saint of England or a king of that name, is known to have existed in the 18th and 19th centuries, but its exact location is unkown. It was, however, probably opposite the **Royal Oak** and could have been in the lane running alongside the garage where a row of cottages was demolished.

Now called Globe House, a building on the corner of Pound Lane was once the **Globe,** a 19th-century beer house. The first reference to it is in 1828 but it was not listed in later commercial directories. The sign may have portrayed a wizard gazing into a crystal ball.

On the corner of St. David's Street with High Street, the **Bull Hotel** was formerly the **Old Bull** probably dating as far back as the early 16th century. The earliest deeds of 1801 refer to the inn 'for many, many, many years under the sign of the Old Bull', and enjoyed a high reputation as a hostelry for it looked onto the market place with the Town Cross and stocks nearby. It was also the scene of bull baiting, an 'entertainment' that continued until the early 19th century. The bull was tethered by a chain to a strong post near the inn and people of all classes gathered round to watch and bet as bulldogs, one at a time, were set to bait the bull. It was quite a profitable business for both the bull's keeper and the landlord. Up until the 1880s the site was called Skin Cross Corner because the tanners brought their skins there.

The **Bull** was rebuilt in the 1820s and extended over the site of the old market square, which originally started from the middle of the present bar. The new building included a garage and petrol pump which was replaced at the end of World War Two by the hotel's own garage. Two large bay windows, one Georgian the other Victorian, were added to the front of the hotel. The licensed area, divided into two bars and an off-licence, was turned into one open-plan bar in the 1960s. It also has a dining room and six bedrooms.

One of the **Bull's** most celebrated landlords was Thomas Burch who had been a great soldier before becoming the landlord in at least 1830. A Sergeant in the Cameron Highlanders, he served in Egypt, the Peninsular War, and

Waterloo and was engaged in 'upwards of 30 battles, sieges and skirmishes'. He died in 1850 aged 68 and is buried in St. Andrew's graveyard. Mr. Burch was landlord in 1840 when the town celebrated the marriage of Queen Victoria with a dinner at the inn. James Meredith was in charge from approximately 1857 to 1880, while William and Annie Burt had taken over in the 1890s. By 1914 William Steiner was landlord and still surviving today is an old spirit quarter bottle marked 'W. Steiner, Bull Hotel, Presteign'. At that time spirits were delivered

Two views of the Bull Hotel in the 1920s

Sporting events at the Bull Hotel

in hogsheads and dispensed in much smaller amounts. The **Bull** enjoyed a reputation as a sportsman's inn with fly-fishing in the nearby Lugg being one of the main activities. This has led to a large number of stuffed fish in glass cases decorating the bar.

In the 1950s and '60s, the hotel was run by Doug James and his wife, who welcomed customers with a board proclaiming: 'Bwyd blasus, cwrw da, cwmni diddan ... lechyd da!' – 'Good food, good beer, good company ... good health!' It went on:

Today you could easily hear the following: How be yer? Kemist! Noo ... ye binna! Any local drinking man will translate. As during the past 200 years 27 inns were open (fortunately not all at the same time) getting kemist presented no problem. There were also many private brewers and cider makers. All for a population of 1,200.

The magnificent black and white building in High Street, now the **Radnorshire Arms Hotel** was originally the country retreat of one of Elizabeth I's favourites, Sir Christopher Hatton, who became Lord Chancellor and died in 1591. It is possible it came into his possession in the 1530s when the property was forfeited to the crown following the Babington plot against Elizabeth.

Among those involved in the plot were several local gentry including the owner of the

Left: The quarter bottle belonging to William Steiner of the Bull Hotel

The Bull Hotel and its sign in 2004

Presteigne property. It was then purchased in 1616 by John Bradshaw 'whose family had great influence on the town' and who considerably enlarged it. 'Erroneously connected with his namesake, one of the signatories of Charles I's death warrant', Bradshaw was forced three years later to sell his manor house and estate. According to a deed:

> John Bradshaw, his wife Sible, Edmund Bradshaw and Roger Bradshaw (his brothers) made a grant on trust to John Reade of London, his mansion house where he dwells, etc, in consideration of £1,200.

The Radnorshire Arms in the 1920s

65

The Radnorshire Hunt meeting at the Radnorshire Arms

Bradshaw spent his last years at his new home, known as Cross House. Later, in 1792, the house became an inn, possibly called the **Crown** to begin with, and then the **Radnorshire Arms**. It quickly claimed importance as a coaching inn and as a county social centre.

With large stables opposite, the inn quickly became a busy posting house on the London to Aberystwyth coaching route, where coaches changed horses. There was a lapse of about 12 years, when the coaches went through Kington, but the Presteigne service resumed in 1833 with the introduction of a 'New Patent Safety Coach,' called the *Prince of Wales*. Passengers to London stayed the night at Worcester before catching the *Aurora* coach next day. The **Radnorshire Arms**, which in 1820 became the first inn in Radnorshire to adopt the title 'hotel', also provided travellers with other conveyances.

Two well known travel writers who stayed at the **Radnorshire Arms** made some interesting comments. In 1801 G. Lipscomb in his *Journey into Wales* wrote:

The plaque commemorating Sir Christopher Hatton

The Radnorshire Arms in the 1960s

> The civil face of our landlady at the Radnorshire Arms, the civilities received from all, compared with that in England was highly disadvantageous to our own countrymen [English].

Then in the middle of the century George Borrow, author of *Wild Wales* and *The Romany Rye*, asked one of the maids at the hotel whether Presteigne was in Wales or England. 'Neither', she replied, 'simply in Radnorshire'.

Among the social events held at the hotel was a celebratory dinner for dignitaries of the town and county to mark the passing of the Reform Act in June 1832. This followed a procession, complete with a band and banners, and the distribution of bread, meat and cider to the townspeople. Another celebratory dinner was held in 1837 when local lawyer and banker Cecil Parsons was presented with silver plate to commemorate his victory to safeguard 'cottagers' rights after buyers of several crown manors in the county wanted to throw out long-established squatters from the holdings. Processions, fireworks and a bonfire organised by Parsons's supporters led to a summons alleging 'riotous behaviour'.

W.H. Howse gave a list of the charges at the **Radnorshire Arms** in 1835:

... breakfast, 1s. 9d. (servants, 1s. 3d.); lunch 2s. (servants 1s. 6d.); tea 1s. 6d.; supper 1s. 3d.; bread and cheese 6d; coffee 1s. 6d.' A bed at the inn cost 1s. 6d. a night. We may assume that the liquor bill was a substantial extra, otherwise the cost of feeding a horse on hay and corn for the night, put at about 8s. would make the animal's expenses more than those of the man. Sherry, port, brandy and rum were the favourite forms of refreshment. Gin and negus (hot, sweetened wine and water) were also fairly common items. Mulled wine was only occasionally asked for and punch and whisky were also in seldom demand.

The Radnorshire Arms Hotel

Above : The heraldic device over the front door

Left : The lounge bar in 2004

In the same year, the hotel supplied rum at 17s. a gallon and gin at 14s. a gallon. Some of the town's concerts were held in the **Radnorshire Arms** instead of in the room over the market hall. In 1830 the landlord was Robert Phillips while in 1844 Harriet Phillips, presumably his widow, held the licence and also ran an excise office. Edward Harley and his son were in charge in the 1850s followed by Thomas Harley, probably the son, in the 1860s.

In Victorian times the premises were considerably enlarged to the rear with the addition of a large dining room, now called the Hatton Restaurant, and more bedrooms. In 1881 the proprietor was Mr. W. Clements who was summonsed for selling '1 quart of adulterated Irish Whiskey in November, 1880 to Mr. J. Wheldon of Pennybont'. He was ordered to pay costs of

The Radnorshire Arms in 2004

45 shillings. In the 1890s, when it was advertised as a 'family, commercial and tourists hotel and posting house', it was run by Elizabeth Baldwin and by 1914 Montague Kemp was landlord. The hotel came to be owned by Trust Houses, later known as Forte, and after the demise of that hotel empire its owners included Grenada and Regal before being taken over by its present owners, Drayton Manor Hotels, in 1996.

Despite modernisation the **Radnorshire Arms** today retains most of its original features including the fenestration and close-studded framing, giving it its black-beamed 'Magpie' appearance, and fascinating chimneys. The front porch, bearing the date 1616, has a heraldic device depicting boars' heads and possibly wool shuttles over the front door, and ancient tiles leading into the foyer. In the early 20th century a box full of tiles was found dating from the Wars of the Roses, with some bearing the name of Sir John Talbot and others the Arms of Beauchamp, and those of the Warwick family. Most of the tiles were framed in the entrance hall, but have now disappeared.

Inside, the fine oak panelling, floors and beams are of interest in themselves. The upstairs lounge, previously the ballroom, boasts a priest's hole. It was during alterations in 1829 that the secret chamber was revealed. Behind its panelling, the diary (since lost) of a Roman Catholic priest who had hidden there for two years, was found. The area is now used as a small

69

An early photograph of the Posting House

library. Tradition speaks of other secret rooms and passages; there is also reputed to be a ghost, a female figure, who sometimes appears either in one of the bedrooms or coming down the stairs. There are now 16 en-suite bedrooms.

A copy of the 1648 Death Warrant of King Charles I was found in the hotel's attic in September 2004 by the head housekeeper, Marilyn Lewis, and now hangs in the reception area. The first signature is that of John Bradshaw, a lawyer, who may or may not have been the same Bradshaw who bought the property in 1616, followed by another 58 signatures, with their seals, including those of Thomas Grey and Oliver Cromwell. It is believed that a copy of the original document was given to each signatory as a keepsake.

The **New Inn** was once a bustling coaching inn where the Posting House now stands. It was open in 1784, if not earlier, and was soon providing changes of horses for travellers and some form of conveyance. One reference to it as the **Posting House Inn** indicates that it was probably used by mail carriers to change their mail bags and perhaps offer other post office facilities. By the end of the 19th century, Walter Evans, described as carriage proprietor, was offering horses and traps. He remained there until the First World War. The building later became the Posting House Garage and today the ground floor is inhabited by a hairdresser's shop.

Two views of High Street showing the Castle and the Lion

The former **Castle Hotel** stood on the site next to the Londis super-market and opposite the butcher's shop. A 17th-century building, or even earlier, it was originally known as the **Falcon** (a reminder that falconry was a royal sport for centuries), but had probably already changed its name when the Great Fire of 1681 broke out. The fire swept along the western half of High Street and up the southern side as far as the inn which was badly damaged. As many as 65 other buildings were, however, completely destroyed.

Once the Castle Hotel

The **Castle** was later re-built, probably in 1685, an almanac of that date having been discovered behind a plaster partition during alterations to the building in 1949. Records of 1743 show that the **Castle** had a malthouse and a barn plus two stables. Up to 1795 the magistrates of Quarter Sessions often adjourned to the **Castle** for the transaction of civil business. In on case in 1788 a woman was whipped on the bare back at the cart's tail from the old Market House to the **Castle** and back again for a minor offence. In 1800 an advertisement appeared in the *Hereford Journal* for the sale of the **Castle**, called 'that ancient and well-accustomed inn' with brewhouse and malthouse, capable of producing 2,500 bushels of malt in a season.

In the 1820s, the *Royal Radnor* London to Aberystwyth coach changed horses at the **Castle**. The coach left at 6 a.m. and arrived in Aberystwyth at 5 p.m. It carried four inside passengers and seven outside, the fares being 21s. inside and 16s. outside. A coach also left the inn for Worcester on Saturdays (market day), starting at 4 a.m., and returning the same evening.

A dinner to celebrate the Coronation of Queen Victoria was held at the **Castle** on 28 June 1838. It was attended by 54 people with Sir Harford Jones in the chair. In 1840 the local Race Ball was held there. That same year the *Cambrian Travellers' Guide* said that the principal inns at Presteigne were the **Radnorshire Arms** and the **Castle**.

From about 1878 to 1883 the **Castle** supplied the refreshments for most of the big functions at the Assembly Rooms. The social event of the season was the County Ball, known as the Hunt Ball in the 1890s. In 1880 it was held at the Assembly Rooms and Mr. Edward Thomas, the host of the **Castle**, (then described as a commercial hotel and posting house) provided the supper, which was laid on the table with much taste and skill, according to the local press report.

Several Coursing dinners and Race Stewards' lunches were held at the **Castle** in the 1870s. In 1875 a celebratory lunch was held there to mark the completion of the railway line to Titley. Sir Richard Green Price, of Norton Manor, who played a leading role in the formation of the company which built the Assembly Rooms and Market Hall and in promoting the railway line, commented on the immediate local benefits – the reduced price of coal and the improved access to distant markets for the products of the area. From 1874 to 1900 and later, the Oddfellows made the inn their headquarters and assembled there for their annual procession to the church. The New Club also met there, from 1895 to 1900.

In 1904, Walter Evans of the **Lion Hotel** paid £500 to James Evan Powell Wilson, a farmer of Hargest, for the **Castle**. Two years later it was in danger of being burnt down again when fire broke out in the **Lion Hotel** only a few feet away. Fortunately, the fire was contained but the **Lion** was completely gutted (see Lion Hotel). In 1912 Evans sold the hotel to Arnold, Perrett & Co. Ltd, brewers of Wickwar, Gloucestershire. Later owned by Southam Brewery, it was being run in 1925 by Willie Edward Davies, described as licensed victualler and builder. In 1968 the **Castle** was bought by Threlfalls, the Chester brewers, who later closed it down. In 1970 they sold it at an auction in the **Bull Hotel** for £3,500 to Kenneth Edwards, of Worcester, with a covenant preventing its future use as a brewery, pub or club. Mr. Edwards turned it into a tea-room.

In 1972, the property was sold for £8,250 to Dr. William Schofield, who changed the bar area into a doctor's surgery with a waiting room. This was appropriate as in previous years expectant farmers' wives would take lodgings there while awaiting the services of a midwife. Dr. Schofield no longer practises but still lives there with his wife. The old stables to the rear have been converted into a house called Castle Barn and there used to be a bowling alley.

Dr. and Mrs. Schofield recall an unusual smell, sweet and sickly, which used to emanate from the lounge and landing, and some strange experiences including the sight of a smoky female figure, who a local girl described as Lady Bluefoot from Stapleton Castle. According to local legend she was meeting her lover when she was discovered by her husband who murdered her. Also, books used to fly off tables and a musical box, which had not worked for years, suddenly started playing.

No. 41, where the Londis shop now stands, is the site of the **Lion**, a 19th-century beer house which later became a hotel. John Worthing was the landlord between 1891 and 1895 when, for a short time, it was called the **Red Lion**. It then became owned by Messrs. Salt and Co. with George Price as tenant, but in the small hours of an October morning in 1906 fire broke out completely destroying the building.

Two views of High Street and the Lion Hotel before the 1906 fire

A local newspaper reported:

It appeared that the fire was discovered between the back stairs and the back kitchen and the inhabitant of the house at once went and roused the captain of the brigade, Mr. T. Smith. In the meantime the occupier of the adjoining premises, Mr. H.J. Sparey, the proprietor of a large grocery establishment, part of which is really under the same roof, and his wife were roused by the crackling, and on looking out through the bedroom

Two views of the Lion after the fire in 1906

window was told by his next door neighbour that the hotel was on fire. Mr. Sparey at once got up and ran round the town, shouting the alarm of fire, and in a very short time the brigade under Captain Smith and Supt. Watkins were at work.

The fire had got a good hold of the back portion of the premises spreading from the back kitchen to the bedrooms and the inside of the house was soon glowing like a heated furnace. The flames gradually spread to the roof, and burst out with fury, cracking the slates like bits of paper. The firemen cut holes in the roof, and the hose played on the fire underneath, but it was impossible to save the house itself, and the brigade turned its attention to the saving of Mr. Sparey's premises adjoining, and cut off that portion of the hotel from the next door premises.

The fire in the meantime had taken complete hold of the side of the Lion next to the Castle, which was close to and only separated by a few feet, and that portion was soon destroyed, the flames bursting out with great fierceness.

Grave fears were entertained that the adjacent hotel, the Castle, the property of Mr. Walter Evans, would be destroyed and this was accentuated when it was found that for a long time the brigade were unable to deal with that side of the premises owing to the insufficiency of hose. At last the two engines were got to work, and they pumped water on to the fire and minimised the danger of its spreading. The brigade were, however, unable to prevent the destruction of the hotel, which was completely gutted.

*Londis now occupies the site of
the Lion Hotel*

*Once the King's Head
in High Street*

In 1909, Richard Davies, a High Street draper, purchased the site of the **Lion**, but it was left to a later developer to fill the site.

No. 44 used to be the **King's Head**, certainly an inn by the early 19th-century inn and possibly even earlier. There is a reference to the **King's Head** in the Session Minutes of 9 October 1811. It was probably named after Charles I, giving stark evidence of the local popularity for the Stuart cause. For some years the inn was associated with a tug-of-war in the streets of

Presteigne, a tradition which survived until the end of the 19th century. From an upper window of the inn, a rope some 60 to 70 feet long was dropped to the waiting contestants – two teams of 12 men.

> One side's objective was the Lugg Bridge, where dipping an end of the rope in the river would signal victory. Their opponents sought to pull the rope down Pound Lane and into the Lugg by West Wall. The story goes that a win for the former team predicted a fall in the price of bread; the converse for the latter.

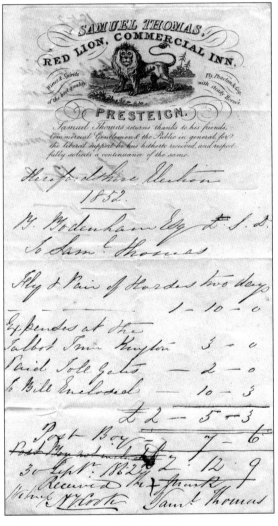

An account from The Red Lion concerning the hire of a Fly and two horses during the Herefordshire Election of 1852

Commerical directories show that in 1830 the licensed victualler at the **King's Head** was Edward Stanton, while in 1868 John Ball was at the helm. But there is no reference to the inn in the directories from 1880 onwards. At one time the publican was apparently also a cobbler, while in the cellar are large ovens. After closing, the **King's Head** became a private house before being transformed into a store and a second hand bookshop.

The exact location of the **White Hart** is not clear but it might have been at No. 2, on the opposite side of the road, close to the Post Office. Now used by the Hamman Agricultural and Pharmaceutical Services, the building dates back to the 16th century and once had a thatched roof. Another possibility is No. 53, although there is no building today bearing that number. At any rate the

*The former Red Lion in
High Street*

*No. 47 High Street may once have
been a pub*

inn was open in the 1760s and in one deed was named as the **White Horse.**
The White Hart was the badge of Richard II; both he and Richard III were
supported by the men of Radnorshire.

At No. 46 was the **Red Lion**, an 18th-century beer house although the
first known reference was not until 1799. The red lion was the emblem of
the early Welsh rulers of Radnorshire and was adopted by many of the
leading families in the county.

Samuel Thomas ran the **Red Lion** for a lengthy period from at least
1830 to 1852, when it was described as a commercial inn and sold 'wines
and spirits of the best quality' and also offered 'fly, phaeton & gig with
steady horses'. In an advertisement Mr. Thomas returned 'thanks to his
friends, Commerical Gentlemen & the Public in general, for the liberal
support he has hitherto received, and respectfully solicits a continuance of
the same'.

That same year, a M. Modenham Esq., paid Mr. Thomas the sum of
£2 12s. 9d. in connection with the Herefordshire Elections including £1
10s. for a 'fly & pair of horses two days' and 7s. 6d. for a post boy. After
the **Red Lion** closed, the **Lion** opened nearby, which also appeared to use
the name **Red Lion** from time to time.

The pretty timber-framed building at No. 47, now functioning as a charity shop, is thought to have been a pub some hundred or so years ago, but its name does not seem to have been recorded.

5 GEO. IV.——Sess. 1824.

AN

A C T

FOR

Making repairing and improving several Roads in the Counties of *Radnor, Hereford* and *Merioneth.*

[ROYAL ASSENT, 3 *June* 1824.]

WHEREAS an Act was passed in the Seventh year of the reign of his late Majesty King *George* the Third, intituled, " An Act for amending repairing and widening several " Roads in the Counties of *Radnor* and *Hereford :*"   Preamble: 7 Geo. 3. cap. 67.

And whereas another Act was passed in the Twenty-fourth year of the reign of his said late Majesty, intituled " An Act to " continue the Term and alter and enlarge the Powers of an " Act made in the Seventh year of the reign of his present " Majesty, for amending repairing and widening several Roads " in the Counties of *Radnor* and *Hereford*, and for repairing " and widening several other Roads in the said Counties :"   24 Geo. 3. sess. 2. cap. 69.

And whereas another Act was passed in the Forty-fourth year of the reign of his said late Majesty, intituled, " An Act to " continue the Term and alter and enlarge the Powers of two " Acts passed in the Seventh and Twenty-fourth years of his " present Majesty, for the amending repairing and widening " several Roads in the Counties of *Radnor* and *Hereford*, in " the said Acts mentioned, and also for amending, widening, " repairing and diverting other Roads in the said County of " *Radnor :*"   44 Geo. 3. cap. 48.

The 1824 Roads Act. Whilst the Wyeside Trustees were to meet at the Swan at Letton and the Aberdovey Trustees were to meet at the Raven Inn at Aberdovey, the poor Trustees of the Radnorshire District were to meet at the Town Hall in Presteigne

79

PRESTEIGNE

1 Duke's Arms *
2 Oxford Arms
3 Old Oak
4 Bridge
5 Grove
6 Fountain
7 Farmers Arms *
8 White Hart
9 Sun
10 Rose & Crown
11 Oxford Arms
12 Apple Tree
13 Barley Mow
14 Masons Arms
15 Machine House

*– Open in 2006
See also page 56

CHAPTER FIVE

Presteigne

BROAD ST., HEREFORD ST. BROADHEATH & NORTON

On the site of the Assembly Rooms next to the Public Library on the corner of Hereford Street and Broad Street was once an inn called the **Black Lion**. It was re-named the **White Hart** and then the **New Oak**, under which name it closed in 1823. The building then became the town's Post Office before being demolished to make way for the new Market Hall, with its Assembly Rooms above, in 1875. A trap-door was discovered in 1995 going down to a vaulted cellar beneath the Market Hall, now in use as the Public Library.

The **Duke's Arms** further down Broad Street dates from about 1480, when it was known as the **Talbot Inn**, making it one of the oldest taverns in Radnorshire. It was probably named after the Talbots — the earls of Shrewsbury — and the sign would have shown a Talbot (a white hunting dog with black spots) which appeared on the coat of arms of the earls. An open gallery, leading to a large room at the rear of the property, was an early feature.

One of the first skirmishes in Wales of the English Civil War took place at the **Talbot** in October 1642. Royalists planned to re-take Hereford which had passed into Parliamentary hands and arranged to meet in Presteigne to finalise the details. News of the meeting reached the Earl of Stamford, Parliamentary leader in Hereford, who decided to raid Presteigne. Accordingly he sent a party of 40 troopers and 20 mounted musketeers under the command of Lieutenant Fleming.

According to local historian Keith Parker:

> Leaving the bulk of his force on the outskirts of the town ... , Fleming, accompanied by five troopers, rode into the town centre, pretending to be a Royalist patrol, to find out the venue of the meeting. By this time the conference held at the home of Francis Richards, the Radnorshire clerk of the peace, had broken up and most of the participants ... had left the town.

A few, including Charles Price and Francis Richards, remained in a gallery at the rear of the Talbot Inn ... Fleming joined them and, pretending to clear his pistols, fired a shot, the signal for the rest of the raiding party to enter the town, while he and his five troopers secured the room, the exterior staircase and the gateway to the building.

The raiding party beat off attacks from 200 or so Royalist troops, killing three, before joining Fleming at the **Talbot**. After seizing weapons and documents, they marched their prisoners, Price and Richards, to Hereford. It is believed that Price, who was released from prison, was stabbed to death at Presteigne by a Colonel Robert Sandys in January 1645.

Later, King Charles and his army twice passed through Presteigne. On the second occasion, in September 1645, after a long day's march he and his soldiers reached Presteigne at midnight, and spent the night there, filling all the inns in the town, the **Talbot** among them (the King himself staying at Lower Heath). After the war, in 1652, Cromwell's committee for seizing Royal estates in Radnorshire used the inn as its headquarters.

The **Talbot** changed its name to the **Duke's Arms** about 1723 after the first Duke of Chandos, who was the Lord Lieutenant of Radnorshire and owned property in Presteigne; it may also at some point have been called the **Chandos**. In the late 18th century the inn was included in the freehold estates of the Marquis of Carnarvon. Mr. E. Meredith was the tenant paying a rent of £11 with the lease expiring in 1774. At the beginning of the 19th century, when Presteigne started to hold an annual race meeting (for 'Horses, Galloways and Ponies') on Broadheath, race entries were taken at the **Duke's Arms** and race dinners were often held there.

In 1829 the inn and two adjoining houses was sold by auction by Thomas Adams. At that time the tenant licensee was Thomas Cooper who was also there in 1830. Among other early landlords was Robert Bore

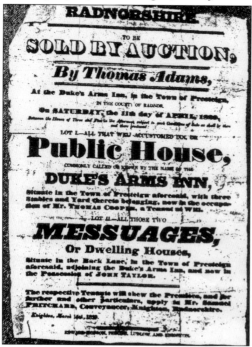

A rare poster advertising the 1829 sale of the Duke's Arms

Two early drawings of the rear of
the Duke's Arms with steps
leading to the upstairs room

in 1857 who also ran an inland revenue office from the inn. Twelve years later the landlord was Quinn Bore, possibly his son, who used the inn as a posting house as well as for inland revenue purposes.

In 1861 the inn began to be called a hotel and in the same year a long upstairs room at the back was opened. This was used by the local Volunteers and was called the Volunteer Hall. Until the Assembly Rooms were built in 1865 most of the town's major functions were held there, including the Sheriff's luncheons, public dinners, political meetings, concerts and balls. The Ancient Order of Foresters used the hall from 1866 to 1884 and again in

The Duke's Arms is on the right of this early 1900s photograph

83

1900 and later years. In 1880 Mrs. Bore is said to have provided an excellent spread for 300 members and their guests.

In the 1860s the timber-framed building was extensively modified, some would say butchered, with purely cosmetic alterations boxing-in or covering over any defects. The main jettied façade was underpinned and bay windows added to both front rooms giving it a Georgian appearance. The roof was raised and a third storey added.

Then the town's most fashionable hostelry, the **Duke's Arms** was bought in 1875 by the colourful Captain Cecil Otway,

Captain Cecil Otway MP

a generous benefactor of Presteigne and the county. He started a stage-coach revival in the late 1870s and early 1880s driving the coach himself and providing the horses. Covering a distance of 64 miles, it was the last mail coach in Britain. The four horse coach started from the **Duke's Arms** and travelled via New Radnor and Rhayader to Aberystwyth with 40 horses stationed along the route to make the change-overs. The service only operated in the summer and started from each place on alternate days. The coach left Presteigne at 10.50 a.m. and was due in Aberystwyth at 6 p.m.

Another flamboyant character was Albert Garrod, the landlord at the beginning of the 20th century. As a side-line he also ran a horse and trap both as a taxi and to collect the mail. According to his grandson, Albert used a big copper water bottle to keep his feet warm when he went to Knighton to fetch the mail which came in at 6 o'clock in the morning. 'He used to go over in the night, put the horse and trap in the Horse and Jockey, sleep in the stable, and then came back in the morning, at six o'clock with the mail'. By 1914 his son, Arthur, who also ran a taxi service, was the landlord.

In 1927 David Williams, of Builth, and Susannah Garrod, widow of Arthur Garrod, 'late of the **Duke's Arms**, proprietor', sold the hotel to Elizabeth Deer, wife of Graham Deer.

At the beginning of World War Two Presteigne was 'absolutely saturated with troops' and the **Duke's Arms**, run by Graham and Elizabeth Deer, was a popular watering hole. It also boosted a badminton hall, in the room where functions used to be held, which was well used. But in May 1941, the War Department took possession of the hotel including the badminton hall and an adjoining cottage which was converted into lavatories. After the war, in 1946, the Deers sold the hotel to Trouncer and Company, the Shrewsbury brewers.

The Duke's Arms in 2004

Outbuildings, malthouse, stables and cottages belonging to the hotel were demolished in 1952-53 and the functions room also came down in 1964.

At some point the **Duke's Arms** stopped functioning as an hotel and, in an arrangement with Allied Breweries of Burton-on-Trent, Reginald and Marilyn Carswell, then running the **Farmers' Arms**, leased the property in 1982 for a seven-year period. They stayed there for less than five years and the inn then remained empty until it was bought by the present owner, John Matthews, of Swansea, in 1987 for £83,200. In 1990 Mr. Matthews wanted to rebuild the front oak-studded wall and jetty to return the façade to its original appearance, but his application for planning permission was turned down. One of the reasons for refusal appeared to be that its Georgian appearance would be ruined! The inn now operates two bars and a pool room and although there are 12 rooms upstairs including two bathrooms and two kitchens, no accommodation is offered. An adjoining building, which used to be the off licence, is now let as a shop selling carpets and curtains.

Ghosts appear to be rampant. Mr. Matthews has felt a hand on the back of his head, while his mother has seen a short man in a long coat. 'I spoke to him on the stairs', she said. 'I had come in with the washing. "Do you want a cup of tea, John", It wasn't until I'd made the tea that I realised it wasn't John. I've also seen him in the bar walking up and down'. She has also seen a tall man with long hair, smelt terrible smells in a bedroom, seen white smoke coming through a wall, windows shaking and a teapot jumping off a wardrobe. 'I've also had a horrible feeling in the cellar — it gives me the creeps going down there'.

Further down, two doors above the Judge's Lodgings, is Harp House, which used to be the **Harp Inn**, a 19th-century cider house.

On the other side of the road is White House which was originally the **Oxford Arms**, first referred to in 1767. At various times it also bore the names **New Inn**, **Blue Boar** and **Bowling Green**, there being a bowling green at the rear which is now a garden. The name **Oxford Arms** was transferred to another building in Hereford Street between 1820 and 1830.

A detailed painting of Broad Street with the Old Oak Inn on the right

The Old Oak is on the left in the early 20th-century photograph

Further along again is Oak House which used to be the **Oak Inn**, once renowned for its sporting activities. Open in the 17th century, it soon became known for its cockfighting. Birds, carefully bred, fed and trained, fought there in matches organised by the local gentry, who wagered heavily on the results. Although the sport was outlawed by Parliamentary Acts of 1835 and 1849, illegal cockfighting continued at Presteigne into the early 20th century, notably at a sawpit near the Burgage.

The Old Oak Inn in retirement in 2004

The inn was the scene of a famous duel in the early 18th century between two local gentlemen while laying considerable wagers on a fight involving a main of cocks. In this eight pairs of cocks were matched, next the eight winners, then four, and finally the last two, until only one was left alive. In his *History of Radnorshire*, W.H. Howse said this provoked 'one of the many fatal instances of ungoverned passion which the partaking of this brutal and barbarious diversion ever fails to kindle and inflame'. High words arose between the two contending parties, the Squire of Boultibrook, Presteigne, and one of the Baskervilles of Aberedw Court, near Builth Wells.

> They withdrew into the yard of the inn to settle their dispute; swords were drawn, and the former gentleman was run through the body, and died on the spot. The bringing of weapons so dangerous to such a place can only be accounted for on the score that a personal combat had been previously concerted by the parties.

Another version states that Boultibrook was severely injured in the groin and died later. At any event the death apparently led to the Baskerville family being the recipients of bad luck afterwards.

The inn became known as the **Old Oak** in the 19th century following the opening of the **Royal Oak**. In 1830 the landlord was Thomas Price and in 1844 James Knowles was in charge. Now owned by the Wrekin Brewery, William Crowe ran it in 1906 and by 1910 the owner/licensee was Harry Crowe.

Described as a beerhouse, most of the drinking was done in the kitchen although there were 12 rooms. Cider was the main drink consumed, together with draught ale and bottled beer and stout. However, in 1912 its licence renewal was refused as part of the County Licensing authority's bid to reduce the number of licensed premises and Mr. Crowe was granted £300 as compensation. The property became a private residence and is still called the Old Oak House.

Adjoining St. Andrew's churchyard and near the bridge over the River Lugg is Bridge House, which used to be the **Bridge Inn**. It was a late 16th- to early 17th-century timber-framed building in an L-shaped block with two stories. The roughcast front is jettied on curved brackets over the ground floor. For a time it was called the **Waterloo Inn,** in recognition of Wellington's triumph over

Napoleon at the Battle of Waterloo in 1815, but it does not feature in commercial directories after 1830. The timber frame was covered in stucco in the latter half of the last century. It was at one time known as Ford View.

Across the bridge in Ford Street is a house on the right where the **Grove Inn** used to stand.

The Bridge Inn in retirement

The Bridge Inn and the bridge over the river Lugg in the early 20th century

The one-time Grove Inn in 2004

It was a cider house in the 18th century.

At Green End, a yellow painted private residence with bay windows at No. 1 was once a beer house that was originally called the **Fountain**. It was open early in the 19th century, if not before, and was then re-named the **Star** and in 1854 it was known as the **Hope and Anchor.** Its first name probably referred to a nearby spring or well; the second alluded either to the star of Bethlehem or to the star that appeared in the arms of the Worshipful Company of Innholders; while the third was another religious symbol, the anchor being the symbol of hope.

Prior to 1867 the **Farmers Arms** in Hereford Street was called the **Blue Boar** (a heraldic reference to the Earl of Oxford, a supporter of the Lancastrian cause), which dates back to the 17th century. For about 30 years during the 19th century the licence was held by the Wimbridge family with records showing that in 1830 the landlord was Hugh Whimbridge, followed

The Farmers Arms with Mrs. Eliza Davies as licensee in the late 19th century

Where Welsh and English meet – fashions in advertising

in 1844 by Grace, his widow and, in 1858, by John, presumably their son. The inn was frequented by pedlars and hawkers on visits to the area. It was also regarded as being a 'very lively' place. One old lady, born in 1868, recounted a conversation overheard by her father in the **Castle** in the early 1860s: 'Let's go to the **Blue Boar** boys, there's fiddling, dancing and Hell's delights!' The proprietor was charged with selling '2 quarts of adulterated beer' in December 1880; he was ordered to pay costs of £4 5s. 4d.

The **Farmers Arms** inn, as it was then called, was owned in the late 19th century by Mrs. Eliza Davies, a spinster, who sold the property in 1890 for £800 to Arnold, Perrett & Co. of Gloucestershire. The firm was taken over by the Cheltenham Original Brewery and in 1925 the inn was bought by George Rawlings, who had been the licenced victualler from at least 1914. Rawlings

The Farmers Arms in the 1990s

90

in turn sold the property in 1938 for £2,250 to the Alton Court Brewery of Ross-on-Wye, which went into voluntary liquidation in 1962. At that time they owned a number of hotels and inns including the **Oxford Arms Hotel**, also in Hereford Street, and the **Crown Inn** at Walton. The various properties were taken over by West Country Breweries Ltd. of Cheltenham.

About 40 years ago, when Ernie Goodman was the landlord, a wall was knocked down and a new serving area made between the lounge and the public bar. The area where the bar and snug used to be, on the original site of the **Blue Boar**, was turned into a restaurant. The present public bar is where a wheelwright used to ply his trade and stables. At one time there was a glass panel in the ceiling for observation purposes from the bedroom above.

The pub was run from 1988 to 2001 by Mrs. Beryl Darsley and her husband Pete. On retiring an article in the local *Broad Sheep* magazine stated:

> For the last 12 years, Beryl (half down to earth mummy, half way new age whacko) and Pete of the suffer-no-fools eyebrows have been the lynch pin of Presteigne's social and cultural life. ... Over the years, the tiny bar has played host to hundreds of musicians from lone classical pianists to full on blues bands ... The bar has always had a piano and Chris Money and Peter Faulkner among others have performed the task of resident pianist with gusto. The regular Wednesday music nights had to be stopped mainly because just too many people came and jammed up the public bar, the hallway to the toilets and eventually spilled out into the street.
>
> If you have never been to the pub you'd be gobsmacked by Beryl's idea of interior decor which manages to combine David Jones' wacky 3D paintings with Rowena Riley's stern and revealing portraits, Titi's diminutive cherries and 1,000 plates, knick knacks and brass elephants into a whole area that makes the average antique shop look like Ikea.

As a reminder of their days as publicans, Beryl and Pete have hanging on

the lounge wall of their home, a 'sculpture' painting of the inn which Beryl specially commissioned from Ludlow artist David Jones. The painting shows photos of customers looking through the pub's windows together with celebrities such as Elvis Presley, Marilyn Monroe, and Mona Lisa.

Beryl also did bed and breakfast and was renowned for her traditional pub catering.

A reminder of the Farmers Arms
Painting — David Jones

Inside the Farmers Arms

She also recalled strange happenings – gas cylinders in the cellar used to be turned off, plates and clocks on the walls would fall off, and a bottle jumped over the bar. The flying plates are attributed to the ghost of Dougann, a 17th-century landlord who sheltered King Charles I on his escape from the Roundheads. This, at any rate, according to Heleneia Brierley, a visionary healer, who on a visit to the **Farmers Arms** in 1995 heard phantom voices and saw three apparitions. One of these, she claimed, was Charles I 'down-dressed though wearing a wig' who said he had stayed at the inn.

> I was spiritually told that this had been the house of Master Oliver, which I understood was the code name of the landlord, whose real name was Dougann.

Dougann was apparently the head of a Royalist resistance movement. King Charles is known to have stayed in the house of a poor farmer at Evenjobb and also spent two nights at Lower Heath, a farmhouse near Presteigne.

The Farmers Arms in 2004

Still hanging in the bars are two Rowena Riley paintings, one of Foxy Morris, who used to be a regular customer and uncle of the present landlord, and Les Griffiths, another long-term regular.

Millfield House on the opposite side of the road was once the **White Hart**, operating as an inn in 1781. Although it was then of some importance, it had closed about the end of the 18th century and certainly before 1820. In 1781 it was advertising its own postchaises with 'good horses and careful drivers to any part of England'. The premises had an old brewhouse attached to them, and other signs of having once been an inn.

On the other side of the road, almost opposite the **Farmers Arms** is Millfield which used to be the **Sun**, (the sign usually showing a circle with a few rays around it, and filled in with eyes, a nose and mouth), which had its heyday in the 19th century. It boasted a large functions room upstairs capable of seating 150 people or more and in the mid-19th century most town functions were held there. The tradesmen of the town and their families met there, for instance, in 1866 to celebrate the opening of the new Market Hall. In 1857 the landlord was John Powell followed by his wife, or widow, Ann, who was

The Sun Inn faced the Farmers Arms in Hereford Street

A late 19th-century view of Hereford Street. The Sun Inn on the left

Hereford Street with the Sun Inn on the right

A rather damp street party between the Sun Inn and the Farmers Arms

in charge from about 1868 to 1880. Mrs. Martha Howells held the licence in 1890 and 1895 when she also described herself as a butcher.

A serious fire broke out in February 1901 destroying the whole of the stabling and outbuildings and causing considerable damage to the inn itself. The *Radnor Express* of 14 February reported:

It appears that Mr. Cadwallader, the tenant of the house, had been in the stable, cleaning his pony, and left the lantern suspended by a piece of string. It is supposed that the string was burnt through, and that the lamp falling to the ground ignited a lot of hay and straw which was lying about, spreading to the building, the old materials of which favoured its rapid spread. When the alarm was given it was evident that the entire premises were in great jeopardy, and ready hands soon cleared out the bulk of the furniture and stock. The flames soon reached a portion of the roof, and for some time the fire engines played in vain upon the burning part. Mr. Jenkins, grocer, of Radnor Buildings, accordingly sent a mounted messenger for the Knighton engine, and those in charge of it are to be congratulated on the quick manner in which they answered the call. In the meantime the fire had extended to the adjoining house, in the occupation of Mrs. Davies, but an engine checked the fire by playing through apertures cut in the roof, and saved the house. During this operation the flames were doing great havoc at the back of the inn, gutting the kitchen and back bedrooms before the outbreak was completely subjugated. The inhabitants of the town are entitled to great credit, especially the ladies, who worked hard in keeping the engine supplied with water; and praise is due to the Fire Brigade, under the command of Captain J.T. Price and Supt. W. Watkins, who did their level best under very trying circumstances. The inn, we understand, is the property of Mr. McNish, of the Leominster Brewery, and is fully insured. Great sympathy is felt in the town for the tenant, Mr. Cadwallader, who must be a heavy loser. The damage is estimated at between £400 and £500.

The **Sun** did not shine much longer, renewal of its licence being refused by the Radnorshire Licensing Committee in 1906 when it was owned by the Leominster brewers, Paxton & Co., with John Clarke as licensee. The Chief Constable said it was not required to meet the wants of the neighbourhood, there being five other houses in the same street. In 1905, 98 barrels of beer, 75 gallons of spirits, 92 doz. bottled beer and 12 hogsheads of cider were sold. Compensation was awarded: £612 12s. to the owners and £59 8s. to the licensee. It became the Millfields printing premises in 1946, but is now a private residence.

Lloyds Bank now sits on what used to be the **Rose and Crown**, although part of the inn still survives. Originally called the **Crown**, it was an important inn in the 18th and early 19th centuries. One of the earliest references is in 1791 when the High Sheriff, Thomas Jones, of Pencerrig, paid 9s. for supper on 19 April after attending the Assizes. As the **Rose and Crown**, it was one of the first inns to provide changes of horse and postchaises for hire. Before the Shire Hall was opened in 1830, the county magistrates would adjourn to the **Rose and Crown** and other inns for dinner and discuss business. Geoffrey Howard

On the right Lloyds Bank replaced the Rose and Crown. Beyond it is the Oxford Arms and, a little further away, the Apple Tree Inn

The one-time Oxford Arms in Hereford Street

was the landlord in 1830, but the inn closed shortly before 1835 and briefly became a private residence before being turned into a bank called Parsons and Co. Lloyds took over in the 1890s and erected a new building on the site. 'Crown' was a popular name for an inn, being easy to illustrate and recognise, while rose and crown indicates loyalty to the monarch.

Next door is Oxford House which at one time was the **Oxford Arms**. Open in 1825 after being transferred from its original site in Broad Street, it was named after Robert Harley (1661-1724), the Earl of Oxford and Mortimer, who lived at Brampton Bryan. One of the first landlords was John Roberts, who was there in 1830, followed by William Norris in 1844, and John Prosser in the 1850s. By 1895 William Stephens held the licence with his widow, Mary, taking over in 1914. At one time the **Oxford Arms** was a focus for footballers with showers and changing rooms at the back. It closed in the 1960s and is now a private house.

Oringally a beer and cider house in the 18th and 19th centuries, the **Apple Tree Inn** at No. 47 closed down in 1912. When the owner/licensee, Richard Hill, applied for a renewal of his licence it was turned down, again on the grounds there were sufficient other pubs in the vicinity. It was stated that the house appeared to be little frequented and the stables were chiefly used by the licensee for his own horses. Mr. Hill was granted £162 compensation. On closing, a sale was held of some of the fixtures and fittings. One former customer, the late Martin Moses, bought a brass bell which used to sit on the bar counter as a memento; it now belongs to his son, John, of Church Street. The pub, which has one bay window and two doors, is now a private residence called Apple Tree House. The sign may have shown a boy scrumping apples.

By the turn of the century an auction yard had been established close to the goods shed where the weekly cattle market was held, while the field beyond Appletree Orchard became the venue for the livestock fairs, previously held in the streets of the town.

An old photograph of the Barley Mow taken in 1905

The **Barley Mow** (a barley stack was one of the earliest signs used to indicate that beer was sold on the premises) closed in rather ignominious fashion in 2001 after quite a long and illustrious history. Certainly open in 1822 and probably much earlier, it offered accommodation with at least six bedrooms and stabling to the rear. In 1830 the business was run by Mary Stephens, and by Evan James in 1844, but its most enterprising landlord was John Weaver, who was there for nearly 30 years. As well as running the inn, he opened a highly successful malting business and a spittletree or spade handle factory at the rear of the premises. Then, with his partner James Mackenzie, of Hill Farm, he also expanded the Nash limeworks and quarry. By then employing nearly 40 workers, Weaver set about housing them in a row of cottages on either side of the **Barley Mow**

An interior view of the closed Barley Mow in 2004

In retirement the Barley Mow still looks like a pub

and in what became known as Gas House Row opposite the inn. When Mr. Weaver died in 1882 at the age of 49 the *Hereford Times* of 4 November wrote: '... if his place is not taken by some competent successor, there will be a loss in the town which will be felt keenly both by the working classes and trade generally'.

Elizabeth Weaver, presumably John's widow, continued to run the pub and was still there in 1895.

Railwaymen used to have a right of way across a meadow behind the stables allowing them a more direct route to the **Barley Mow**. In 1914, Frederick Hetch was the landlord and about 30 years ago a new bar counter was installed. Unfortunately, the pub later became notorious for drug-taking and its licence was eventually withdrawn. It was bought privately and has now been turned into a non-denominational Christian centre. A cartoon appeared in a local paper at the time with the caption: 'Apparently they're licensed to sell lay spirits'.

Today, the interior is still the same with the bar counter retained between the two bars and the bar furniture still *in situ*. Even the old beer pumps, although dismantled, are still there. The spittletree building still exists as well as the old malthouse, while the big mash container is in the garden sporting a fir tree. A new sign proclaims the **Barley Mow** but now there is the outline of a fish underneath.

On the opposite side of the road at No. 14 was the **Masons Arms**, a beer house from the 1860s until its closure in 1906. It might have been named after the Company of Masons, who cut stone into shape for building purposes, and was granted a coat of arms in 1473. The property consisted of a sitting room, kitchen and back kitchen with four bedrooms, two available for visitors. There was a two-stall stable. Apparently most of the drinking was done in the kitchen. But in 1906 last orders were called when the pub's licence was not renewed and the owner/licensee, Shirley Price, was granted £125 in compensation (including £20 16s. 8d. to the tenant). The **Masons Arms** was not required, the Chief Constable said, there being 13 licensed premises in the town, or one to every 95 persons including women and children.

The British Legion Club in Hereford Street was once the Machine House

At No. 9, at the corner with Back Lane, was the **Machine House**, which was operating as a beer house in 1882; its name probably derived from some connection with the town's fire brigade. Next to it was the old auction yard. The building was later used as council offices and is now the headquarters of the local British Legion Club. A car park has replaced the auction area.

Across the border into England and at either end of Broadheath, which used to be common land on the B4362 road to Leominster, are two old houses both of which were once pubs — the **Cat and Fiddle** and the **Cricketers Arms**. The former was probably named after the nursery rhyme beginning 'Hey diddle diddle, The cat and the fiddle ...' which appeared in a collection produced in the mid-18th century and the sign may actually have been a cat fiddling. Although the building is between 400 and 500 years old, it is not known when it became a pub or cider house. It certainly existed in the 19th century but had probably closed by the turn of the century. There used to be a forge with a smithy's cottage at the end of the grounds, and it is likely that passing coaches would have stopped if their horses needed re-shoeing. A green lane which passes to the side may have been used by drovers. Another source of trade would have been the annual race meeting held on Broad Heath, which was a popular event from the time of George III until the 1880s.

The one-time Cat and Fiddle

The property was bought in 1911 by a Miss Coates, of Combe House, by which time it had long ceased to be a cider house, and she restored it and turned it into a private house. Today, a sign on the iron gate leading to the front porch of the two-storey house still bears the name **Cat and Fiddle**. Inside some of the original beams can still be seen as well as the inglenook fireplace with a bread oven. In the beam over the fireplace are two holes into which once fitted a weaver's frame. At the back of the house is a hatch leading down into a large cellar.

At the other end of Broadheath, which was enclosed for agricultural purposes during the Second World War, stands another old building, once a beer house called either the **Cricketers** or **Cricketers Arms**. It was apparently built in 1851 to cater for Presteigne's great interest in cricket. A report in the *Hereford Journal* of that year states:

> Cricket – liberally supported by the gentlemen of the town and neighbourhood and under the patronage of Mr. F. Evelyn (landowner), J.G. Cooper and J.R. Ince esqs. Twice weekly practices are being held on the Broadheath preparatory to the grand match which is to come off on Friday. The ground has been levelled, recently turfed and is equal to any in the kingdom. A new tent will be purchased by the members and a commodious inn is about to be erected near the cricket ground.

No doubt later the inn would have staged the customary dinner party after matches with 'the jovial accompanyment of toast and song'. Originally a much smaller building, customers came in through an iron gate with vertical bars which came from the old Presteigne prison, now the Shire Hall, then across an open yard to a front door leading to a snug on the right with a side entrance. Behind the snug was a hatch, under the stairs, leading to the cellar. Outside was a urinal and a dairy room.

Records show that it was called the **Cricketers Arms** in 1868 when Job Strangwood was landlord. He was followed by John Taylor in 1880 and Edwin Taylor in 1895. An old photograph of the property shows a board above the front door which reads 'The Cricketers, H. Meek'. It was then run by James Taylor in 1914 followed by Sergeant Price and then in 1924 was bought for £526 by

William Prosser. When his licence was renewed that same year Mr. Prosser said that while there there were few customers, business was improving. His wife managed it while he went out to work. But in 1929, when Arthur Taylor was the licensee and occupier, he offered the licence be

Behind the ivy was once the Cricketers Arms

The cricketers sign and padlock on the old prison gate

referred for compensation owing to poor trade and 'no drinking being done at my place'. Trade in 1928 was one barrel of beer and four bottles of spirit per fortnight. The double-fronted building of stone and slate consisted of a bar, parlour, back kitchen, passage and cellar, and store-house. Outside was a cowhouse or stable, fowl house and trap house with one and a quarter acres of land. The licence was not renewed and Mr. Taylor received £100 compensation.

It was then bought by Mr. Boden, agent to the Arkwrights of Kinsham, who turned it into a private residence adding two new wings, one including a new main entrance. Today, the road entrance has been closed off and the old prison gate relegated to the rear garden. The front of the building, where the old front door has been rein-stated, is now covered with creepers.

There is a theory that the **Cricketers** may have been built on the site of an earlier beer house mainly serving drovers using a subsidiary route to avoid the turnpike gates, and thus paying the toll due. While the drovers enjoyed the hospitality of the house, their animals would be safely secured in a nearby enclosure on the common.

NORTON

Straddling both sides of the B4355 road to Knighton is the village of Norton, which at one time boasted two pubs and a hotel. The latter still survives, but is a far cry from its former glory days. There used to be a square when the main road skirted round the church and before a 15th-century house was demolished.

Opposite the church is a house called Castle Bank which stands on the site of the **Castle Inn**. Records show that this ancient hostelry was in existence in 1809, again in 1823-29 and in 1868. After meetings at the church it was customary apparently for villagers to walk the short distance to the **Castle** to quench their thirst. The inn was demolished in 1880.

Further down the road towards Presteigne was once another pub called the **Maypole**, near a farmhouse and opposite School Lane. Nothing is known about the building, but it would be nice to conjecture that it actually possessed a maypole and that dancing around it was held on festive occasions.

Continuing down the road, but on the opposite side, is a sign proclaiming the **Norton Manor Hotel** with a mile-long driveway across arable land leading

The Norton Manor Hotel in 2005

to what used to be the old neo-Jacobean manor house, a building which has led somewhat of a chequered life since it was built by Richard Price in 1858. In 1861 the property and estate was left to Richard Green, a Knighton solicitor, who played an important part in modernising that town and in the construction of the Central Wales railway line between Craven Arms and Llandovery. Assuming the additional name of Price by royal licence, he moved to Norton and started transforming the village. He arranged the restoration of Norton church by Sir Gilbert Scott, built a new school and houses for his estate workers, also built the Norton vicarage and the Gables, and was instrumental in enclosing 720 acres of farmland. Together with all this local work, he served as an M.P. for Radnorshire.

In 1885 the manor house was left to Sir Powlett Milbank, who had married Edith, one of Sir Richard's daughters. Just after World War One it was sold and the estate, including four farms, was split up. Under the new owners it became an hotel in 1925, but was then requisitioned by the army during World War Two. They left it in poor condition, but some time afterwards it again opened as an hotel. A succession of owners followed and at various times the building was threatened with demolition, became derelict, its acreage was fragmented, whilst its remaining land became the sites for a complex of retirement homes. Despite all this, **Norton Manor** operated spasmodically as a hotel with some 20 bedrooms leading off a grand staircase, a restaurant, bar and ballroom. Eventually it closed, but the new owners hope to reopen. Meanwhile the previous owners intend to restore the west wing as their residence.

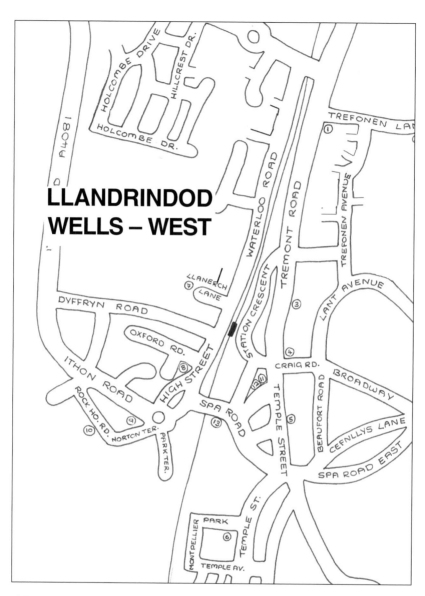

LLANDRINDOD WELLS – WEST

1	Middleton Arms *	8	Elephant & Castle
2	Trefonen	9	Gwalia *
3	Kincoed *	10	Rock House
4	Hampton *	11	Glen Usk *
5	Metropole *	12	Lansdowne
6	Montpelier *	13	Commodore *
7	Llanerch *		

– Open in 2006
See also page 128

CHAPTER SIX

Llandrindod Wells – West

> Let England boast Bath's crowded springs,
> Llandrindod happier Cambria sings,
> A greater, though a modern name,
> By merit rising into fame.
>
> (*Gentleman's Magazine,* October, 1748)

The Llandrindod Wells area was of some importance during the Roman period with a road running just to the west of the town centre and a fort at Castell Collen some 2 miles to the north-west. In addition, there was a series of what have been identified as 'practice camps', a short distance to the south of the town.

Until the 1730s there was no town of Llandrindod Wells. The only buildings of significance were the small 13th-century Holy Trinity church, the independent Cae-bach Chapel, the 16th-century **Llanerch Inn** and a few isolated farmhouses. There was also a chalybeate spring, known as Rock Water, used 'from time immorial' and known by the Romans. Then, in 1736, Mrs. Jenkins of Bach y Craig Farm found a saline spring and a sulphur well. After curing her daughter's ulcerated head, she treated many local people for various ailments and began selling the waters to travellers and visitors staying in nearby farmhouses. Thus came into being the Spa town which soon grew in popularity following the publication in 1747 of *A Journey to Llandrindod Wells in Radnorshire* and a poem in the *Gentleman's Magazine* of 1748 (quoted above). In 1754 a German scientist, Dr. Diederick Linden, visited the town to find a cure for his scurvy that 'soured my juices and irritated them on every occasion'. It must have worked because he analysed the mineral contents of the waters and two years later published a glowing *Treatise on the Three Medicinal Waters at Llandrindod*. The town now had a national reputation.

Visitors were initially accommodated at farmhouses until 1749 when William Grosvenor, a businessman from Shrewsbury, converted a deserted farmhouse near Holy Trinity into a splendid hotel called **Llandrindod Hall**. This flourished for 30 years before being suddenly closed by its new owner after hearing of its dubious reputation as a gambling centre, and later it was destroyed by fire. However, it was not until the 1860s, with the construction of the Central Wales railway line from Knighton and the enclosure of common land, making it available for building, that development of the town began in earnest. A new spring was discovered near Rock Water and a pump room and bath-house with gardens were erected in an area called Rock Park. It was around there that the centre of the new town grew with hotels, shops, private houses and a new Holy Trinity Church.

Up until the beginning of the First World War Llandrindod Wells was a boom town with an expansion of building work. The season as a fashionable Spa lasted from May to mid-September with visitors – some 80,000 a year – entertained by orchestras while queuing outside the pump rooms at the Rock Park and the **Pump House Hotel**, sited on Mrs. Jenkins farmhouse. Both pump rooms charged 6d. per day for any amount of water which varied from two to six glasses at a time, often starting before breakfast. Sports facilities followed with golf, swimming, tennis and croquet, together with horse racing on the Rock Ddole, a meadow near the river Ithon.

The Spas declined after the 1950s although Rock Park stayed open until 1972. The town's fortunes were restored, however, as it became a more general holiday centre and the administrative centre, first for Radnorshire and, since 1974, for the new county of Powys (an amalgamation of Brecknock, Radnor and Montgomery).

Tremont Road leads northwards from the town centre. The **Middleton Arms**, on the corner of Tremont Road and Trefonen Lane, was named after Edward Middleton Evans, a 19th-century landowner and benefactor. He donated sites for the Cottage Hospital, the Convalescent Hospital

A coach outside the Middleton Arms

for the poor, and the Holy Trinity Church. He was High Sheriff of Radnorshire in 1849 and Middleton Street was named after him. There was land to the rear of the **Middleton Arms** including a blacksmith's which was probably owned by Mr. Middleton. Known as Middleton House, the main entrance

The stone frontage of the Middleton Arms;
the original entry was on the side

to the building was originally in Trefonen Lane. When the railway line was being built through the town in the 1860s, the pub was frequented by many of the workers who were mainly Irish. As trade increased, the bar was extended by knocking down a few walls – there is still an original railway sleeper used as one of the beams. In 1904 the landlady was Mrs. Mary Powell who, according to a local inhabitant, 'ran a very tidy public house and there was never any trouble there'. He also recalled that Mrs. Powell had a daughter called Kitty. 'She had a lovely dolls house and lots of dolls kept in a little shed at the back and I used to go round there to play'. At that time the bar area consisted of a hall with a serving hatch for off-sales, a door on the left leading to a small bar, and another on the right leading to two small bars. One of the most popular drinks was scrumpy cider sold from the barrel. Bottles of scrumpy were left on the front doorstep for regulars to pick up on their way to work, while the milkman exchanged milk for cider.

In 1946 the hotel was owned by David Williams (Builth) Ltd. and the tenant was Ernest Rees. At that time a smith's shop, a smithy and stables still adjoined the premises. A former landlord committed suicide by shooting himself in the head while behind the bar; there was reputed to be a big blood-stain on the ceiling behind the counter leaving a mark which came back even after re-decoration. Apparently, the tragedy occurred on the day he was leaving after owing money to the pub owners. The most famous person to visit the **Middleton** and enjoy a drink was Bill Clinton, the future President of America, as guest in the 1960s of local school-teacher, Lyn Jones, both men having attended Oxford University.

Having always been owned by brewers, in 1991 the present owners bought it off Whitbreads and it became a free house for the first time. They carried out extensive alterations making the main bar area open plan and including a pool room. The present landlord is also a self-employed builder and a motor-bike enthusiast.

Trefonen House in 1775

Further along the lane on the right-hand side is a modern house with the name Treffonen, which is on the site of **Trefonen (Trevonen) House**, one of the oldest buildings in Llandrindod Wells. It was the home of the Jones family, prosperous squires, since the mid-17th century and was the birthplace of Thomas Jones (1742-1803), the celebrated artist. The house possessed seven bedrooms, three sitting rooms and a 'farmery with cowhouse, barn, stable and hovel'. It was leased in the 18th century by Mr. Grosvenor, of Llandrindod Hall, as a supplementary hotel. In a letter Jones explained that

> the influx of Visitors of all descriptions, the Infirm, the Rich, the Gay, the Idle and Dissolute ... was so great, that it became an intolerable Nuisance to the Neighbourhood – On which Account, My father resolving to quit it, let Trevonen ... as a Supplementary Hotel, and removed to Penkerrig.

One year a company of comedians run by a Mr. Ward attended from Brecon and performed in a barn at Trefonen which had been fitted out as a theatre. Mr. Ward's grand-daughter was the celebrated actress, Mrs. Sarah Siddons, who no doubt 'exhibited her infantile talents in the barn'. It later became a dairy farm, but after falling into disrepair **Trefonen House** was demolished in about 1980.

Temple Street is the southern continuation of Tremont Road. On the east, and near the hospital is the **Kincoed Hotel**, which has 10 bedrooms, a dining room and a licensed bar. It was originally a private house and possibly a private school, before becoming a hotel. The owner's motto is: 'Arrive as a guest, leave as a friend'.

The Hampton Hotel in 2005

A little further southwards and on the corner with Craig Road is the **Hampton Hotel**, which offers 30 bedrooms together with two main bar areas. There is a separate café at the front. It was originally built as two residential houses and when the owner Thomas Lunt, who also owned two quarries, died in the 1930s he left the property to the town to be used as a Youth Hostel. It was run by the Y.M.C.A. in the 1950s, but was then sold and converted into a hotel with Mr. Kermode as the first proprietor.

The site of the present **Metropole Hotel**, near the Memorial Gardens, was bought in 1870 by Edwin Coleman, the post-master from Howey. He then erected a three-storey building and divided it into two semi-detached houses; one half – Templefield House – was let, whilst the other became **Coleman's Hotel**, which opened in 1872. The licence was held jointly by Coleman and his friend, James Owen, a farmer of Llandrindod Hall, and then by Coleman's son John. On the death of Coleman Snr. in 1877, the hotel was sold for £2,500 possibly to William

Coleman's Hotel in 1888, later to become the Bridge and then the Metropole

109

Lewis, a wheelwright, with the licence remaining with John until 1884. The hotel probably accommodated up to 40 guests and its licensed bar was well patronised, with only the **Llanerch**, the **Pump House**, the **Rock House** and later the **Middleton Arms** and the **Ridgebourne Arms** holding on-licences.

In 1885 the hotel was sold for £2,200 to John Wilding, of the **Severn Arms Hotel** in Penybont, who regarded it as an investment for his wife and seven children as Llandrindod was enjoying a boom at that time. However, he died on the very day that the ownership was transferred. The Wildings changed the hotel's name to the **Bridge** as the building lay near the Arlais brook running under the road to Builth. While Mrs. Wilding remained at the **Severn Arms**, four of the children ran the **Bridge**. Although there was

a vegetable garden, meat and other fresh food was supplied from the family's farm at Cwmtrallwm.

In 1890 a lioness escaped from Bostock and Bailey's Travelling Menagerie and Circus, which had moved to open ground opposite the **Bridge**, and:

Two views of the Bridge Hotel in the early 1900s

110

made for the hotel's bar door which was quickly shut in her face. She then made for the private entrance and walked into a drawing room and jumped through a window on to the verandah, where the keeper and his assistants, in close pursuit, threw a coil of rope over the lioness's head, recaptured her and led her back to her wagon.

At that time a gentleman visitor was sitting alone in a chair outside. 'Though suffering from chronic rheumatism, the invalid visitor sprang from his chair with astonishing agility and flung himself into the hotel'.

In 1891, enlargement plans for the hotel were carried out which including a slate-covered verandah running the length of its front. A wisteria was trained to grow up it and is still flourishing today. In 1892 a second coach house was built and in 1894 a billiard room and laundry were added. In

Guests outside the Bridge Hotel, later the Metropole

111

Mrs. Elizabeth Miles, the founder of the Metropole

1897, Mrs. Elizabeth Miles, 'a business woman of great ability and enterprise' and owner of the New Inn Hotel at Pontypridd, bought the **Bridge Hotel** for £7,850. She eventually held the licences of 10 inns and hotels in South Wales. Over a period of 26 years she enlarged the building by about five times making it the largest hotel in Wales accommodating up to 200 guests. In 1909 part of the hotel was converted into a Hydro with staff offering a wide range of treatments including Professor Bergoni's (of Bordeaux) latest system of treatment of obesity, gout, cardiac derangements, insomnia, neurasthenia, etc. The creation of an imposing main entrance, with green copper turrets, terraces and steps, at the east end of the hotel was short-lived when a scheme for the proposed Beaufort Road never materialised.

In 1911 the hotel was given the more fashionable name of the **Metropole**, and in 1914 it was described on a postcard as being 'a Centre for Motorists with Garage for 25 cars and Excellent Roads', and 'recommended as Centre for American Tourists'. Boarding terms in 1921 were 18s. per day and 126s. per week. Other facilities included lawns for tennis, croquet and bowls. It

The Metropole in its garden setting in the '30s

112

The Metropole in the 1950s

*Front and rear elevations of
the Metropole in 2004*

expanded further in 1923 with the purchase of the adjoining Templefield House, the ground floor of which became a ballroom. In 1925, Mrs. Miles sold the hotel for £32,000 to the Hotel Metropole Company, which was very much a family affair, consisting of herself, her son Francis and other relatives. It was Francis who, in 1935, built a 120 feet long swimming pool in the garden of Templefield.

During World War Two the hotel was requisitioned by the Army for use as an Officer Cadet Training Centre and afterwards was left in a run-down condition. However, Mrs. Miles' great-grandson, David Baird-Murray, took over and the hotel's fortunes revived. Marketing was improved by joining the Interchange Consortium which later became part of Best Western, one of the largest marketing consortiums in the world. Mr. David, as he was known, became chairman of Best Western UK in 1976. The number of bedrooms was increased to 138, many of them with private bathrooms. In the 1980s the old swimming pool was replaced by a leisure complex including a heated pool. With managing director Justin Baird-Murray continuing the family line, the **Metropole** now has 122 *en suite* bedrooms and offers many other facilities including a purpose-built conference centre.

The **Montpelier**, on the western side of Temple Street and on the corner of Montpelier Park, has been a hotel since at least 1906. Originally a private house with large quarters for servants, it became a hotel under the name of **Mostyn**. In 1920 the proprietors were Mr. and Mrs. J. Watson Armitage. In the town's official guide of 1928 the following description appeared:

> The Mostyn Hotel is a modern building which has been newly furnished and decorated throughout. It has excellent accommodation for visitors and contains a commodious coffee room (separate tables), lounge, smoke room and private sitting rooms. The Hotel is lighted throughout with Electric light and the Sanitation is perfect.

The Montpelier Hotel was originally called the Mostyn

The name was changed to **Montpelier** on the closure of another hotel of the same name and today offers eleven *en suite* bedrooms, a dining room and a bar open to non-residents. On the other side of Montpelier Park in Temple Street once stood the original **Montpelier Hotel** which is now a block of flats. An impressive three-storey building with a distinctive turret on one corner, it operated for about a hundred years. By 1921 it was a listed RAC hotel 'Recommended for Quiet and Comfort' offering an electric lift and tennis and croquet lawns. It was 'Renowned for Warmth,

Comfort and Excellent Cuisine'. The hotel stopped trading in the 1980s and was converted into an Evangelical church before being demolished in 1999.

High Street runs parallel to Tremont Road and Temple Street, on the western side of the railway. The **Llanerch Inn**, just off the High Street in Llanerch Lane, is one of the oldest buildings in the town, dating from the 16th century. It was

The Llanerch in 1874

The Llanerch Hotel in the 1930s

115

*Marstons ales were once sold at
the Llanerch Hotel*

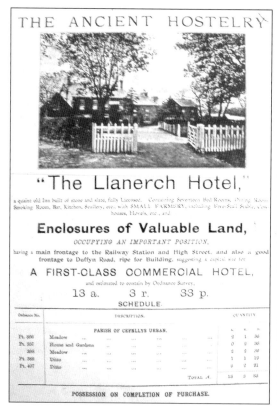

*An early 20th century sale notice for
the Llanerch Hotel*

formerly a coaching inn known as the **Llanerch y dirion Inn**, the name referring to its original position in a 'pleasant glade or clearing'. In the 18th century, there was no town of Llandrindod Wells, not even a village and the roads through the area were notoriously bad being in many places little better than tracks. Despite this, people began to visit Ye Wells early in the 1700s. Visitors lodged at farmhouses on either side of an extensive common. Lying close to the turnpike road, which ran across the moor between Builth and Penybont, the **Llanerch** was one of the few places offering accommodation at this time. Llandrindod Common, which made up the surrounding area contained a number of 'island' enclosures, of which the appropriately named **Llanerch Inn** was the most important.

Towards the end of the 18th century, the inn was owned by Thomas Jones of Pencerrig, who also owned the **Pump House**. In 1813 it belonged to Mr. Middleton Jones, a local attorney, and by 1828 it had passed to Edward Middleton Jones, who retained ownership for

The Llanerch Inn in 2004

many years. In the 1840s and '50s the **Llanerch** was run by Joseph Betts and was described as a neat and comfortable boarding house. To increase the accomodation, the next door Waterloo Cottage was incorporated into the establishment. By the 1860s, it was kept by Mr. Dawson, who also ran the **Refreshment Rooms** at the Railway Station. With farmland attached, the **Llanerch** was able to provide its own meat and vegetables for all its customers.

In the late 1800s, the building was renovated. The front of the present building is mainly early 19th century, but the interior retains some reused and original timbers with beams and staircase dating from the 17th century.

The **Llanerch** is described as a 'first class commercial hotel ... with 13 acres of land' in an undated, but probably early 20th century, sale notice hanging in the bar. 'A quaint old inn built of stone and slate ... containing 17 bedrooms, dining room, smoking room, bar, kitchen, scullery etc. and small farmery including five stall stables, cowhouses, hovels etc'.

Memories of the **Llanerch** in the 1920s were recalled by local inhabitants:

It used to be run by the Lewis family who had several sons and daughters, all employed on helping to carry out the duties of running a public house ... The Llanerch used to keep their own pigs for ham and bacon to use in the meals for the visitors. They employed a man to go around the hotels to collect waste food for the pigs. ... The beer was good and only cost four-pence-half-penny and cider was three-pence-half-penny, and my five woodbine cigarettes were only a penny.

Lewis the Llanerch, as he was known, remained at the helm until the 1960s or '70s. The **Llanerch** now has a dining room for special occasions and Sunday lunches, 12 *en suite* bedrooms, and an outside patio and beer garden with a children's play area.

In his article *Radnorshire Inns of 1941*, the Rev. D. Stedman Davies wrote that

There are the remains of a house in High Street nicknamed the Elephant and Castle, at the back of the Electric Works, of which only the end wall and chimney remain, the rest being boarded up and used as a shed. Tradition says it was an ale house; that is, it had an occasional day licence during the Races in the early 20th century.

Today, there is no trace of wall or chimney and the Electric Works is empty awaiting re-development. It is on the site of the old Market Hall, gutted by fire in 1957, demolished and a depot built for Hancock's Brewery.

Norton Terrace continues the line of High Street south-westwards from the Ithon Road/Park Crescent roundabout. The former **Gwalia Hotel** stands on a corner site in Norton Terrace close to Rock Park. It was started in 1889

The Gwalia Hotel in the early 20th century

118

The Gwalia Hotel in the mid-20th century

The name and the revolving doors linger on, although the building is now used as the County Hall

at the corner house, then known as Brynhyfryd, but very soon extensive structural additions had to be made to meet the demands of a rapidly developing business. These extensions culminated in the new premises which opened to the public in 1899. Edward Jenkins, who also owned the Gwalia private hotel in Tavistock Square, London, was the managing director. He was still there in 1904. The hotel, which was enlarged in 1908, has an architectural style blending Queen Anne with Edwardian baroque. Shaped as a 'V', it has an impressive entrance with a glass and iron canopy and white stone-work above. Its three-storey brick front is framed by octagonal, domed turrets with nine-panelled circular windows. The building has retained its revolving hotel entrance door leading into a fine entrance hall with two-level galleries incorporating iron work banisters. The hall has a stuccoed and panelled ceiling and there are period fireplace surrounds in many of the rooms.

Amongst its famous visitors have been the former Prime Ministers David Lloyd George and Neville Chamberlain, and the composer Sir Edward Elgar. Lloyd George caused something of a scandal when, shortly after the First World War, he stayed there with his secretary who was widely believed to be his mistress. On one occasion when he left the hotel, he was greeted with a chorus of boos from an outraged crowd. Agatha Christie also stayed there and mentions Llandrindod Wells in her novel *The Caribbean Mystery*.

During World War Two the **Gwalia** was one of the many Llandrindod hotels to be requisitioned by the Army for use as an Officer Cadet Training Centre; it never recovered, closing down soon after the war. In 1951 it re-opened as Radnor County Hall complete with council chamber and is still used as local government offices.

Near Rock Park is Rock House Road where once stood the splendid **Rock Park Hotel**, also known as **Rock House Hotel**, now demolished and replaced with a housing development. It was originally an inn with a thatched roof in the reign of George III with Edward Tompson as landlord in 1816. In 1821 it was described as 'that capital and well accustomed inn', and was called a neat and pleasant boarding house in 1825 when it was kept by David Smith. Built entirely of stone, it 'contained two parlours with commodious and lofty bedrooms'. Mr. Smith was still there in 1859 when the terms were: 'Bed 7s. a week, Cooking 1s. per week per person, public sitting room 1s. per week and private parlour 10s. and 12s. per week'.

An early view of the Rock House Hotel

Above: A stagecoach in front of the Rock House Hotel

Right: An early 20th-century advertisement for the hotel

The site was developed by Sir Richard Green-Price after the sulphur well was discovered in the mid-19th century. In the 1860s, it was run by Mr. Philip James, who had previously been landlord at the Severn Arms, Penybont. In the 1880s it was very popular under the charge of Mrs. Careless. Captain Cecil Otway's coach, on its way to and from Aberystwyth, was a big attraction as was the croquet lawn. In 1904 the proprietor was Morgan Walters.

Standing in its own beautiful grounds of a hundred acres, Rock Park was by now a large hotel with 100 bedrooms, together with private sitting rooms, recreation room and a ballroom. It also offered golf, tennis, billiards, fresh water bathing and seven miles of fishing. There were daily

The Rock House Hotel in the 1920s

The Rock Park Hotel in the 1930s; it has since been demolished

conveyances to the Birmingham Water Works in the Elan Valley. Sanitation was described as 'perfect' and there was 'excellent stabling' and a 'lock up for bicycles'.

In 1947 a fire, caused by an electrical fault, damaged the ballroom, dining room and some bedrooms. However, the hotel continued trading until it finally closed in 1995 while under the management of Bill and Elizabeth Higginson. After being sold to property developers, the building, boarded up after acts of vandalism, was demolished in 1997 and nine two- and three-storey houses are being built on the site.

South Crescent is in the centre of the town, leading south-westwards from Temple Street to Spa Road. The **Glen Usk Hotel** was formerly the **Brynawel Hotel**, which opened in 1897 with the conversion of what had been five large, terraced houses in South Crescent. In 1904, when Jeffrey Jones was propretor, the hotel boasted electric lighting throughout and the facilities included a large billiard table, a tennis

*The Prince of Wales taking the waters
at Llandrindod on 6 August 1926.
Lord Glen Usk is on the extreme right;
Mr. Jones of the Brynawel Hotel is on the left*

The frontage of the Glen Usk Hotel, previously the Brynawel

lawn and a bowling green. In 1920, by then called the **Glen Usk**, it advertised: 'For those who enjoy riding we have our own stables and riding school, five miles of our own Trout Fishing and our own Shoot'. The hotel offered 84 bedrooms, all with 'H & C' water and interior spring beds, an indoor cinema and games room. Terms varied from 6 to $8^1/2$ guineas. Later, an open-air swimming pool was built opposite in Temple Gardens. Mr. Jones was still the owner in 1926 when he was photographed with the then Prince of Wales drinking the 'waters' in the town. Also in the photograph was Lord Glen Usk wearing scout uniform. It would appear that the relationship between the two men may have had some bearing on the hotel's name being changed to **Glen Usk**. A major refurbishment was carried out in 1985 by its then owners, Mount Charlotte Hotels, who took over in the mid 1970s. The pool was filled in in 1990.

In recent years the **Glen Usk** has been owned by various hotel groups, including Thistle Inns, Grace Hotels and, for the last five years, Grand UK Hotels. Today, the hotel features a spacious bar, lounge and restaurant and a function room where dinner dances, entertainment and conferences are held. There are 79 bedrooms, all *en suite*. It is planned to refurbish the decorative iron balconies along the hotel's frontage.

A delicate feature of the original stained glass windows at the Glen Usk Hotel

The Glen Usk Hotel in 2004

The Lansdowne Hotel is now the Conservative Club with flats above

Next door to the **Glen Usk** is the Conservative Club which used to be the **Lansdowne Hotel**. The town's official guide of 1928 stated that the hotel had recently undergone very important alterations, including 'A new recreation room for dancing, whist drives and games; increased accommodation in the dining room; the cloak room has been enlarged and a silent telephone box has been added'.

With Mrs. Cook-Jenkins as proprietor, the hotel offered accommodation for 70 guests. When the hotel ceased trading in the early 1970s, the ground floor was taken over by the local Conservative Club and the upstairs was converted into the Lansdowne flats.

The **Commodore Hotel** in Spa Road was originally built as the rectory for the nearby Holy Trinity Church in 1882-4 by the newly-appointed Archdeacon, Henry de Winton. The building was set within two acres of gardens and included a stable and a coach house. An unusual feature of the rectory was a room in the north wing which was large enough to hold some 200 people. This became the Parish Room and was used for church functions. After the Archdeacon's death, the rectory was sold for £6,300 in 1896. The building was enlarged and converted into a private hotel called the **Plas Winton**, after the archdeacon. In 1904, with Mr. J. Sheen as proprietor, it contained some 60 rooms with a garage and cycle house. In 1921 Miss Sheen was the proprietress. Like all other large hotels in the town it was taken over by the army for use as an Officer Cadet Training Centre during World War Two. After the war the hotel was refurbished by

The Hotel Plas Winton later renamed the Commodore

Proposed refurbishment plans for the Plas Winton

The Commodore Hotel in 2004

a private company and renamed the **Hotel Commodore**. Described as 'the latest achievement in the hotel industry', it offered 'all those 4-star amenties you always dreamed about in your ideal hotel'. The managing director was Mr. J.F. Ritchie. The building is designed in the Arts and Crafts style, 'a movement inspired by the idea of simplicity, truth to materials and the units of craft and design which flourished from about 1880 to 1910'.

Interesting features include the fishscale terracotta tiling and, on the second floor, oriel windows under small hoods. Among the guests staying at the hotel have been royalty including the King of Jordan – one of the bathrooms was specially designed for him. Today the hotel is owned by the Baverstocks, a seventh-generation family of hoteliers. It has 51 *en suite* bedrooms and two bridal suites with four-poster beds. The ballroom caters for up to 180 guests for wedding receptions, conferences and meetings. A restaurant and two bars are also featured.

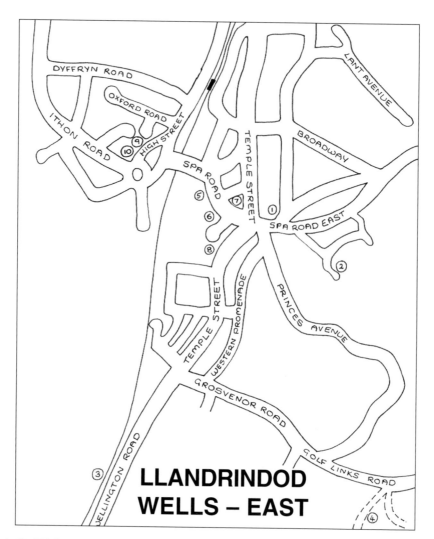

LLANDRINDOD
WELLS – EAST

1 Ye Wells
2 Pump House
3 Ridgebourne Arms
4 Llandrindod Hall
5 Lindens

6 Belgrave
7 Manor
8 Lyndhurst
9 Duggan's
10 Clovelly

None open in 2006
See also page 104

CHAPTER SEVEN

Llandrindod Wells – East

Spa Road continues eastwards across Temple Street where it becomes Spa Road East. This is where one of the most luxurious hotels in the town – **Ye Wells Hotel** – was built in 1907. It was owned by Mrs. Bryan Smith who was always called Madam by the entire staff. It offered 100 bedrooms, large lounges, and smoke, billiard and recreation rooms. As recorded in *Voices of Llandrindod Wells* by Joel Williams, one of the housemaids, Ellen Phillips, imagined Llandrindod 'must be like London', when she first arrived from Leominster to start work aged 14.

Construction of Ye Wells Hotel in 1906

129

Ye Wells Hotel presented an imposing sight to visitors

> I arrived just before the season started and we had to light fires in every
> room to 'air' all the mattresses and pillows – no central heating in those
> days! This took a whole fortnight and then all the rooms had a thorough
> cleaning to be ready for visitors.

She earned 2 shillings and 6 pence a week for working from 6.30 a.m. until
8 p.m. with two hours off in the afternoon. She also did late duty till 11 p.m.
three times a week. At 9.30 a.m. all the staff had to assemble in the staff hall
when Madam read prayers.

> We would all have to kneel on the floor with our heads on a chair.
> Everybody was there, waiters, boots, billiard markers etc. And she always
> knew if anyone was missing. Madam was quite strict.

Many wealthy and well known people stayed at **Ye Wells**, she recalled:

> I remember one couple from Liverpool (he owned a factory). We called
> his wife the Queen of Diamonds. When she came down to dinner she
> wore them everywhere – rings, necklace, brooches, earrings and in her
> hair. One of us always had to wait to help her undress, so we got a good
> look at them. Dame Clara Butt [the famous contralto singer] often stayed
> at the hotel and even had her own private staircase entrance [which was
> specially constructed and led directly to her suite]. Other guests included
> an Indian princess whose brother was a famous cricketer, Mr. and Mrs.

130

Wallis who owned a chain of shops in London (she played golf all day) and I remember also seeing Mr. Lloyd George in town, wearing his 'Inverness' and raising his hat to the ladies.

A local inhabitant also remembered Dame Clara Butt. As a boy in 1922 he was privileged to hear Dame Clara sing for the guests:

> She sang *Ave Maria* and *Land of Hope and Glory* and the people passing on their way to the Pump House band stand stopped to listen to the impromptu concert.

The hotel was not licensed, but 'visitors may bring their own wines etc, or these can be obtained from local wine merchants through the head waiter. There is no charge for corkage'. Meal charges were: breakfast 3s.; lunch 2s. 6d. to 3s. 6d.; tea 1s. to 1s. 6d.; dinner 4s. to 6s.; and supper 3s. 6d. A large garage for the use of customers was adjacent. When the hotel was full, extra accommodation could be provided at the Old Country Club House in Beaufort Road, a small private hotel. Guests could also take advantage of two tennis courts and two croquet lawns, while greenhouses and vegetable gardens provided the hotel with fresh produce.

A distant view of Ye Wells

With the decline in the popularity of spas, large hotels like **Ye Wells** were no longer needed and the building became part of a School for the Deaf (together with the **Pump House Hotel**). Later it became a College of Further Education – *Coleg Powys*.

To the south of Spa Road East and on the site of the modern County Hall, headquarters of Powys County Council, once stood the **Pump House Hotel**, described as the largest and finest of the Spa hotels in Llandrindod Wells. Sited beneath a wooded hillside it boasted its own pump house for the Spa waters and even a bandstand. It all started with the discovery in 1736 of the saline and sulphur spring by Mrs. Jenkins of Bach y Craig Farm. By

Bach y Craig farmhouse which eventually became the Pump House

1820, with the growing number of visitors, Bach y Craig Farm had become a large boarding house known as the Pump House. This was described in 1824 as 'a modern sash-windowed, brick dwelling house', where the previous tenant had made 'an ample fortune retailing the waters!' At some point it was run by Elizabeth Collins, described as a 'licensed brewer and dealer in the finest spiritous liquors, ale, porter, cider and tobacco'.

The house was later enlarged into a hotel which operated a two-tier tariff for first and second class visitors. This led to the hotel being designated 'The House of Lords' and 'The House of Commons' – an arrangement which continued for a generation or more. Canon W.E.T. Morgan, who stayed there during the winter months when it was kept by Mr. and Mrs. Morgan, recalled that 'There was very little intercourse between the two sets of visitors'. Canon Morgan used to go shooting with Mr. Morgan and his son, Lewis. He also remembered the rows of hams hanging from the ceiling in the old smoking room:

> No one who ever stayed at the Pump House can ever forget the cook, Jane, and the ham which she prepared for us, cooked as I have always understood in boiling fat. Woe betide the luckless intruder who ever entered the kitchen uninvited, and incurred her wrath, for when she was angry her language became somewhat sulphurous.

Weekly charges in 1827 were two guineas for first-class visitors and 31s. 6d. for second class ('servants or any who join them' were charged 21s.). By

1859 the charges had only gone up to 52s. 6d. for the 'Lords' and 42s. for the 'Commons'.

In 1868 Edward Middleton Evans of nearby Llwynbarried Hall, Nantmwel, inherited the Trefonen Estate on which the hotel stood. Encouraged by the rapid growth of the town as a resort, he rebuilt the **Pump House** as a grand Victorian hotel and also created a 14-acre lake, which became popular for boating and weekend regattas. Then in 1888 it was replaced by a bigger luxury building and further enlarged in 1897. An advertisement of 1906 said the hotel was the largest in Wales, capable of accommodating some 200 people, and the most comfortable in Europe

Visitors to the original Pump House

The Pump Room about 1900

The rebuilt Pump House with its 14-acre lake

133

The Pump House in all its glory in 1909

Left: The concierge at the Pump House

Above: The Pump House tariff about 1939

with such luxuries as hairdressing departments. It was at this hotel that Keiller's Austrian Orchestra gave daily concerts. The hotel's ornamental grounds covered a hundred acres on both sides of the present Princes Avenue, including tennis courts, croquet lawns, the present boating lake, and promenades in the grounds and surrounding woods. A private 9-hole golf course was later added onto what is today called the Common.

Middleton Evans built himself a private residence next to the hotel, which survives today as Southfields. Visitors usually arrived by train and were met at the station by conveyances from the hotel. A local inhabitant recalled:

> It was a fine sight to see the horse bus with its two fine horses, the driver with his smart black coat and cockaded top hat. On the back step stood Otto, the Swiss footman (6ft. 4in. tall), in his top hat, long camel-coloured coat and matching trousers. The luggage float would follow behind.

134

Two views of the Pump House Hotel in its heyday

He also remembered that as a boy a great treat was to see the arrival of the Earl of Coventry with his retinue in his own special train. The Earl's hunters were transported in horse boxes and once the fox hounds came as well. In 1904 the manager was Mr. E.M.P. Duffield.

In 1929 the **Pump House** was acquired by Lady Honeywood Hotels Ltd., with a reputation for status and clientele to match the best hotels in the south of France. During World War Two it became a military hospital and was also used as an Officer Cadet Training Unit. It ceased trading as an hotel in 1947 and became an Emergency Teacher Training College until 1950, and was then part of the residential school for deaf children up to 1971. In 1974, the building was purchased by Powys County Council for use as its headquarters, but in the late 1980s the building became structurally unsound and was eventually demolished. The new County Hall was opened in 1991. Perhaps the only reminder of the **Pump House** today is the ornate glass canopy that graces the down platform at the railway station – it was originally part of the hotel.

The Ridgebourne Arms in 2004

The **Ridgebourne Arms**, located on Wellington Road, the road leading south towards Builth Wells, was originally part of a row of early 19th-century terraced town houses. A Foresters Club was opened there in the 1860s and Henry Wheatstone was the landlord in 1904. The inn was completely refurbished in 1999 just prior to its re-opening with Charlie and Maggie Cutler at the helm. It has a centrally-sited bar counter with a public bar to one side and a lounge bar on the other with a restaurant leading off. Accommodation, small by Llandrindod standards, comprises one double, one twin and one twin/double *en suite*.

Grosvenor Road leads eastwards from Wellington Road towards the boating lake. Beyond the lake and on the site of a deserted farmhouse by the old Holy Trinity church once stood the town's first ever hotel. It was known as **Llandrindod Hall**, or Mr. Grosvenor's Great House. The farmhouse had been converted in 1749, with many additional buildings, by Mr. William Grosvenor, an enterprising businessman of sporting tastes from Shrewsbury, who saw the potential of accommodation for 'the more genteel sort of folk'. Eventually the hotel had dancing rooms, billiard rooms, bowling greens and fish ponds, while the grounds were laid out with plantations, shrubberies and a cockpit. A barber from Bath came specially every season.

A description of the hotel in 1750 reads:

> Here were accommodations for the invalid of whatever rank and distinction, field amusements for the healthy ... balls, billiards and regular assemblies varied the pastimes of the gay and fashionable. The grounds were ornamented in a style of elegance. There were fishponds ... a cockpit ... race grounds. The utmost regularity and systematic management prevailed in the interior of the house ... Like a *metropolitan* hotel, it had attached to it both neat and handsome shops for milliners, glovers, hair-dressers, and all descriptions of person likely to be useful to the visitors. In short Llandrindod Hall bore some resemblance to a market town.

In a letter of 1760, the Welsh poet and literateur, Lewis Morris, wrote:

> The best company stayed at Grosvenor's Hotel near the Church, which provided a Ball Room for ladies and a Bowling Green for men ... That it allows breakfast, dinner and supper but perhaps it would not be amiss to take a little generous liquor in the evening.

Morris took the water and a 'wonderful cure' was effected, for after 10 days he could put on his shoes and stockings which he had not done for six months previously.

Mr. Grosvenor put his brother-in-law and sister, Mr. and Mrs. Robert Ingall, in charge of the internal arrangements, while he and his daughter, Lucy, looked after the out-of-door activities – cockfight-ing, horse racing and

The present farmhouse on the site of Llandrindod Hall

hunting the hare, fox, otter and even deer. The hotel could accommodate as many as 300 guests while as many as 1,000 people danced in the Great Ball Room. Balls during the Horse-Racing and Buck-Hunting week were held at the hotel during the 1750s – the earliest big dances in Radnorshire. During the Race week of 1756 it was reported that a ball was given each night and 'it was judged that near a thousand persons were in the Great Ball Room on Monday night when two sets danced without interruption'. Although it contained more than a hundred beds, Mr. Grosvenor took a lease of Trevonen as a supplementary hotel. According to the Rev. D. Stedman Davies:

The influx of visitors of all description, especially during the Horse-racing and Buck-hunting week became a nuisance, so these sports were discontinued after 3 or 4 years, partly from the remonstrances of the Landlord of the Inn [hotel], who experienced great losses by the numbers of sharpers who attended on these occasions, but principally on account of the inhabitants rising, and with scythes and pitchforks protecting their harvests from the ravages of the sons of Nimrod.

Later the hotel became a popular rendezvous for gamesters and on one occasion £70,000 was won and lost in a day there. But a new owner, influenced by the Methodist Revival, came along, and so scandalised was he at what was going on, that he closed the place down. After the owner, Thomas Jones, the artist, failed to let it, it was converted in 1794 into a House of Industry for the employment of the able-bodied poor. This venture failing, Llandrindod Hall was razed to the ground. Later, Llandrindod Hall farm-house was built on the site of the hotel's old kitchens. Today, the farm is still thriving with about 100 acres put to sheep, cattle and horses. The bowling green to the rear of the building is still discernible.

THE BELGRAVE, LLANDRINDOD WELLS.
Mrs. INGRAM MUIRHEAD, Proprietress,
Close to Pump Rooms, Common, and Golf Links.

Three failed Llandrindod hotels:
Above: The Belgrave in Spa
Road in the 1920s
Above right: The Lindens, also
in Spa Road
Right: The one-time Manor
Hotel in Lindens Walk

Top: High Street with the Clovelly Hotel on the left.
Left: The Clovelly, boarded up in 2005
Right: The statue of Hygiea

Up until World War Two, Llandrindod Wells abounded in other hotels most of which have since closed and either been converted into other usages or demolished. Examples of these include the **Lindens Hotel** in Spa Road which is now an office block; the **Manor Hotel** in Lindens Walk which became an old people's home, but is now awaiting re-development; the **Belgrave** in Spa Road, now turned into flats and a solicitor's; the **Lyndhurst** in Temple Street; and **Duggan's Hotel** in High Street. Established in 1877, this latter hotel was described in 1904 as a commercial and boarding establishment with private apartments, billiard room and croquet. The proprietress was Mrs. Thomas Duggan. Another well known, old establishment in High Street, which boasted at least half a dozen hotels, was the **Clovelly Hotel**, which closed after the war with the ground floor becoming a café. Now empty, it too is awaiting re-development. The stable doors are still visible as is a statue near the roof depicting Hygiea, the Greek Goddess of Health, which is also the symbol of Llandrindod Wells.

Llanwyre is a village some 1½ miles to the north-west of Llandrindod Wells. Close to the village church is the **Bell Inn** built in 1888 on the site of a much older hostelry after it was demolished by its owner, Mr. Gibson Watt, of Doldowlod Hall. The Old Bell probably dated back to 1667, which was the date engraved on an oak panel just inside the present front door. A carved oak pew in the church bore the same date and was supposed to have been occupied by the landlord's family. Welsh drovers on their way to markets in England and local farmers were regular customers.

Mr. G.E. Body lived there as a child in the 1870s and '80s and in his book *The Old Fashioned Inn*, written in the 1930s, described the **Bell** as having

> a thatched roof, and I remember, when I was quite young, watching the sparrows and other birds going to roost in the crevices in the thatch. The living room was a large one, used for cooking and all domestic purposes, with a large, old, chimney corner which provided seating accommodation for some of the customers, and in addition there was room to hang a ham or flitch of bacon on each side. The mantelpiece bore all kinds of pewter and copper plates and pans, which were polished every week. There were many beehives in the large garden in front of the house, which was filled with all kinds of flowers, fruit trees, vegetables and herbs. ... Old countrymen in smock frocks sat in the chimney corner smoking their long clay pipes and drinking their well-earned Bass or Worthington, which came direct by rail from Burton to Llandrindod Wells.

The inn, he recalled, was 'built of wood, with large oak beams for support, and in stormy wintry weather the old house would shake and the beams creak until you were afraid the whole place was coming down'. He had to carry spring water from a well nearly half-a-mile away.

Mr. Body states that the landlady was Mrs. Gredby, immortalised by Miss Braddon in her novel *Hostages to Fortune*. However, a Llandrindod Wells guide of 1890 says that 'for 54 years a celebrated old lady, named Mrs. Body kept this house'. The guide also quotes from Miss Braddon's novel that the licensee was Mr. M.A. Gredby and the landlady was Mrs. Gredby. As she called the **Bell** the New Inn, these are obviously fictitious names. Whatever their proper name, they

The Bell Inn about 1900

were both larger than life characters. According to Mr. Body, the landlady often visited the hotels at Llandrindod. She was 'gifted with a beautiful voice and the power of expressing herself admirably, she had no difficulty in entertaining a number of visitors, who in return invited her to their homes in London and other large towns when the season was over'. Mr. Gredby, 'a man of a fearless turn of mind,' often travelled 'for miles at night, after collecting money for insurance companies and debts due to the local doctor'. He would even on dark nights 'accompany policemen who were afraid of going alone to track suspicious or dangerous characters'.

In winter, fox-hunting was a favourite sport and people came from miles around to take part, usually calling at the **Bell** for refreshment on their way to the meet. Another popular sport was greyhound coursing. 'Those farmers around who kept greyhounds arranged to meet at the Bell, each one bringing his greyhounds, of which they were all very proud'.

An occasional visitor, usually with the Vicar, was Squire Watt, from nearby Doldowlod Hall, 'a close relative and descendant of the gentleman who found out the power of steam by watching a boiling kettle. The squire had in his possession the original kettle which first suggested the idea to James Watt'.

The Bell Inn suitably decorated for the Gibson-Watt marriage in 1914

Mr. Body added:

> There was no policeman living near the Bell, but one came periodically
> from Newbridge-on-Wye, three miles away. Named Bird, he was like an
> illustration out of Dickens. He had a flowing red beard which reached to his
> waist, and was addicted to biting off lengths of tobacco, and saying to any
> transgressor: 'Dos't thee know thou comes under the penalty of the law'. ...
> He used to drop in casually at the Bell, but never came when there was a
> jolly good fight, which occurred frequently 50 or 60 years ago, as each
> one learned to use his fists in self-defence. ... Seldom did it happen,
> however, that they struck each other in the Inn. They would challenge
> each other to go outside.

Inns in those days, he recalled, were open from early morning until late at
night, and if travellers called at night, they were open even then, as far as
offering accommodation and refreshments went.

One of many eccentric characters who visited the **Bell** was a former
huntsman who had followed the hounds all his life and

> after a few glasses of beer from the wood he would grow quite jolly and
> elated ... When in conversation, he would break out into his old call to the
> hounds, 'Tally ho, hark away!' and could be heard singing a hunting song
> as he returned home.

Gypsies and tramps wandered about especially during the summer. The
gypsies often camped on waste land near the inn and after eating would sing

Two views of the Bell Inn at Llanwyre in 2005

and play the violin and other musical instruments and 'have what we call a jolly time ... '.

Mr. Body left the district for a few years and on his return:

> I walked a few hundred yards in the direction of the old Bell Inn, which had been replaced by a well built stone house and the old church had been pulled down and replaced by a new one.

At the turn of the century John Hamer was the landlord. During the Second World War the **Bell** was run by Mrs. Mackintosh while her husband

An aerial view of the Bell Inn

was serving in the Royal Air Force. At that time the pub had a large garage, stables, a pigsty, French barn and a large vegetable garden, together with two fields along the lane on part of which houses have since been built. From being a small country pub, the **Bell** was considerably extended in the 1970s with a second bar built around a new serving

Local residents outside the Bridge End Inn, which closed in 1916

counter and a restaurant behind. The stables, which had been demolished, were replaced by another restaurant appropriately called Stables, complete with the Stables Bar. Accommodation upstairs was refurbished and there are nine 'luxury' bedrooms with a separate entrance.

Now a free house and called the **Bell Country Inn** it has been run since March 2004 by Shek, assisted by his son Duke, who has up-graded the hostelry even further and increased the dining area. Shek, who worked at Guy's Hospital in London as a psychiatrist for 30 years, also aims to expose the old chimney corner in the original living room.

A few hundred yards along the road from the village to Newbridge on Wye is a row of four cottages, the end one of which used to be an old alehouse called the **Bridge End Inn**. Also known as **Tophouse**, it was run for a number of years by the Pritchard family at the end of the 19th century and beginning of the 20th century. Built of stone with a slated roof, the inn had stabling for three horses, a cowhouse, two pig-sties, hay bay and French barn, together with one and a half acres of land. However, in 1916, when the licensee/owner was Lucretia Pritchard, who had taken over from her husband, the late Thomas Pritchard, the renewal of its licence was refused by the Radnorshire Licensing Committee. She was awarded compensation of £270, of which £250 went to the mortgagee. Her son, Thomas, told the committee that in 1915 the inn sold 45 barrels of beer, 50 dozen bottled beer and stout, and £33 16s. 8d. worth of spirits.

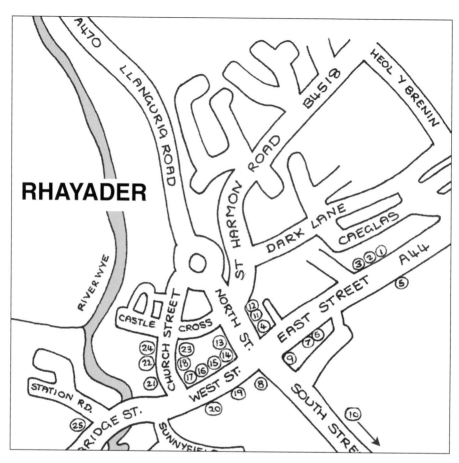

RHAYADER

* – Open in 2006

CHAPTER EIGHT

Rhayader
EAST ST., SOUTH ST. & NORTH ST.

The people of Wern Marteg (Pantydwr)
To town they will come,
Some of them are at the Lamb,
And others, at the Crown,
The people of St. Harmon
Will fill the Oak and Harp
and ride upon the Railway Train
And get home before it's dark.

(Edward Hope of Rhayader early in the 19th century)

Originally known as Rhaiadr Gwy or 'cataract on the Wye', Rhayader came into being because of its position as an important crossing of the river, first by fords and then by a bridge. In the 12th century Rhys ap Gruffydd, prince of South Wales, in order to guard the crossing, built a castle which was captured and destroyed several times during its brief history. Another smaller castle was constructed overlooking the Wye ford in Cwmdauddwr to the south-west. At that time the main focus of the settlement was the river crossing and the main road was Bridge Street. During the 13th century Rhayader was captured by the Norman lord, Roger Mortimer, and it was then that the medieval town took shape. This consisted of two principal streets running roughly north-south and east-west, East Street being a short continuation of Bridge Street.

When the Act of Union of 1536 joined Wales to England, Rhayader hosted the new Courts of Law alternately with New Radnor, but shortly afterwards the town was raided by the Plant Matt, a notorious gang of robbers, who broke into the gaol to rescue one of their group and then murdered the Assize judge who was about to try him. As a result the Assize court was afterwards held solely in New Radnor.

The town developed as a cloth-making centre with a large sheep population on the surrounding hills and it became well known for its sheep sales, markets and four annual fairs. Other crafts such as weavers, millers and saddlers also thrived. Rhayader was also very much a cattle market centre with a main drover's route passing through the town. Not surprisingly there were a number of hostelries – amongst the most substantial buildings in town – to cater for their needs. In fact, the Council of the Court of the Marches complained in 1575 that there were too many alehouses. Rhayader Feast was long notorious for its scenes of drunkenness and disorder and liquor flowed freely at celebrations held by local landowners. This probably was the case, too, at Easter 'heaving' when men heaved the women (in a chair) on Easter Monday and the women heaved the men the next day. This ancient custom was practised up to about 1840.

Travellers had to contend with an open stream, the Bwgey, which coursed down the streets giving the town another nickname of 'Bwgey'; the stream was 'buried' in 1877. In the 1840s Rhayader got caught up in the Rebecca Riots in which terror was spread by armed men with blackened faces, wearing female attire. Although protesting mainly about economic conditions in South Wales, the rioters vented their pent-up fury against toll gates, which levied excessive charges on travellers using the turnpike roads. Probably named after Rebecca in the Old Testament (she was told by Abraham 'let thy seed possess the gate of those who hate them'), the rioters descended in October 1843 on Rhayader, which had six toll gates. They wrecked two of the town's gates and were on their way to a third gate on the Wye Bridge when they were intercepted by police-sergeant Shaw and six special constables outside the **Bear** public house.

According to Pat Malloy in *And they blessed Rebecca* it was

> an astonishing sight. Two hundred men, their faces blackened, wearing petticoats, shawls, bonnets and straw hats, marching in step 'with a slow and measured pace' in the standard four-abreast military formation, the front and rear files with shouldered muskets and those in the centre carrying swords, hatchets, sledgehammers, saws and more guns. Words of command rang out and were instantly obeyed as the silent column struck down with the butts of their muskets those special constables who ventured near. Desperately, Sgt. Shaw placed his unarmed men across the street to oppose the 200 marchers, and shouted to them: 'My men, I hope you will not fire'. But without a word they wheeled around the Lion and Castle and to the roar of nearly a hundred blank cartridges which they fired towards the police officers, disappeared into the darkness on the Aberystwyth road.

The men went on to destroy the stone-built Wye Bridge toll house and later destroyed the remaining three. While peace was soon restored the name

Rebecca continued, this time in connection with salmon poachers after a new act made salmon fishing in the Wye illegal. Customers of the **Bear's Head** recalled the days when Rebecca and her daughters returned to Rhayader in the form of gangs of salmon poachers when illegal bait was sold in old jam jars. Hen salmon were gaffed and the eggs stripped out, which, after being dried and mixed with other ingredients, were put in a jam jar and sold for £1 a jar. Trout found the bait irresistible.

Although the building of the railway in the 1860s brought to an end the isolation of mid-Wales from the rest of the country, it meant little change for Rhayader. In 1876 Captain Cecil Otway, who still ran a coach service from Presteigne to Aberystwyth, described the town as 'a quaint old place, a crumbling relic of the past that ought to be put under a glass case and kept for ever'. However, a complete transformation came about in the 1890s when the nearby Elan Valley dams were built. Following an Act of Parliament in 1892, Birmingham Corporation were allowed to build four reservoirs by damming the valleys of the Elan and Claerwen rivers. Thousands of workers from all over the country were employed and many were housed in a specially built 'model village' in Elan. The work brought many jobs and prosperity to Rhayader, which about that time boasted 17 inns.

The high point of Rhayader's prosperity probably came in 1904 when King Edward VII and Queen Alexandra offically opened the dams. A fifth and largest dam and reservoir, the Claerwen, was inaugurated by Queen Elizabeth II in 1952. 75 million gallons of water a day is conveyed through 12 miles of tunnel, 23 miles of 'cut and cover' and 38 miles of pipe lines to Birmingham.

However, according to local old-timers, the pubs of Rhayader were in their heyday in the 1960s when they voted to open on Sundays. People from neighbouroughing counties, which were still 'dry', descended on the town. 'It was like the Wild West', said one veteran. Today, the Elan Valley, with its now mature lakes, has become the focus of tourists who come to the area via Rhayader which continues as a busy market town.

East Street is the main approach road (A44) to the town from England and continues to the cross-roads where the war memorial stands. On the northern side of East Street, entering the town from the Leominster direction, stands the **Bear's Head**. The first mention of it is in the Minutes of the Radnorshire General Quarter Sessions for 1823-1829. The landlord between 1830 and 1835 was John Hamer, succeeded by David Edwards. According to the census of 1841, Edwards lived there with his wife Mary, both aged 30, and their children, Mary, 6, Margaret, 4, and Elizabeth, 2. They had a busy house for also residing there at that time were Margaret Gold, a 15-year-old servant; Thomas Morgan, 30, relieving officer; Mary Morgan, 40, grocer, and four children; William Mann, 35, mail coachman;

East Street looking east about 1900; the Bear's Head is on the left

Catherine Prees, 20, servant; Elizabeth Jones, 12, servant; and Robert James, 85, independent, with his wife Mary, 75, and daughter Catherine, 40. Edwards was still the landlord in 1843 when Rhayader became involved in the Rebecca Riots.

In those days the front door of the **Bear's Head** opened onto a passage with stairs leading to accommodation above. On the right, a door opened to a room with an open fireplace and a serving hatch to the bar. To the left of the passage was a snug. At the side of the building were stables with three or more horse bays while at the rear was a yard, garden and large field.

In 1902 the licensee was Price T. Griffiths. Some 40 years later, in 1946, the **Bear's Head** was bought by the David Williams brewery in Builth and Mrs. E. Griffiths became tenant. It was then sold to Evans Bevan of the Vale of Neath Brewery, Swansea and in about 1947 Noel Lewis became landlord. His son, Alan, recalls that spittoons were provided under the benches in the bar and that there was a hard earth floor in the kitchen. Boxing matches, between locals, which took place in the back yard, were a popular feature with the pugilists including Lewis himself and Fred Dore, who ran a china shop opposite. Noel is also remembered for blasting the dart board with a shotgun in order to show the other players where the bull was! An advertisement in the town guide of 1950 describes the **Bear's Head** as having 'H. & C. water in bedrooms' and offering 'fishing, shooting and riding'.

Harold Turner took over as landlord in 1955 and it was during his early tenure that the premises were modernised. The bar became open plan with the

The mounting block at the Bear's Head

serving hatch removed and the old fireplace replaced with a stone front. The date, 1956, was carved in stone with the initials H.T. for the landlord, M.T. for his wife Margaret, and R.T. for their son Richard. The fireplace was later blocked and wall seating installed. Other improvements included inside toilets and, at a later date, the stables and coal shed were converted into a restaurant. Early travellers are remembered by the large stone mounting block for horse riders that survives outside the pub. The Vale of Neath Brewery was eventually taken over by Whitbreads from whom Turner bought the **Bear**. Turner, who also worked as a driver for Rhayader Quarries, advertised it as a hotel in the 1960s. Before drinking on Sunday became legal, a special bus was laid on to take customers to the Tram Inn at Eardisley. The **Bear's Head** eventually became the first pub in Rhayader to obtain a seven-

The Bear's Head in 2005

day licence although drinks could only be served with food on Sundays. Mr. Turner stayed at the **Bear's Head** until 1985 when it was sold to Mr. Wymss and then to David Howells, who sold the field at the rear to a local builder for housing development.

At one end of the **Bear's Head** was once a separate beer house known as the **Esam Fach**, its name appearing in the Minutes of the General Quarter Sessions for Radnorshire during the period 1823-1829. The name probably came from the Esam family who are recorded as living in Rhayader as early as 1696. Ownership eventually passed to the **Bear's Head** and it became a shop but is at present empty.

Next door to the **Bear's Head** is the Mount Guest House in the front garden of which once stood the **Borough Inn**. It was sited a little way back from the road and probably included stables and a field in which to keep animals. During the 19th century it was run for a long period by the George family; according to the 1841 census, the publican was Thomas George, aged 45, who lived there with his wife, Jane, also 45, their children Elizabeth, 10, Ann, 8, Thomas, 6, and William, 3, together with Elizabeth Mills, a 20-year-old servant. Thomas was still there in 1844 but by 1891 the landlord was William George, in all probability the 3-year-old son mentioned in the census. He was one of numerous local people who signed a letter of thanks to country veterinary Edward Thomas for his valuable services including, presumably, to some of his own animals. The **Borough** closed about 90 years ago and the building was then demolished. The present driveway originally led to the pub.

At the corner of East Street and North Street is the **Castle**, which used to be called the **Lion and Castle**. Remains of a timber-framed gable end wall and timber partitions date back to about 1800. In 1830 Richard Evans was landlord and was still there in 1835 when, according to *Pigot's Directory*, 'The *Tally-Ho* coach from Hereford called in at the inn every

A 1960s advertisement for the Castle Hotel

Tuesday and Thursday afternoon at one o'clock on its way to Aberystwyth and again on the return journey'.

The 1841 census showed that Joseph Betts, 25, was publican of the **Lion and Castle**, with his 20-year-old wife Elizabeth. Also staying there were Elizabeth Collins, aged 7; Elizabeth Lewis, 30, servant; William Wallice, 30, land surveyor; and Charles Bate, 25, also a land surveyor. By 1844 there was another landlord, David Davies, and the inn was again referred to as the **Lion and Castle**. In 1902, Richard Jones ran the **Castle**, then described as 'a family & commercial hotel & posting house'.

Mr. and Mrs. D.H. Price were licensees in the 1950/'60s when it was a free house with 'H. & C. in all rooms'. At one time it became the home of Rhayader Football Club who, together with their opponents, used the upstairs facilities as a changing room, despite there being only one bath. Music lessons were held there as well. A previous landlord allegedly saw the ghost mentioned in one of H.L.V. Fletcher's novels of the 1950s. Cwmhumphrey, once a baker's shop next door in North Street, was later incorporated into the hotel. A wall was knocked down and the baker's shop converted into another bar with a pool table and game machines. The bar counter was extended to serve both the new room and the existing lounge bar.

By the 1990s the **Castle** fell on hard times, being in need of structural repairs, and closed down for a spell. In 1997 it was described as 'Rhayader's most distressing eyesore, the more so because it is the most prominent building in the town centre, only too obvious to travellers from any direction'.

The Castle Carvery and Bars in 2005 after restoration

Its ground floor was boarded up for security reasons, the yellow boarding contrasting glaringly with the green building, making its dereliction still more obvious. The plaster render — especially on the North Street frontage — was in need of repair, both frontages needed repainting, while the roof and many of the windows and surrounds required attention. A saviour was to hand, however, in the form of Michael Lloyd, who also runs the funeral parlour at the next door Alma's showroom. Having bought the premises, he converted the upstairs accommodation into five flats, and installed a tenant to run the **Castle** as a pub with a large restaurant. The landlord Phil Woosnam continued the football connection. A member of the Welsh Football Association, he welcomed players and fans *en route* to Cardiff. Now there is an unofficial Wednesday Club when old-timers meet up for a chat and a drink and an annual tippit competition is held. The ghost still re-appears, in female form, and is said in prior life to have hung herself from one of the upstairs beams after being jilted. A distinctive smell of violets has been noticed and on one occasion a wine glass mysteriously burst into smithereens with the noise of a gun shot.

The former Unicorn in 2005

Towards the east and on the southern side of East Street there used to be a public house called the **Unicorn** which was opposite the **Bear's Head**. It closed down at the end of the 19th century or in the early years of the 20th century and became a private residence and later was divided into shops. One is Rhayader Books and the other was bought five years ago by Clive Powell, who owns the Cwmdaudder Arms, and let out to Richard Bryan, who ran a car finance business, and since January, 2005 houses Watson Associates, a mortgage company.

Further along the street towards the clock is the **Royal Oak Hotel**, which at the time of writing is closed, but is understood to be re-opening at some future date. A former coaching inn, the building dates back to the early 19th century although the remains of a 17th-century stone-built house are still visible at the rear. At some period the timber frontage was demolished and re-built in brick with an extra floor added. Stables at the rear accommodated a dozen horses with a large dormitory above.

The Royal Oak with its boarded front. The Market Hall is on the right

According to the *Universal British Directory (1793-98)*, the victualler was John Jones whilst in the mid-19th century it was run for a number of years by Evan Lewis. The 1841 census records that Mr. Lewis, who was 45, lived there with his wife Ann, also aged 45, and their children Ann, 15; John, 13; Charlot, 11; James, 8; and Evan, 9. Also living there were three servants: Catherine Pugh, 20; Thomas Price, 15; and David Price, 15. On the death of Mr. Lewis, his widow took over and was still running the business in the 1890s. In memory of her late husband, she presented the clock in the war memorial tower situated at the main cross-roads. On her death, Mrs. Lewis left the **Royal Oak** to Llandrindod Hospital, which later sold it. In 1902 it was decribed as a family and commercial hotel with Ernest Hilliard as landlord.

The Plaque on the war memorial tower

The hotel was taken over in 1922 by Charles Futcher, on leaving the Army, and has remained in the Futcher family ever since. Mr. Futcher had been a First Lieutenant in the Royal Garrison Artillery

155

serving first in India and then in France and Belgium during the First World War. In 1916 he was awarded a medal for long and meritorious service together with £10 annually. Further light on his military service came in a *News of the World* article dated 13 November 1960 which stated:

> Lt. Futcher knew the secret of the Unknown Warrior tomb in Westminster Abbey, himself a casualty of WW1 torn by shrapnel and gassed on the Western Front as an artillery officer. Soon after the end of the war he and another officer were detached to the singular mission of finding the unknown warrior. They were sworn to secrecy. They began their strange quest on the Belgian battlefields where vast, communal graves were being reopened so that the dead could be buried with honour in the military cemeteries in Belgium and France. Among the bodies, many still in recognisable uniforms, they found one whose uniform bore no insignia of rank or regiment. His tunic bore 'universal' buttons. The body was sent home with three bulky sandbags containing Belgian soil and in which he is still buried. He told his family 'If I ever told the full story people would hardly believe it'.

On Mr. Futcher's death in 1939, his widow took over the licence. During World War Two the hotel was commandeered by the Army and used as a Sergeants' Mess. Mrs. Futcher died in 1953 and the **Royal Oak** was taken over by William, one of her four sons, who all served in the armed forces during the last war. The bar area remained more or less as it was well over a hundred years ago and in 2000 was placed on CAMRA's inventory of historic pub interiors. There are just over two hundred British pubs in the list including only six in Wales. The hotel closed two years ago on the death of William and his widow lived there until her death in 2005.

The sole surviving brother, David, who grew up there, recalled that there were three bedrooms on the top floor and three on the floor below with a

large room for various functions including wedding parties and darts competitions.

Another activity associated with the hotel was pigeon flying with a pigeon house in the rear garden. In the stables was a pit in the floor where work was carried out underneath the coaches. He also remembered impromptu musical evenings in the hotel

Local fox hunters outside the Royal Oak   bar, which still retains its

Left: David Futcher behind the bar of the Royal Oak in 1968.
Right: The sign still has the Futcher name as licensee

pewter top counter, when the singing was led by a police inspector conducting with a matchstick. A police sergeant remained discreetly outside.

Next to the **Royal Oak** used to be the **Welsh Harp Inn**, which is now a shop with a flat above. In 1811 it was known simply as the **Harp** or **Old Harp**. The licensee in 1835 was Ann Jones and the 1841 census showed that she lived there with her children, John, a 20 year-old shoemaker; Thomas, also 20, an apprentice shoemaker; and Ann aged 15; together with Jane, an 87-year-old independent; and Ann Edwards, aged 22. Ann Jones was still there in 1844. In 1902 the

The Royal Oak in 2005

About 1900 the Royal Oak and the Welsh Harp stood side by side

The one time Welsh Harp 2005

landlord was Price Worthing, but by 1911 it was owned by Mrs. Annie Worthing, of the Sun Inn, St. Harmon, with David Mason as the licensee. But when its licence came up for renewal in 1912 it was refused by the Radnorshire Licensing Authority on the grounds that there were 12 licensed houses in Rhayader for a population of 961, or one pub for every 80 people. Described as an alehouse, the property had 14 rooms and stabling for five horses. Compensation paid amounted to £282 10s. to the owner and £27 10s. to the licensee. The building has since been run as a retail premises and at present is a gift shop called *By Design*.

The Red Bull (Stag) once filled this gap in South Street

Turning the corner from East Street into South Street, on the right-hand side is a large gap to the south of No.2 where once stood the **Red Bull Hotel**. It was also known as the **Stag** in 1816 and, from time to time, simply as the **Bull**. In the early spring members of the Hafd y Mynach angling club used to meet there in:

> solemn conclave to arrange the programme of the season's outings and again at Christmastime, when around the festive board, the scenes and incidents of those outings are in their flowing cups freshly remembered.

The inn was used as a club for all sorts of meetings, transaction of business, discussions of local and public affairs, and for clinching bargains after a sale of livestock. It often became the resort of fortune-tellers and showmen of freaks, for the house was common to all. At some point it ceased

The Fleece Temperance Hotel about 1900

trading and had become the Red Shop by 1941. The building was later demolished with only the outline of three fireplaces remaining on the wall of the adjoining property.

On the opposite side, an empty shop and a two-storey, stone-built private house was once the **Fleece Hotel** and originally an inn. The name refers to the important local wool trade, rather than being a place where a customer would be fleeced. The **Fleece** appeared in the Minutes of the General Quarter Sessions for the period 1823-1829. In 1830 Evan Powell was landlord and in 1832 the Baptists held their early services there before its church was opened in 1838. At the turn of the century it became a Temperance Hotel, both private and commercial, with Thomas Morris as proprietor. He was nicknamed Morris the Fleece and also known as Foot-it. The latter name resulted from his custom of crying out 'foot it' to passengers in one of his horse and traps when approaching a hill and making them get out and walk behind the trap. The **Fleece** later stopped trading; the two pillars on the front were removed and it became a private house and a shop.

Continuing along South Street towards the outskirts of town lies an imposing three-storey building which is now the **Brynafon Country House Hotel**. Built in 1878, it started life as a workhouse owned by Rhayader Rural District Council and run by a Board of Guardians. The first floor was used as a maternity ward and the second floor accommodated single and unmarried women. At the rear was a separate building for

The former Fleece Hotel in 2005

The Brynafon Country House Hotel in 2005

vagrants and tramps, who were given breakfast providing they first broke rocks for use in road repairs. To monitor their efforts, the crushed rock had to be passed through a grille. With social welfare changing, the workhouse was no longer needed and it closed in 1935. The building re-opened as a school for the deaf, and then became a factory producing car accessories. This subsequently closed and the building was left derelict. About 25 years ago it was given a new lease of life when it was bought by André Gallagher and transformed into seven large holiday apartments. He sold it after about eight years and it was then converted into a hotel by Winston Collins who ran it with his family for 15 years. In 2004 it was taken over by Linda and Gerard Wilkinson. Today the **Brynafon**, far removed from its workhouse origins, boasts 20 *en-suite* bedrooms, a licensed bar,

The grille at Brynafon used for quality control of road stone

restaurant and conference facilities. The bar is situated in a conservatory full of plants and a sunken fish pool.

In the opposite direction from the War Memorial and on the east side of North Street is the **Lamb & Flag**, a name signifying the Holy Lamb or Jesus Christ and a banner used in heraldic signs. At one time it was referred to as the Preacher's Pub since hundreds of them were accommodated there on their journeys. It was originally a timber-framed house of about 1700, but has been much altered although some timber framing remains. In 1830 Richard Mills was the licensee and again in 1841 when he was 45 years old and

Old shops being demolished for an extension to the Lamb and Flag

The Lamb and Flag in 2005

worked as a saddler, living at the **Lamb** with his wife Elinor, also 45, and three children. Also living there were an agricultural labourer and a plumber. In 1844 Elizabeth Bevan was in charge.

In 1902 Mrs. Elizabeth George was described as both licensee and butcher. The **Lamb and Flag** was later bought by David Williams of the Builth brewery. In 1946, when the inn was transferred from Williams' personal ownership to his brewery, the landlord was Gordon Griffiths. The premises then included a boot shop, stabling and out-buildings. Bed and breakfast was being offered in local press adverts in the 1950s and '60s.

At some point a large wooden building on the far side of the pub, that had housed the stables and a shoe shop, was demolished to be replaced by a new building that now forms the restaurant. Alterations were carried out in the 1970s making the bar area open plan. Previously a passage led from the front door to a staircase and the bar counter was in the rear lounge. The washroom behind the present bar was a snug with a piano. A massive oak beam above the bar fireplace gives some indication of the inn's age.

When Mr. Mosen was landlord about 20 years ago panelling dating back to the 13th century was found but it has since been sold. At one time the **Lamb and Flag** was the only place in Rhayader which had a legal betting shop. The licence was issued to a shed in the garden which was regularly manned and bets were phoned through by the landlord while monitoring a TV in the bar. The present owners bought the free house property in 1995. There are five letting bedrooms and the inn is a favourite watering hole for local rugby players.

Further along North Street and opposite the Smithfield Market is the **Black Lion**, a favourite haunt of local farmers. A plaque used to be displayed on the frontage bearing the date 1742 and the initials D.J. (Daniel Judd). This could indicate the date the pub was first built or be a record of a later refurbishment. David Thomas was listed as victualler in the *Universal British Directory (1793-8)* and in 1811 the inn was being called the **Old Black Lion**. In the 1841 census Thomas Hope, aged 40, was publican and lived there with his wife, Ann, 35, and children Mary, 8, Elizabeth, 4, Ann, 2, and Thomas, 11 months. Also living there were two servants, Elizabeth Cleaton, 20, and Elizabeth Lewis, 14. In 1844 the licensee was Rees Powell, while in 1902 Mrs. Sarah Hughes was at the helm.

A horseman outside the Black Lion in the 1940s

The Black Lion in 2005

163

In the 1930s the **Black Lion** was bought by David Williams of Builth and in 1946 the tenant landlady was Mrs. E.A. Hamer. The story goes that her husband originally held the licence and also worked on the railway. On being told by British Rail that he could not carry out two jobs at the same time, Mr. Hamer transferred the licence to his wife. At that time the premises included outbuildings, stable yard, garden, and a piece of land of over 2,000 square yards. There were also two buildings or sheds (formerly occupied as cottages) adjoining the inn.

Mike and Mary Griffiths were in charge in the 1980s, when an extension was built at the rear providing a new kitchen, indoor toilets and a cellar. The pub was then the headquarters for pony trekking which had become popular in the area. John McAndrew took over until about 1994; then owned by Bass, the pub was closed for about a year before the present landlord purchased the property in 1997. When he took over, the downstairs was divided into two rooms, only one being used as a bar, the other being a private lounge. The central staircase was moved, and the dividing wall knocked down and the two rooms became the bar. Upstairs there are eight bedrooms which, after refurbishment, are planned for letting.

On the other side of the road, next to the Chinese restaurant is, in 2005, an empty building that once used to be the **King's Head**; it started life as two

The former King's Head, which may soon be demolished

164

The Crown Inn about 1920, with the landlady, Mrs. Jones, in the doorway

private houses. In 1835 the landlord was Morgan Jones and, according to Pigot's *Directory* of that year, it was a port of call for the *Prince of Wales* coach from Cheltenham to Aberystwyth passing through every Tuesday and Thursday evening at 5 p.m. On the return journey it called at the **King's Head** every Monday, Wednesday and Friday morning at 10 a.m. The service only ran in the summer. The present owners have applied for planning permission to demolish the building, now in poor condition, and replace it with a three-storey town house.

On the other side of the Chinese restaurant is the **Crown**, believed to be a 16th-century building, which has always been an inn. Although linked with the stabling of horses, it was never a coaching inn. Richard Evans was licensee in 1830 and he was still there in 1844. In the 1841 census,

The 1939 Crown darts team

165

Evans, aged 55, lived at the inn with his wife, Ruth, aged 60, and their children John, 20, an apprentice joiner; William, 20, also a joiner; Jane, 20; and a baby called Mary. In 1902 the landlord was Richard Rowlands and in the 1920s Mrs. J. Jones was in charge.

From 1953 until his death in 1978 Major Patrick Stancomb was the landlord. A member of the Wills tobacco family, he was an eccentric character who seemed to run the place more as a hobby than a business. He could be seen sitting on a bench outside the bar telling potential customers, 'I wouldn't go in if I were you. I'd go to the Lamb across the road'. And if a coach party appeared he would simply lock the front door. He excelled as a tennis player and could do the *Times* crossword every day in 20 minutes.

During his tenure, the **Crown** got the reputation of being the scruffiest bar in Britain. Under the heading 'So proud of his scruffy boozer', an article by Jim Lawson appeared in a national paper in the early 1970s.

> With a cloth that would have passed as a mechanic's rag the landlord of the Crown polished my glass. Then he placed it, smeared and greasy but complete with gin, on the bar which was covered in black slime — leftovers of beer spilt long ago. Reaching for the tonic water the landlord must have sensed my revulsion. 'Don't worry', he explained, 'the dirt will not do any harm, old boy'.
>
> As I gazed around the dust-covered bar strewn with empty soda syphons, old bottles, overflowing ashtrays and bits of paper I had my doubts. And I could not believe that mine host, with his grubby nicotine stained hands, was a former British army major. Somewhere along the line since his days with the Welch Regiment, Patrick Stancomb has done a slovenly about-turn. His studious disregard for hygiene has produced a public bar possibly the scruffiest in Britain. And as far as I could establish he has only one regret — that it isn't in London. 'Customers tell me that if I could transport my pub, untidy and dirty as it is, to London, I would make a million', he said. As it is, on both occasions that I visited the Crown Hotel — it was empty. To be fair the snug at the back was clean, comfortable and tidy. There was no bar in this room.
>
> Why has the major, 56, allowed the public bar to get so bad? 'A doctor friend says there is nothing wrong with spiders webs and dust as long as the glasses and tables are spotless', he said. 'This is a hotel where conversation is valued and everyone can state their opinion. I cannot be bothered with pubs which have become hospitalised with disinfectant and washing-up liquid. It does more harm than a bit of dirt. I have no intention of changing my pub. It's always been like this. I like it and so do my customers'. No doubt they enjoy his excellent beer.

Major Patrick Stancomb behind the bar at the Crown

Major Stancomb and some of his customers

The Crown Inn still thrives in 2005

Despite changes in the early 1980s, much of the internal timbering is still visible; the linen-fold bar front was saved from a demolished house. A small room at the front used to be the office of the local National Farmers' Union. The old stables have been converted into a storage room with three bedrooms above.

In the 1990s the inn was closed for a time until it was purchased in 1994 by Alan and Pauline Lewis, who sold it in 1999 to Brains Brewery. It is the only tied house in Rhayader. A feature of the pub is a large collection of photographs helping to preserve the town's history; many have been supplied by regulars.

CHAPTER NINE

Rhayader
WEST ST., CHURCH ST. & BRIDGE ST.

On the right-hand side of West Street going towards the bridge is the **Lion Royal Hotel**, formerly the **Red Lion**, a coaching inn dating back to the early 17th century. It was described in Ogilby's *Britannia*, published in 1675, as the town's principal inn. According to historian W.H. Howse, the **Red Lion**

> became a well known coaching inn from the time when coaches first penetrated into this part of the country. The turnpike road from Presteigne and Kington to Rhayader was completed in 1779 and by about 1790 the road had been carried through to Aberystwyth. Before these roads were made, very little wheeled traffic of any kind passed through Rhayader, but by 1781 the **Red Lion** had its own postchaises, and the coaches followed soon afterwards.

A 6-horse wagon service between Rhayader and Kington was instituted in 1781, performing the weekly journey of 26 miles in 12 hours. In the *Universal British Directory (1793-98)*, the **Red Lion** was described as 'the most respectable inn, where a post-chaise may be had', with Stephen Evans as the victualler. When the Rev. Richard Warner visited Rhayader on a dark night in 1797 the only glimmer of light he could see was a rush-light in the window of the **Red Lion**. He soon forgot the darkness when he entered the inn and joined a throng of Welshmen greedily eating at a table 'covered with rounds of beef, loins of pork, cheeses, etc'.

Another traveller, G. Lipscomb, stayed at the **Red Lion** in 1799. In his *Journey into Wales*, published in 1801, Lipscomb wrote that Mr. Evans, the landlord, was 'a well-informed man, and a good-humoured Welsh girl, with no knowledge of English, was the only attendant, but possessed genuine politeness'. For supper he and his friend were served with 'a couple of roasted fowls, ham dish, veal cutlets, piece of cold roast beef, excellent tarts, and a quart of strong beer per man, for only a shilling each. A tolerable fare for what one traveller had described as a miserable place'.

The **Red Lion** was well established as a coaching inn by 1814 and was mentioned in Cary's *Traveller's Companion* of that year. In 1815 it was described as 'a bow-sashed house', where post horses could be hired at 1s. 4d. per mile. The stage coaches continued to use the old road to Aberystwyth by way of Devil's Bridge up to the end of 1820, but only in the summer. The road via Llangurig did not come into use until about 1830. The Royal Mail coaches began to come by Rhayader to Aberystwyth in 1835, a run made daily on this road, summer and winter alike until 1858. Other coaches continued to use the Aberystwyth road up to 1864, when the railway was completed to make a direct connection with Aberystwyth through Llanidloes.

Probably the most enterprising landlord of the **Red Lion** was James Lantrow, who died in 1825. He ran his own coaches from the Bull & Mouth, London, through Oxford and Worcester, to the King's Head at Kington, extending the service weekly in the summer to the Talbot Inn, Aberystwyth. He also ran a goods wagon between Rhayader and Kington, where it connected with wagons for London and other places. In 1816 the coach took 28 hours to get from Kington to London and 13 hours from Kington to Aberystwyth. Rather better times were made in 1825, owing to an improvement in the roads. In 1835 the Royal Mail left Kington at 1.23 p.m. and was in Aberystwyth at 8.13 p.m.; returning, they left at 5.30 a.m., reached Rhayader at 9.30 a.m. and arrived in Kington at 12.44 p.m. So punctual were these coaches that people set their clocks by them.

When Samuel Meddins was landlord in 1835, the *Sovereign* coach from Worcester on its way to Aberystwith stopped at the **Red Lion Hotel** every Monday, Wednesday and Friday afternoon at 3 p.m. On the return journey, it called in on the same days at 10 a.m. In the census of 1841, Meddins, aged 45, was still landlord and lived at the hotel with his wife, Elizabeth, 30, together with Samuel, aged 20, and Mary, 15. Also living there were Howard Greenhouse, 30, ostler; Samuel Norris, 15, post boy; Thomas Lawrence, 15, post boy; and five servants – Mary Jones, 25, Elizabeth Hope, 25, Mary Price, 20, Elizabeth Lewis, 15, and John Lawrence, 15.

Two barristers appointed to revise the list of voters in the election of a Knight of the Shire, met at the **Red Lion** in 1842. Two years later the licensee was Elizabeth Meddins, the pub being then called the **Red Lion Royal Hotel**, which boasted an excise office. In 1845 the celebrated Ira Aldridge, known as the *African Roscius* and described as the 'only Actor of Colour that was ever known', appeared for one night at the hotel. The programme included a *Defensive Lecture on the Drama* by Aldridge followed by several songs such as *Miss Lucy Long and The Negro Hunt*, or *Oppossum up a Gum Tree*.

RED LION HOTEL, RHAYADER.

POSITIVELY FOR THIS NIGHT ONLY.

On FRIDAY, OCTOBER 3, 1845,

The following are a few of the DISTINGUISHED PATRONS *of Mr. IRA F. ALDRIDGE, the AFRICAN*

ROSCIUS *in Great Britain and Ireland:*

His Royal Highness the Duke of Gloucester
Their Graces the Duke & Duchess St. Albans
His Grace the Duke of Rutland
Their Graces the Duke & Duchess de Revigo
His Excellency Prince Esterhazy, Austrian
Ambassador to the British Court
F. M. His Grace the Duke of Wellington
Colonel Clarke and Officers, 76th Regiment
Rev. John Herbert, Rector, Killarney.

The Marquess of Kildare
His Grace the Archbishop of Tuam
Right Rev. Dr. Kyle, Bishop of Cork
The Marquess of Granby
The Right Hon. Earl & Countess of Glengall
The Ladies Butler
Lord Dundas   Lord Petre
The Hon. Stewart & Lady Emeline Wortley
Col Cairnross and Officers, 64th. Regiment
Col Badcock and Officers, 15th. Hussars

Major and Lady Elizabeth Wathen
Viscount & Viscountess Boyle
The Earl of Uxbridge
Sir J. and Lady Burgoyne
Sir James and Lady Stuart
Admiral Hon C. Elphinstone Fleming
Major Gen. Hon. Sir Hercules Packenham
Lieut. Col. Sir Walter Scott, 15th. Huzzars
Col Myddleton & Officers, 42nd Highlanders
Rev. Dr. Llewellyn, Dean of St. David's

Dr. Valpy
Mrs Hemans

The Nobility, Clergy, Gentry, and Inhabitants generally ... informed, that the celebrated

AFRICAN ROSCIUS,

A NATIVE OF SENEGAL, (AFRICA)

Will have the honor of giving one of his

Fashionable Classical Entertainments, in Three Parts, on the above Evening.

As the AFRICAN ROSCIUS is the only Actor of Color that was ever known, and probably the only instance that will occur, and having been acknowledged by the Press of England, Ireland, Scotland and America, to possess histrionic talent of the highest order, the following sketch of his life may not be unacceptable :— The African's progenitors, down to the Grandfather of the subject of this memoir, were Princes of the Foulah Tribe, whose dominions were Senegal, on the banks of the river of that name. The father of the present individual was sent for his education to Schenectady College, near New York, in the United States. Three days after his departure from his native shore, an insurrection broke out among the tribe, arising chiefly from a wish on the part of their King, to exchange prisoners taken in battle, instead of adopting the usual barbarous custom of selling them for slaves. His humanity however interfered with an established perquisite long possessed by some of his principal officers. The Grandfather of the present African Roscius, through their interested policy, fell a victim to his mutinous subjects. Deprived of the means of ascertaining his birthright, and to a certain degree cast upon the world as a cosmopolite, the father became a clergyman and officiated in New York. The subject of this memoir was born July 24, 1807, was destined for the same profession, but preferring the sock and buskin, he departed his father's roof, and wended his way to the shores of Old England.

PROGRAMME OF THE ENTERTAINMENT.

DEFENSIVE LECTURE ON THE DRAMA

Written and delivered by the AFRICAN ROSCIUS containing the opinion of many distinguished Divines Writers, viz Archbishops Tillotson and Secker, Dr. Isaac Watts, Martin Luther, &c. &c.

ANECDOTES OF EMINENT PERFORMERS.

Song—*West Indian Courtship*—"LUBLA ROSA, SAMBO COME" *Spanish Guitar Accompaniment.*

Passages from the early life of the African—THE CORA OF HIS OPENING NIGHT.

A DESCRIPTIVE NEGRO SONG

"MISS LUCY LONG,"

GUITAR ACCOMPANIMENT.

MATTHEWS'S WELL-KNOWN "TRIP TO AMERICA."

"To be or not to be."—"Hamlet the Dane, or Opossum up a Gum Tree."—An Anti-Tragic Audience— Melpomene at a Discount—Unqualified submission to the Gods.

Song, "*The Negro Hunt, or Oppossum up a Gum Tree,*"

Drawing to a close—the African's reception in England—Tour through Ireland, Scotland, &c.

AN INTERVAL OF FIVE MINUTES TO ELAPSE BETWEEN EACH PART.

PART SECOND.

SONG, "THE NEGRO'S ADDRESS TO HIS MISTRESS,'

OR, THE

MIDNIGHT SERENADE,

Air, "Fanny Ellsler's Cachouch

Part of an 1845 poster advertising an event at the Red Lion

171

The Red Lion Hotel on the left in the 1880s

West Street and the Lion Royal in the early 20th century

Reserved seats cost 2s. Another form of entertainment was visiting circuses and in 1848 an elephant of Hylton's Menagerie broke out of its stable at the **Red Lion** in the night and raided the baker's shops. Shouts of 'go home' from bedroom windows had no effect whatsoever!

At the consecration and opening in 1865 of the new church of St. Winifred in Cwmdauddwr, a 'superb luncheon' was laid on regardless of expense by Mr. and Mrs. Morgan of the **Red Lion** at 3s. a ticket. Mr. D.T.M. Hope Edwards was the licensee in 1885, when he was also a wine and spirit merchant, and the hotel advertised a billiards room which had previously been used for courts, tribunals, and meetings.

The hotel was enlarged when the Elan Valley dams were being constructed and the excise office became the **Vaults**, frequented by dam workers. Solomon Selman Fisher was the proprietor in 1902, when it was described as a family and commercial hotel and posting house. At some point its name was changed to the **Lion Royal**.

In the 1930s Mr. J. Shufflebottom was in charge, but during the last war the hotel was requisitioned by the army, with the **Vaults**, which had long since closed, being used as the troop office. In 1947 William Collard, who had been at the **Royal Oak** from 1906 and at the **Severn Arms**, Penybont from 1920, took over. Mr. Collard was a well-known sports personality owning race horses, winning greyhound coursing trophies, and refereeing top boxing matches.

A 1960s advertisement

In 1955 Wilfred Pickles came to Rhayader for his *Take Your Pick* programme and stayed at the **Lion Royal**. The Rebecca Riots were re-enacted including salmon poaching. After the broadcast in the Bethany Hall, Wilfred was hoisted up, like a salmon, and carried to the hotel. The drinks were on him, he declared, but on leaving the following morning it is uncertain whether the bar bill was ever paid!

The Rebecca poachers at the Lion Royal in 1955 when Wilfred Pickles visited

Past times at the Lion Royal:
Above: Early beer handles
(Gaskell & Chambers Ltd)
Left: Service bells

The Lion Royal continues to serve travellers in the 21st century

After Mr. Collard's death in 1967, his nephew Elwyn took over the licence. Elwyn hunted for 25 years and was Master of the Afonwy Foxhounds. On his death in 1997, his widow, Mary, took on the business. A motor-cycle enthusasist – she once took part in scrambles and hill trials and also bought and sold bikes – Mary now finds that most of her trade is accommodating participants in the sport with hill trials being held six miles away on 600 acres of land. She also arranges pony trekking. In 2006 she celebrated her family's centenary in the hotel business.

The old Lion Royal sign

Today the hotel's long and interesting frontage, with its portico and archways, remains architecturally one of the best features of Rhayader. The gates shutting off the arched entrance to the yard came from the market hall; the **Vaults**, on the far side of the archway, is now a wool shop. The Lion Yard, where the main stables were once located, has since been built over with private houses.

Further down the road is the **Cwmdaudder Arms**, once a public house but now a mountain bike shop. The licence has been retained, however, allowing it to run as a licenced café. The original building dates back to about 1600 and was first registered as a pub in 1655. It was then called **Ty wrth Pen y Porth** and was sold by Morgan Evan, a gentleman of Nantmel, to Howell Powell, a gentleman of Nantgwilt. In 1744, by then called **Llayn Pen y Porth**, it was leased for 20 years by Lewis Morgan, also of Nantmel, to Hugh Morris, of Rhayader, inn holder. In 1794 the lease was sold for £71 by Lewis Morgan to Margaret Lewis Lloyd, a widow of Nantgwilt, for 999 years at a rent of one penny *per annum* if demanded. Mrs. Lewis Lloyd sold the property two years later for £21 to Thomas Price, mercer, of Rhayader. He in turn sold it in 1801 back to Mrs. Lewis Lloyd for £100 for the remainder of the lease, having built a dwelling house, outbuildings and office on the site.

A draft deed of 1795 refers to **Llayn Pen y Porth** being occupied by Diane Jones. The property passed from Margaret Lewis Lloyd to her daughter Elizabeth Mary and husband John Lewis in trust, then to their son Thomas Lewis Lloyd. Two deeds of 1825 show that **Llayn Pen y Porth** (otherwise **Cwymtoyddwre Arms Inn**) was occupied by Jane Evans as licensee. She was still there in 1835. The property eventually passed from Thomas Lewis Lloyd to his only son Robert Lewis Lloyd. In 1885-1888 it was rented by Elizabeth Edwards and was sold at auction in 1890 for £810. In 1902 Thomas Williams was the landlord.

175

The Cwmdaudder Arms in 2005

In 1906 the inn was sold for £910 to Meredith Powell, who ran a coaching business from behind the **Royal Oak**. Then in 1917 it was almost closed down by the local licensing committee but for a petition signed by 102 farmers in favour of the licence being retained. At that time it had a large yard, a large stable for up to 16 horses, and a smaller stable for six, together with a large coach house. Mr. Powell said he had had as many as 80 horses in the stables and yard and in the summer had flocks of sheep in the yard every week. The licence was renewed.

From the 1950s to the 1970s the **Cwmdaudder Arms** was run by Bill Powell and his wife Hilda, who also owned the **Cornhill**. They were the first to introduce pub food in the town and were also the first and probably only publicans to keep pet foxes. Called Dai and Cymro, the foxes were at least kept out of harm at the back.

The last landlord was Neil Reid Worilow, who owned the pub for about five years before leaving in February, 2002. The present owner, Clive Powell, bought it in July 2002 and turned it into a mountain bike shop. The two-storey building, half in whitewashed rubblestone and half in weatherboard with a slate roof, still looks the same from the outside. Internally is a different matter. Where the bar counter used to be is now the shop counter and the old bar area behind is now a display room for mountain-bikes. There is, however, still the snug with an open fire place and original flagstones. While Clive runs the shop and arranges mountain bike weekends in the Elan Valley, his wife, Francine, cooks for the café.

Next door is the **Cornhill Inn**, believed to date back to about 1540 and which for many years had a blacksmith's forge at the rear. In 1844 the landlord was Oliver Edwards and in 1902 John Price was the

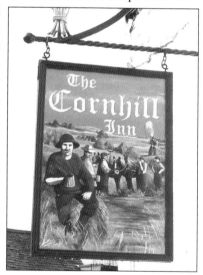

The Cornhill sign, made by local craftsmen

The Cornhill Inn in 2005

licensee. In 1911 it became a tied house being bought by Salt & Co, a brewery based in Burton-on-Trent. The front door used to be at the side leading into the low-beamed bar. Eventually a dividing wall, behind which had been a private living room, was knocked down to provide more bar space. The original staircase was removed and what had been the snug now comprises a darts room and toilets. The old smithy at the back has been converted into a self-contained cottage with five bedrooms.

Many stories of the supernatural are talked about at the **Cornhill**. Two ghostly figures have been seen – one of a man in military uniform in the rear cottage and the other an old woman who creates mischief in the bar. The man is said to be the blacksmith's son who, after returning from the war, hanged himself from a hook which is still in the cottage, while the woman is believed to be his mother who was the landlady. She has been seen walking where the old staircase was and delights in moving things. On one occasion, a diary, on a shelf above the bar, suddenly flew off and hit the barmaid on the back of her head. The old woman is thought to be buried in the nearby churchyard.

Another weird incident occurred about 13 or 14 years ago. The landlord was woken at 3 o'clock in the morning by a party of four bikers who were sleeping in the back cottage. He had to get their bags for they were too frightened to go back inside. One of the rooms in the cottage has a reputation for always being freezing cold. The **Cornhill** was closed for four or five months before the present landlord took over in 2003.

A painting by G. Mallet from an engraving c.1670 of the Old Swan Inn

West Street with the Old Swan on the right.
The Market Hall of 1762 was replaced with the present
clock tower war memorial in 1923

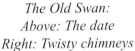

The Old Swan:
Above: The date
Right: Twisty chimneys

On the other side of West Street, by the main road junction, is a fascinating building complete with twisty chimney stacks which once housed the **Old Swan**, and which today is divided into a health shop and Carole's Café. A corner post supporting the jetty beam over the front porch is inscribed with the date 1683, but this probably refers to a later refurbishment rather than when it was first built. This was much earlier, for it was mentioned in 1676 as being one of the two inns in Rhayader. Henry Williams was listed as victualler in the *Universal British Directory (1793-8)*, and in 1830 it was run by Edward James who was still there in 1835.

During the 1860s it stopped trading as an inn and in later years it was used as a variety of businesses. First it was a hardware shop, then in the 1900s a saddlers owned by Mr. Lewis. Afterwards it became a butcher's shop, 'purveyors of Welsh mutton', run by Augustus or Gus Collard. His son, Edward, who was born there, took over the business in 1952. There used to be an abbatoir at the rear (originally the inn stables), with the back room used for hanging the meat. A lower building to the right, which might have been a blacksmith's shop or stables, was demolished and a new brick building constructed which is now Rowlands Pharmacy. Until about five years ago the main building was the home of the Tourist Information Centre before becoming the Wild Swan wholefood shop. Nine years ago part of the **Old Swan** was incorporated into Carole's Café and is now known as the Old Swan tearooms. The Swan's exterior wall was knocked down and a passage dividing the two properties included.

The Old Swan in 2005

Now clad in stucco, the **Old Swan** was originally made of weatherboard and lath and plaster on a stone base. Its partly stone-slabbed roof supports a heavy stack of triple chimney. Its two-storeyed, jettied porch still survives and a wooden corbel has been preserved under the eaves of the west front. Most of the original timber framing is visible inside as are the old, locally-quarried flagstones.

Further down the street is the **Elan Hotel**, which started life as a row of five cottages, probably dating back to the 18th century. In the 1880s or '90s four of the cottages were converted into one big house, occupied at one time by a police inspector who married the owner's daughter. The fifth cottage, nearest the bridge, became a general store. The building did not become a hotel until 1938. In the 1950s it was known as **Curtis's Elan** private hotel with Mr. E. Curtis as

The Elan Hotel in 2005

proprietor. In 1972 the general store was demolished and the site rebuilt as an extension to the hotel providing a restaurant and more letting bedrooms.

The present owners, Dave and Denise Mackie, discovered wallpaper in the reception area under six other layers believed to be at least 70 years old and featuring military looking men on horseback. One section of the wallpaper has been varnished and framed. Today the **Elan Hotel** offers 10 *en suite* bedrooms, a restaurant for evening meals and another room for tea and lunches. Old fireplaces at each end of the hotel are a legacy of its cottage origins.

Church Street joins West Street to the northern end of North Street and on the church side is the Horseshoe Guest House which was once the **Butcher's Arms**. It was built in the early 19th century by a butcher, Thomas George, who used half the building to ply his trade and the other half as a pub. George was still landlord in 1835. Mrs. Mary Ann Jones was licensee from at least 1891 to 1902. In 1891 she was one of several local residents who signed a letter of thanks to the country vetinerary, Edward Thomas, of Llanfadog, for his 'valuable services'. The inn kept stables at the rear, which were later converted into a garage, complete with petrol pump. Cock-fighting was held in the yard

The Horseshoe Inn (once the Butcher's Arms) is now a guest house

whilst inside, customers congregated in the kitchen around a square table by a big fire and enjoyed Tippit, a game played with a coin or a button. They also used to place bets on horses with a runner going to the local 'bookie'.

For many years the pub was run by Dick and Flossie Richards until 1952 when it was taken over by Welsh Brewers of Cardiff. The garage was later demolished and a private house built on the site. After being closed for some time, in 1977 it was purchased from the brewers by Alan Lewis, who changed the name to the **Horseshoe Inn**. It was sold again in 1984, when a dining room was built on, but ceased trading in 1994 and was converted into a guest house. Only a wooden frieze remains of the bar counter and the bar is now the owner's living room.

Just before the church is the **Eagles Inn**, originally known as the **Spread Eagle**, part of a row of cottages believed to date back to the 16th or 17th

Church Street in the early 20th century with the Eagles Inn on the right

centuries, and trading in the 17th century. The name is probably derived from a noble family who incorporated the spread eagle, the national emblem of the Romans, after a trip abroad. Between at least 1835 and 1844 the licensee was Michael Price, who was also a mason. The 1841 census records that Price, aged 40, lived there with his wife Sarah, aged 35, and 7-year-old son William. In 1902 another Price – Thomas – was the licensee. He operated a coal merchants business from the same address.

When the Elan Valley dams were being built from 1892 to 1904, workers frequented the pub which then had a wooden servery with beer being served through a hatch, a custom in most of the pubs in Rhayader. Frequently, however, **Eagle** customers served themselves from jugs into their own tankards and put their money through a slot. One local inhabitant, Mike Pugh, recalled going into the pub in the 1940s, where his grandmother did the cleaning, and being seated

The Eagles Inn is at the end of a row of cottages

on the bar by the landlord, Haydon Lloyd, and told to drink a glass of gin. He was then given a chocolate as a reward. Another story from the 1950s involved the bread man, who delivered bread in a horse and cart. Stopping for refreshment, he would collect any cigarette stubs he could find and feed them to his horse.

In 1959 when another Lloyd – Arthur – was landlord, the next door cottage nearest the church was incorporated into the **Eagles**, the thick dividing wall being knocked down and the new area turned into a restaurant. An outer door serving both properties and an inner door into the pub by the fireplace were both sealed up. The pub,

The Eagles Inn sign

which already boasted the first lounge bar in Rhayader, was refurbished in the 1980s with additional dining space whilst the rear stables were turned into a children's room with game machines.

The head of an eagle carved in granite stone, which for many years was boarded up and was at one time part of the fire mantel, now has pride of place on the front of the bar counter. It was made by local sculptor Ben Lloyd in the 1960s. A reminder of times gone by is a wood-burning Honeywell boiler over a hundred years old, made of cast iron with brass pipes, which used to provide central heating for the whole building. Among functions held in the **Eagles** is a newly-instituted hunting horn competition.

At the northern end of the street, on the opposite side to the **Eagles**, is a garage built on the site of the **Cock Inn**. An ancient wooden building, it was demolished in 1920 by Mr. Harris, the garage owner. Where Smithfield Market now stands was an open field named after the inn.

Another inn which once traded in Church Street was the **Plough and Harrow**. In the 1841 census, David Evans, aged 35 and described as a schoolmaster, lived there with his wife Jane, also aged 35, and their children William, 11, Jane, 9, David, 7, Mary, 4, and Ann, 2. To help in the house they had a 15-year-old servant called Elizabeth Lewis. In 1844 the inn was run by John Pugh.

Bridge Street is the continuation of West Street and, opposite the police station going towards the bridge, is a three-storey stone building which was once the **Railway Inn**. It is thought to have been built in the 19th century and given its name shortly after 1863 when the railway arrived at Rhayader. By the turn of the 20th century the alehouse was owned by John Jones, a blacksmith, who put

The one-time Cock Inn was a timber-clad building

in tenants including Thomas Bennett who was there in 1902. After the completion of the dams in 1904 and the exodus of the workers, trade dwindled and in 1907 renewal of its licence was refused by the County Licensing Authority. The Chief Constable said the premises were not structurally adapted for use as licensed premises and the licence was not required to meet the wants of the neighbourhood. Compensation of £310 was paid to the owner (including £285 19s. 6d. to his mortgagee); £40 to the licensee, Samuel Turner, brewer, and £25 to the lessee.

The Railway Inn:

Left: In operation about 1900

Above: Now converted to two houses

The mists of time have drawn a veil over the location and details of some other public houses which were all trading in Rhayader during the 19th century. For instance the **White Hart Inn**, possibly called the **Sun** at an earlier date, was listed in Pigot's *Directory* of 1835 as one of the main inns in the town. The landlord then was Edward Hope. Then there was the **Tanner's Arms**, with John Morris as landlord in 1830; the **Barley Mow**, mentioned in 1838; and the **Radnorshire Arms**, with Elizabeth Lawrence as licensee in 1844.

CHAPTER TEN

Around Rhayader
CWMDAUDDWR, CWMYSTWYTH RD., ELAN VALLEY, GAUFRON, DOLDOWLOD & NANT-GLAS

Llansantfraed Cwmdauddwr is at the south-western end of Rhayader, across the river Wye. Cwmdauddwr, meaning Parish of the Two Waters (the Wye and Elan), is credited with having had six pubs, but not all of them can now be identified. Although only a small village, looks can be deceptive, for Cwmdauddwr has had two entries in the *Guinness Book of Records*. One entry states that it contains the largest common in Britain, another that it is one of the richest parishes. This latter claim apparently involves Birmingham Corporation's ownership of the Elan Valley dams and reservoirs.

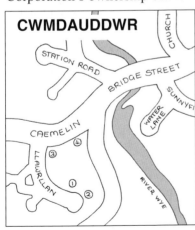

1 Triangle *   3 Parkstile
2 Bell   4 Fox & Hounds
        * – Open in 2006

The sole surviving inn is the **Triangle**, unsurprisingly occupying a triangular site between the old bailey castle and the river. There has probably been an inn here as far back as the 16th century, if not the 14th, under such names as **Three Angles**, **Inn on the Ford**, and **Tavern-yr-Rhydd**, but the present timber-framed building dates from the 18th century. It was favoured by cattle drovers on the Aberystwyth to Hereford drive and by monks travelling between Abbey-cymhir and Strata Florida. The drovers were able to avoid paying a 10d. toll for a score of cattle at the toll gate leading into Rhayader by crossing a ford on the Wye to the south of the town.

An early view of the Triangle

Conveyances, mortgages, and wills from the early 19th century provide documentary evidence of previous owners and landlords. The landlord in 1830 was John Morris, but according to a will of 1831, the **Triangle** had been owned since 1765 by the Rev. John Jones of Denbigh, who passed it on to John, Mary and Edward Jones. According to the 1841 census John Jones, aged 75, who was also a carpenter, lived there with William Jones, 39, a clergyman, and three female servants one as young as 10. In 1843 it was sold to Richard Wood, of Rhayader, who took a mortgage of £41 16s. 6d. on the premises, which then consisted of a house, stable, brewhouse, gardens and about six acres of land. It was run by Thomas Morgan and his wife, Mary, daughter of John Jones, before being sold for £400 to William Davies. Another mortgage was taken out in 1860 to the spinster Mrs. Ann Whitcombe. At the consecration and opening of Cwmdauddwr's new church of St. Winifred in 1865, the choir enjoyed dinner, at the vicar's expense, at the **Triangle** and the nearby **Bell Inn**. By 1873 the property was valued at £864 when it was bought by William Evans, a builder from Rhayader, with a £500 mortgage. At the beginning of the next century the **Triangle** was owned by Mrs. Jane Hamer and, on her death in 1924, it was sold to John and Jessie Parry with a mortgage from David Williams, brewer of Builth Wells, in consideration of their buying his beer and spirits.

George and Martha Pugh were the licensees in the 1920s, when workers on their way to nearby quarries used to call in at 5.30 in the morning to pick up jugs of beer that had been left out for them on the counter. They returned the jugs on their way home and settled up at the end of the week. In 1922, the Pughs had a son, Will, one of seven children, who didn't look as if he would survive. They called in the vicar who christened him by the window looking towards the church. Today, Will Pugh is in his 80s and still going strong after working for 49 years with British Telecom and its predecessors.

In 1938 David Williams finally bought the property and in 1946 it was transferred to David Williams (Builth) Ltd. In the 1940s the stables across the lane were converted into toilets. In 1970 the inn was bought for £3,000 by Mrs. Lily Garbett, one of the Parrys' daughters, who had already been running the business with her husband, Bill, who also worked on the filter beds. Seymour Price, one of the Pughs' grandsons, recalls as a youngster sitting on the staircase, which used to go up from the front door, and watch Mr. Garbett provide a 'silver

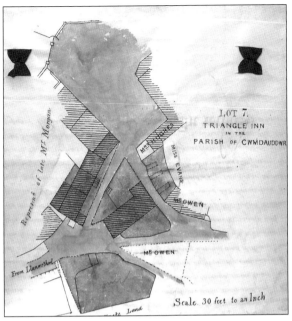

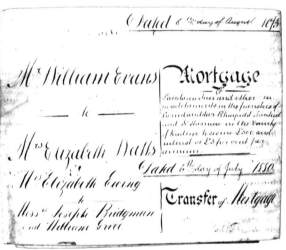

1873 plan and mortgage for the Triangle

service', taking drinks to the table, for the 'elite' customers in the Blue Room on the right. 'But he would kick your feet if you got in the way', he said.

The inn was bought by Denis and Marion Price of Rhayader for £7,000 and they sold it two months later for £10,800 to Rowland Carpenter, of Twickenham who borrowed £6,000 from Whitbread Wales Ltd with a proviso about buying the brewery's beer and spirits. James and Cecily Beilby were landlords from 1974 to 1978 and in 1982 John Knell paid £61,999 with a £25,000 loan from Bass Wales & West. By 1991 the price had gone up to £160,000.

The staircase has since been removed and the bar is now a standard open plan. A trapdoor to one side of the bar counter provides a unique feature – when darts are played the trapdoor is opened and reveals a pit in which the players have to stand as the ceiling in the room is so low that the board cannot be hung at the regulation height. This has led to the inn being given another name – the **Pit**. In the 1980s the licensees, John and Norma Knell, kept and bred ducks, including some exotics, on the river. The welfare of the ducks is maintained to this day, with a collection box on the counter to buy them wheat.

The Bell Inn when Sarn and Lizzie Conway (on right) were the licensees.
Also pictured are Evan Davies (in doorway) and Jack Pencalhaidd (left),
renowned for taming horses

Between the **Triangle** and the churchyard is Bell cottage which at one time was the **Bell Inn**, also known as **Pound Ale House**. Probably deriving its name from the church bell, the two-storey stone building comprised a parlour, kitchen, back kitchen, bar and cellar together with three bedrooms and stabling for three horses. It was run by Mr. and Mrs. Webb towards the end of the 19th century and by the turn of the 20th century was owned by George Morgan with Samuel Conway as licensee. In 1911 Mr. Morgan leased the inn to the Lichfield Brewery. However, in 1914 its licence was not renewed by the County Licensing Authority. While Mr. Conway said he was doing a good trade, with 41 barrels of beer, 30 gallons of spirits, and 60 dozen bottled beer sold in 1913, seven police visits revealed only one customer on the premises. Compensation was granted – £200 to the owner, £120 to the lessees, and £18 to the tenant.

Beer was delivered into the cellar below through a trap door, which still survives near the front door. The internal layout was similar to the **Eagles** with separate snugs and a panelled bar area containing a serving hatch. On the churchyard side of the inn is an old blacksmith's forge in front of which is a pound for lost animals. Now it is only used once a year when a farmer leaves his horses there in the summer. The property was refurbished in the

188

1970s when the stairs were re-positioned and a bathroom installed.

On the corner of the main B4158 road leading from Cwmdauddwr into Rhayader is Parkstile House which, according to its owner, Seymour Price, who was a milkman for 43 years, could have been another inn. Seymour said that when he bought the property 30 years ago, he was told that an old sign had been found, with the words '**Parkstile Inn**' and 'Licensed to sell Porter', but has since been lost. No inn of that name has been recorded, but it could conceivably have traded under another name. The house is believed to be as old as the **Triangle**, and the remnants of a fireplace are apparent in the ruins of an even older property at the rear. At the bottom

Was Parkstile House ever an inn?

The one time Fox and Hounds

of the garden access can be gained to the castle ruins, originally surrounded by a moat or ditch and overlooking the Wye, below which there was once a ford. It was probably used as a look-out post for occupants of the main castle in the town.

Returning back towards Rhayader, on the same side of the street is a private house, now called the Old Fox, which at one time was the **Fox and Hounds**. How far the building dates back is unclear but the earliest reference as an inn is the 1841 census, when 45-year-old sawyer John Jones lived there with his wife Jane, aged 50, and their sons John, 15, and Thomas, 12. The inn

A 19th-century painting of the Hill Gate Inn showing the toll gate

was owned for many years by the Rev. William Prickard of Dderw, who leased it out at a rent which did not change for 30 years. It stopped trading as a licensed house in 1910, as surplus to requirements, with £220 being awarded as compensation including £24 10s. for the licensee, Mary Edwards, a widow. The present living room is where the bar used to be and although the old inglenook fireplace has been boarded over there is still a glass screen at the back through which drinks would have been served. Behind the screen is an area which may have once housed a large bread oven. At the front of the house is a grating, or cellar door, down which beer barrels were delivered to a rear cellar, since covered up. Margaret Hughes, who now lives at the Old Fox, was at the **Bear's Head** from 1955 to 1958 when married to Harold Turner.

On the Cwmystwyth road, not far from Rhayader, can still be discerned the foundations of **Hill**

The old inn sign for the Hill Gate Inn

Hill Gate Inn about 1920

Gate Inn, also known as **Trumpeg Y Mynydd** (Turnpike on the Mountain). As the name suggests **Hill Gate** was both an inn and a toll house with a gate across the road which was the main route to Aberystwyth in the 19th century. In the 1840s it was run by carpenter Thomas Hughes and his wife Anne, who also looked after a 70-acre farm. Twice a year Mr.Hughes took the toll money raised to Presteigne, walking there and back in a day. The toll gate was one of the first in Rhayader to be destroyed by the Rebecca rioters who arrived in force one night in 1843. The story goes that a frightened Mrs. Hughes opened her bedroom window and called down to find out what was happening. She was told by the leader to go back to bed and she would not be harmed. It was only the gate that they wanted to smash. She wisely retreated and the gate was then destroyed. By 1861 Mr. and Mrs. Hughes had left and were running another pub, the Severn Arms in Dolhelfa, and an 80-acre farm. The old inn sign with the words 'HILL GATE INN, THOMAS HUGHES, Licensed to Retail Ale, Beer and Porter' is still in the possession of great-grandson Richard Hughes, of Rhayader. The last licensee was Margaret Rees who was there in 1947. It then closed down and the building became derelict before being demolished when the road was widened in the 1960s.

Two miles west of Rhayader on the B4518 is the **Elan Valley Hotel**, built and opened in 1895 by the Thomas

A 1930s advert for the Elan Valley Hotel

family of nearby Lower Llanfadog. Mr. and Mrs. Bath of Carmarthen were the first guests arriving by rail at Rhayader and then travelling by horse to the hotel. In 1896 Mr. and Mrs Walters, of the Rock Hotel, Llandrindod Wells, were frequent visitors as were members of the Marston Cycle Club who cycled over from Birmingham. Work on the dams was still in progress during this period and the hotel's three bars proved a popular watering hole for the workers. To facilitate trade Mr. Thomas even built a footbridge across the river to the workers' village. Beer was delivered by rail from Burton-on-Trent to Rhayader and arrived the day after it had been ordered.

FULLY LICENSED   FREE HOUSE

The Elan Valley Hotel

TWO MILES WEST OF RHAYADER

Visited by H.M. Queen Elizabeth II and H.R.H. The Duke of Edinburgh

A.A. ★ ★ R.A.C.

A FINE CENTRE FOR TOURING MID-WALES

Fishing over a very large area

With the Compliments of the Proprietors

Mr. and Mrs. NOEL LEWIS

Telephone Rhayader 448

TERMS ON REQUEST

A 1960s advertisement

On 21 July 1904 King Edward VII and Queen Alexandra arrived by royal train at the Elan filter beds for the opening ceremony of the first four dams. The Elan line, specially constructed to transport equipment, materials and men to the dam sites, was lined with soldiers and policemen drafted in for the occasion. After the ceremony, the Royal party and guests adjourned for lunch which was held in a large marquee opposite the hotel. On completion of the dams, the hotel was bought

The Daily Express *National Motor Rally at the Elan Valley Hotel*

by Birmingham Corporation and was booked for one weekend every year by the city's Lord Mayor and councillors for their annual visit to the estate.

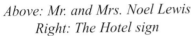
Above: Mr. and Mrs. Noel Lewis
Right: The Hotel sign

Another royal occasion followed in 1952 when Queen Elizabeth, making her first visit to the principality since her accession to the throne, came with the Duke of Edinburgh to open the new two million pound Claerwen dam and reservoir. The **Elan Valley Hotel** was headquarters for the day and the Queen returned there after the opening ceremony. A big sign of 'Welcome', composed of hundreds of garlands, hung across the road approaching the hotel and school children waved flags. The Queen and the Duke enjoyed Welsh cakes made by the wife of the proprietor, Mr. H. Foster-Smith. Later that year the *Daily Express* national motor rally used the hotel for one of its stage stops, taking advantage of its garage and petrol pump facilities. Noel and Blodwen Lewis

The Elan Valley Hotel in 2005

took on the lease of the hotel in 1959, joined by their son Alan and his wife Pauline in 1969, who eventually sold the hotel in 1987. Welsh Water took over the estate, including the hotel, in 1974. Today, the hotel offers 11 *en suite* bedrooms and a restaurant. The three bars have been turned into one and the garage, originally built as stables, has now become a functions room. The hotel is headquarters of the Elan Valley Angling Association.

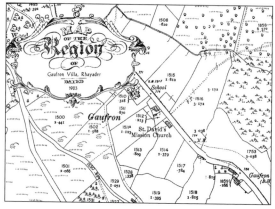

1903 map showing the Gaufron Inn

A pub was among the facilities provided in the purpose-built village of wooden huts constructed by Birmingham Corporation to house most of its workers on the site of the present Elan Village. The pub was part of the canteen and sold only beer; no women were allowed. Also provided was an accident hospital, school, and bathhouse. A guard or bridge-keeper was employed to look out for unauthorised visitors and the illegal importation of liquor, which was banned.

In the village of Gaufron, on the main A44 leading from Rhayader to Crossgates, is Gaufron Villa, which used to be the **Gaufron Inn**, a stone building with slate roof believed to be well over 150 years old. The census has no mention of it being licensed in 1861 when it was occupied by a retired farmer, Edward Williams. However, ten years later it was described as a public house with John Harris as landlord. In the 1881 census it is called a beer shop, and as an inn in 1891 with Harris listed as an agricultural labourer and his wife, Sarah, as innkeeper. The census for 1901, however, has Harris, now aged 71, as the innkeeper living there with Sarah, aged 60, and their children Thomas, a 27-year-old farmer, and Minnie, 16.

The inn's busiest period was probably towards the end of the 19th century and beginning of the 20th when the pipe taking water from the Elan reservoirs to Birmingham was constructed. At that time Harris is believed to have given some of his several acres of land for the building nearby of a prefabricated chapel, demolished some two years ago.

At the beginning of the 20th century, the inn was run by John and Elizabeth Lewis, but in 1912 renewal of its licence was refused on the grounds of redundancy. Described as a beerhouse, it had a small grocers shop attached and five acres of land. Mr. Lewis, who paid an annual rent of £20, said trade for the last 12 months was valued at £76 12s. in beer and £12 in bottled beer and stout, with 60 gallons of cider also being sold. Compensation was awarded – £100 to the representatives of the late John Harris and £10 to the licensee.

The front door was at the rear of the inn with a hillside extending almost down to the premises. Inside, the bar was on the right with a cellar behind,

The Gaufron Inn is now a private house

later to be converted into a domestic dairy. To the left was the landlord's living quarters. Both rooms had inglenook fireplaces. Outside was an adjoining three-bay stable with accommodation above, which later became a chicken house. In the front garden was a barn used as a taylor's shop and then as a farrier's.

After World War Two, Gaufron was the home of Mr. and Mrs. Aubrey Evans for 50 years, during which time they installed new windows. The present owners have cut away the bank of earth and rock at the back and built a retaining stone wall with new stables behind. The old stable has been converted into a games room while the chicken house has become a study. The barn has been converted into an annexe.

An early picture of the Vulcan Arms when the landlord,
Mr. P. Middleton, had a six-day licence

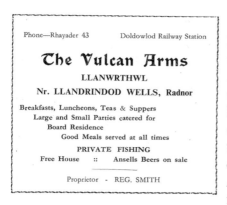

*A 1950s advertisement for
the Vulcan Arms*

At Doldowlod, near the village of Llanwrthwl on the A470 running south from Rhayader, is the **Vulcan Arms**, a country inn which started out as three cottages. One was occupied by a blacksmith, who also made coffins, another by a midwife whilst the third was a private house. It was originally called the **Middleton Arms**, after the Middleton Evans family whose seat was at Llwyn-parriad, but was known locally as the **Man Trap** for several reasons: one because the landlord had several daughters; two, it was frequented by men on their way to work; and three, as one former customer noted, 'the men-folk used to congregate there to have a jolly old time and the wives knew where the men were'. Over the years the inner walls were knocked down to open up the whole building and in the early 1950s it was run by Reg Smith. In the late 1950s and '60s the **Vulcan** operated both as an inn and as a modern motel with Mr. and Mrs. Doug Woodman and Mr. and Mrs. Don Faulkner as proprietors. Later it stopped trading, became semi-derelict and a home for hippies. Eventually it was bought and the new owner took the opportunity of a complete refurbishment to increase the dining facilities and install features such as bookcases crammed with books which adorn two of the rooms. The pub

The Vulcan Arms, once the Middleton Arms, was locally known as the Man Trap

196

Mr. Griffiths at the Glanrafon Inn

The old sign for the Glanrafon Inn

The New Found Out is now a private house called Glan yr Afon

chain Punch purchased the property four years ago.

The **Vulcan** is apparently something of a gateway for spirits of a more incorporeal nature, which cause a certain amount of mischief including bottles, glasses and other objects falling off shelves. The cleaner heard a child crying over the noise of vacuuming; a customer, who is psychic, was nudged by the building's guardian, an old Welsh gentleman, asking for the place to be 'cleaned'; even the landlord Roy Rowland caught glimpses of something in the corner of his eyes. A professional was called in and 'rescued 34 souls and 15 dark entities' with subsequent clearances of darker forces. Loved ones from the spirit world were sent to collect the crying child and a broken ley line and spiritual gateway were repaired. The energies in the **Vulcan** are now supposed to be good.

In the village of Nant-glas, lying between the A470 and the A44, is a house called Glan yr Afon which once traded as the **Glanrafon Inn** and nick-named **New Found Out** and **Rag and Louse**. The licence was held for many years by Eleanor Griffiths, who was licensed to sell beer, porter and cider to be 'consumed on, or off, the premises'. Eleanor, née Bufton, married Thomas Griffiths in 1908, both aged 39. Thomas died in 1947, aged 81, while Eleanor died in 1951 aged 86. They are both buried at Nantmel Church, where they had been married. The **Glanrafon** probably stopped trading as a pub in 1947 and became a private residence.

* ——————————————— *

1 Radnor Arms *	4 King's Arms
2 Eagle *	5 Swan
3 Cross	6 Oak

* – Open in 2006

CHAPTER ELEVEN

New & Old Radnor

Silver John is dead and gone,
So they came home a-singing;
Radnor boys pulled out his eyes
And set the bells a-ringing.

The name Radnor is derived from the Saxon 'readan-ofre', meaning red bank
or hill side, and is mentioned in a charter of King Offa of Mercia, dated 774.
The church at Old Radnor, re-built in the 15th and early 16th centuries,
contains a pre-Norman font and was probably originally dedicated to the
Welsh saint Ystyffan of the late 6th century. According to W.H. Howse the
deeply ditched site near the church was once a castle destroyed by Griffith ap
Llywelyn in 1052, but this is disputed by later historians who think the site

The 15th-century Harp Inn, Old Radnor in 2003

was not a castle at all but somehow connected to the church. First appearance of the word Old being added to Radnor was in 1252, almost 200 years after the founding of New Radnor.

Near the church is the **Harp Inn**, with a sign showing the Welsh harp, reputed to have been built in the 15th century. According to CAMRA it ranks among the ten most important public houses in Wales of historical and archaeological interest. In the 1841 census Evan Worthing, aged 35, was the innkeeper and lived there with his wife Sarah, aged 30, brother,

The Welsh harp is on the inn sign

and three sons. Also staying there were seven other people including a nine-day-old baby. Evan Worthing was still the licensee in 1859 and in the early 1900s the landlord was Mr. Ellway. Mr. and Mrs. Griffiths ran the inn in the 1950s when Dolyhir Football Club took over the bar as a changing room with a tin bath placed on the flagstones, filled with hot water and then used by all the team in turn. One of the players was Doug Inseal who, with his brother Jim, continued to frequent the **Harp**, as customers, until their deaths within a few days of each other in 2002.

In 1972 the Griffiths family sold the inn to the Landmark Trust, a building preservation charity which rescues historic and architectually inter-esting buildings and after restoration gives them a new life by letting them as holiday homes. In the Harp's case one of the urgent requirements was a new roof together with extensive internal renovation. However, period features have been retained such as the slate-flagged floor and beamed ceilings. The bar, which has an open fireplace, contains antique settles and a reader's chair. There is also a newly refurbished restaurant and, on the first floor, are five letting bedrooms. After the Trust sold the property in 1983, it has been run as a free house. Presteigne's Vintage Sports Car Club meets there every month.

According to W.H. Howse, Harold Godwin (afterwards King Harold) is believed to have been the founder of New Radnor, and to have built its first castle in 1064, although another likely contender is William Fitz-Osbern. Standing on one of the main routes into central Wales, the castle became bound up with Welsh history. The first castle lord was Philip de Braose who helped develop a flourishing borough beneath its walls. But in the 80-year period from the end of the 12th century Radnor castle changed hands 12 times and was 'destroyed' four times, including in attacks by Welsh leader Rhys ap Griffith and King John. Then in 1401 both castle and town were left in ruins after an attack by Owen Glyndwr, rebelling against the rule of Henry IV. The castle garrison of 60 men were apparently all put to death. Finally, the castle was destroyed by the Parliamentarians in 1644 during the Civil War.

With the union of Wales and England in 1536 New Radnor became the county town of the new county of Radnorshire, a status which passed to Presteigne in the 18th century. The market was held on the ground floor of the town hall with Quarter and Petty Sessions courts on the top floor. Four fairs used to be held annually, with Royal charters dating back to 1305. Most recently was the 29th October fair for cattle and horses, which was known as the 'goose fair' with goose being on the menu at one of the local hostelries. Today, the town's layout remains very much unchanged from the 13th century and is still overlooked by the ruins of the castle, now a steep mound covered in grass. At one time, the town boasted six or seven inns of which only two remain open – the **Eagle** and the **Radnor Arms**.

On the left-hand side of Broad Street is the **Radnor Arms Hotel**, probably built in about 1700 and believed to have been in the hands of one family for well over a hundred years. Thomas Jones was the licensee in the 1850s, James Williams in 1895, and James Niblett in 1906, who later went to the **Eagle**. The hotel was expanded with the acquisition of an adjoining cottage and petrol pumps were installed. During the Second World War, the **Radnor Arms**, with Bill Swain at the helm, was a popular venue for British troops stationed at nearby Harpton Court and Downton, and for Americans from Kington. The troops were also attracted by a Naafi run by local ladies in the village hall. Soon after the war Mr. Swain emigrated to Australia. In the early 1960s when Bill Bacon was landlord, the hotel was badly damaged by two fires within four months. The first one broke out in the early hours of Christmas Eve, 1961, destroying the back part including a new dining room. Then in April 1962 a second fire destroyed the two bars, lounge and four bedrooms in the former cottage and the roof collapsed. 'Firemen had to pump

The Radnor Arms in 2003

water from the nearby streams', a local paper reported, 'while villagers carried buckets of water as a guard against the petrol tanks holding 700 gallons of petrol, at the front of the hotel'. Since these disasters the pumps have been taken away and a new one-storey restaurant was built on the site of the old cottage. The former dining area at the rear of the main building was turned into a games room with another bar, while the main bar area was enlarged. Then, in December 1976, yet another fire almost completely gutted the hotel. The blaze severely damaged the roof and upstairs floor, including several bedrooms and the landlord's living quarters, according to a report in the *County Times and Gazette*. Miss Cheryl McKeon, joint licensee with fiancé Kevin Dufton, were operating a bar at the Badminton Club dance in the village hall when the alarm was raised. 'There were a lot of young people at the dance and they rushed to the hotel and dived in to rescue whatever they could', said Miss McKeon, who had been at the hotel for four years. 'The whole village was marvellous'. With the hotel suffering its third major fire in 15 years, she added: 'It seems to have got a jinx'. As a result of the damage, the **Radnor Arms** was closed for several weeks.

David and Kath Dent were the owners from 1979 to 1987 taking it over from a consortium. Now owned by Alan Spencer of Worcester, the hotel has been run for the last 10 years by Nigel Pullen.

The roof caved in after the fire at the Radnor Arms

Today the **Radnor Arms** supports a number of local events including the annual cricket match between the Old Codgers and Radnor Valley C.C. Although the hotel put up the Old Codgers cricket cup for the event in 2001, it has yet to be won by them. Another popular event is a duck race on Boxing Day, organised by the local football club, when as many as 750 plastic ducks are floated down the stream from beneath Smatcher Hill to the town's bridge. Needless to say, the day's fun is continued in the **Radnor Arms**.

On the other side of the road is the **Eagle Hotel**. Originally an important coaching inn, parts of the building date back to the 15th century. On the side opposite the town hall the wall is two-and-a-half feet thick and, in

The Eage Hotel in the early 20th century

203

A poster of 1875 announcing the opening of the railway line to New Radnor. The festivities were completed with a public luncheon at the Eagle Hotel

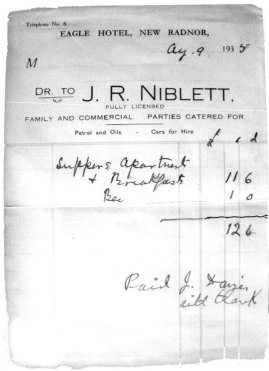

A 1935 invoice from the Eagle Hotel

the 18th century, this section (now one of the bars) was used as the borough goal and court administration centre, with the cellars below acting as dungeons. A gallows and stocks stood in what is now the car park. With the courts being held in the town hall, justice was seemingly confined to a small area of the town. Interestingly, the town hall had, on top of the building, two stone sculptured eagles. This dates back to the days when these royal birds denoted the pre-eminence of law and justice. Sometimes the Quarter Sessions adjourned for lunch at the **Eagle** until 3 p.m.

The Eagle in the 1930s

The Eagle Hotel in the 1950s.
Top: Dining Room
Middle: Central bar
Bottom: Residents lounge

In 1830 the landlord was Herbert Morgan and in 1844 the licensee was Stephen Evans when the inn also acted as the excise office. The licence was then held by Elizabeth Evans, presumably his widow, up to at least 1859 when it was described as being 'commercial'.

In 1875 a public luncheon was held at the **Eagle** to celebrate the opening of the new railway to New Radnor. The other attractions included the distribution of 'a Fat Ox to the deserving poor', tea for the women and children, athletic sports, a brass band and a grand display of fireworks. Landlord in the 1880s and '90s was Thomas Morgan, but by 1906 Thomas Gailey was in charge. Later, probably at the end of the First World War, James Niblett, landlord of the **Radnor Arms**, took it over. An invoice of 1935 shows that Mr. J. Davies paid Mr. Niblett the sum of 11s. 6d. for 'suppers, apartments and breakfasts' and 1s. for beer – the inn at that time being described as 'fully licensed, family and commercial'.

At some point a garage and petrol pump were installed to cater for the increase in motorised transport. The annual Horse Fair not only attracted

Two recent views of the Eagle Hotel.
Top: in 2003
Bottom: In 2005, no longer with gabled windows. Taken from Castle Hill

The Eagle sign

horses by the score to New Radnor, but numerous customers to the **Eagle** for their famed goose meals. In the late 1960s fire destroyed the gable ends of the building which meant that a new roof had to be constructed. Afterwards it was run for some years by Angela Hoye, who built up a successful restaurant trade. About six years ago it was bought by Michael and Catherine Campbell-Jones, who also ran a para-gliding centre. Since the beginning of 2004, however, it has been closed, opening only on the occasional weekend. Planning permission to convert the **Eagle** into three houses was obtained, but in June, 2005 it was sold and the new owner intends to carry on running the hotel as a going concern.

Facing down Broad Street is a large building now divided into two private houses, one called the Cross and the other the Forge. This was once an important inn called the **Cross**, mentioned in 1785, but which probably closed in the following century. The name derives from the fact that crosses were erected at the roadside, particularly at a cross-roads, to comfort travellers.

A snowy scene in New Radnor with the Cross Inn central

The former Cross Inn at New Radnor

Just opposite the Cenotaph in High Street and near the church is a large building, now divided into two houses, which was formerly the **King's Arms**. The middle section may date back to medieval times. John Griffiths was the landlord in 1830, while in 1841 it was run by Thomas Powell, aged 45, who lived there with his wife, Martha, 35, and their 10-year-old son, William, together with a 50-year-old female servant and a cattle dealer. In 1844 the licensee was John Morgan who was still there in 1859.

Caroline Meredith who, with husband Charles, ran the King's Arms from the 1890s to the late 1920s

In the 1890s it was taken over by Charles Meredith, licensee of the **Radnor Arms**, on a day when three pubs changed hands (the third being the **Eagle**). The inn was owned by the Lewis family of Harpton Court who, after the First World War, sold it off. Charles, now the owner, had 10 children, one of whom tragically drowned in a drinking trough when only a toddler. In the 1930s he left the inn to his daughter, Gertrude, and son, Gilbert, who ran it between them. When pubs in Wales were still closed on a Sunday, patrons of the **King's Arms** would go to a cow shed at the back where beer would be brought out in large jugs. After Gilbert's death in the early 1950s, Gertrude continued at the helm for a while and then left it to Mr. and Mrs. Meredith, who ran it for a short time before deciding to close it in 1955 and divided it into two houses which they put out to let. On their death it was left to their two daughters. One of the houses has been occupied by Caroline, now Mrs. Price, for the last 40

years. The other house continued to be let out but has remained empty for the last 12 years. The Prices' lounge used to be the bar with bench seats round the walls. The bar counter and shelf behind has been removed and that area now leads into a new kitchen. An internal door, now walled up, led into a room with a cast iron range where customers used to eat. But on busy days such as the Radnor Fairs further dining space was available upstairs. Outside were stables and a butcher's slaughter place.

The Radnor Fairs attracted an influx of animals and men and extra trade for pubs like the King's Arms. On the far right is the Old Parsonage also known as the Steppes or the Old Oak

The one-time King's Arms, New Radnor

Next door is Swan House which used to be the **Swan Inn**, erected in the 15th century and one of the oldest buildings in New Radnor. It was originally built as a hall house or meeting place and had a thatched roof, which has been since raised twice. It is listed as:

New Radnor about 1800

211

One and a half storeys, incorporating the truncated portion of a high quality, late medieval cruck-built house comprising part of a two-bay hall and the upper end bay. Nineteenth century rubble stone refacing, central front gabled dormer. ... two fairly complete cruck trusses of large scantling are exposed, mainly on first floor.

In addition to the two bays there are two inglenook fireplaces, one in each living room on either side of the front entrance. Some of the stones around the fireplaces are believed to have come from the castle, while added timbers were reclaimed.

Ted Davies at the entrance to the Old Swan

It is not known for how long the building operated as an inn, or more likely as a 'watering hole', but it was mentioned in the *Hereford Journal* of 1830, when John Griffiths was the landlord. John Morgan was the licensee in 1844 and was still there in 1859. The **Swan** was still open in the early 20th century and probably closed after the First World War. The adjoining cottage was added about 150 years ago.

Opposite the **Swan** is a picturesque house with steps leading up to the front door which used to be the **Oak Inn** in the 16th century. Yet another inn was the **Duke's Arms**, mentioned in the *Hereford Journal* of 1771, but its location is not known.

The former Swan Inn, New Radnor, which closed about 80 years ago

The Oak Inn
Left: In the early 20th century.
Above: In 2005

Midway between New and Old Radnor is the hamlet of Yardro reached by a minor road off the A44 and through Harpton. Nearby is a farm called Lett ne fford, which used to be an old drovers' inn. Around it hedges frame a series of small paddocks that were once used to separate sheep and cattle.

Continuing westwards along the A44, the hamlet of Llanfihangel-nant-Melan is reached and the roadside hostelry called the **Red Lion**, which began life as a 16th-century drovers' inn. The inn will always be associated with the story of John Lloyd, a bonesetter and animal healer known as Silver John. A frequent fixture in the **Red Lion** bar, where he transacted a lot of his business, he would not take money for his work, but instead silver buttons which were stitched to his coat. One customer added a pair of silver buckles, while another gave him a heavy silver-knobbed stick. So heavy did his coat become that he only wore it on high days and holidays, when attending anyone with broken bones, and on trips to Builth Wells. And it was one such jaunt, on the road to Builth Wells Fair, that was to be his last. He set off after a warming drink with passing drovers at the **Red Lion**. Eventually his horse brought his cart or gambo back, but there was no sign of Silver John. Despite strenuous searches he could not be found – until the Radnor Candlemas Fair was held on the nearby Llyn Hilyn lake, frozen over in the great frost of that year. Under the ice was discovered the glacial form of Silver John. The old man had been murdered, stripped of his silver, and thrown into the waters of Llyn Hilyn.

The Red Lion in the early 1900s

Over the years, on cold misty nights, it has been said that the wails of long-dead injured animals can be heard echoing round the hills behind the inn as they wait in vain for Silver John to set their broken bones. Even recently, a former manageress of the **Red Lion** claimed to have seen the ghost of Silver John, a 'grey figure walking through the pool room when the pub is closed'.

In 1841 the landlord was John Vaughan, aged 65, who lived there with 25 year-old shoe-maker James Adams and his wife, Hannah, and their two young daughters. Edward Jones was the landlord in 1857 and in 1859. At the turn of the 20th century, the inn was owned by Lewis and Agnes Williams, who, after the First World War, converted the stables into a garage and installed a petrol pump. During their stay, accommodation, luncheons and teas were provided, while 'picnic and tourist parties were catered for'. The growing tourist trade, particularly cycling, was of considerable importance and the hotel was NCU and CTC appointed. The Williams stayed until the early 1930s. Later the garage was converted into three bedrooms, while an area to the front, which at one time had been used as a granary, was transformed into a dining room. The **Red Lion** changed hands several times until the early 1970s when it was bought by Dr. Stephen Roggendorf, a doctor of engineering, who made extensive alterations. The works included knocking down internal walls, changing the position of the staircase, and providing a new kitchen and toilets. The front verandah, which is now used as a restaurant,

The 1938 golden wedding of former Red Lion licensees Lewis and Agnes Williams. Both are buried in the nearby churchyard

was also erected at that time. He stayed there for six or seven years, since when there have been several different owners. Stabling facilities are still available at the rear which come in useful as the **Red Lion** is connected to FreeRein, a horse trekking and holiday business. It was a popular spot – an old visitor's book recorded the comment: 'Called for a pint, stayed for a week!'

The Red Lion in 2003 showing the verandah style restaurant constructed in the 1970s

The Forest Inn when owned by Henry Price

Just a few hundred yards further along the A44 at the junction with the A481 to Builth stands the **Fforest Inn**, one of the oldest and highest inns in Wales. Signs of much earlier civilisation can be seen all around including a 5th-century BC stone circle, a tomen marking the fortified dwelling of a 12th-century warrior, and a tumulus. The inn was probably built in the 16th or 17th centuries and was originally a drovers' watering hole, with ground at the back for their animals, before becoming an important coaching house. It also has the distinction of being the main subject of a novel – *Forest Inn* – written in 1946 by Nantmel author, H.L.V. Fletcher, but set in the period immediately after the Battle of Waterloo. The story mainly revolves in and around the inn and although his description of the interior of the building is made up, Fletcher's rendering of the exterior would have been truthful. A coach arrives in a snow-storm and:

> Half-way up the hill the Forest Inn came in sight. It was a long, two-storied building standing on the left-hand side of the road, surrounded by a group of bent, tired, complaining pines. The Inn was roofed with grey slates, its walls whitewashed and its woodwork painted black. At one end an absence of windows showed where the barns and stables and animals' quarters were, for it was a farm as well as hostelry.

Like the **Red Lion**, the inn is also associated with the legend of Silver John Lloyd, bonesetter and animal healer, who must also have enjoyed its hospitality. A short distance from the inn towards Builth is Llyn Hilyn lake and it was here in the 1830s that the landlord's daughter, Mary, found the

The Forest Inn in 2005

murdered body of Silver John. This was when Radnor Candlemas Fair was being held on the lake, frozen solid during a great frost. Hot cider and cakes were enjoyed and hundreds skated and played games on the ice. Mary, who had gone sliding to the far end of the lake, suddenly slipped and fell face downward on the ice. Her cry of horror brought a crowd and looking through the thick ice they saw the body of Silver John. Only after the ice had melted was the bonesetter's body removed, when it was found he had been stripped of his silver adornments. Interestingly, the 1841 census shows that John Price, aged 65, was the publican of the **Fforest Inn** and that also living there was Mary Jones, aged 20, described as a wife. Was this the same Mary, now married, who discovered Silver John? In the 1850s, Elizabeth Owens was the licensee. The inn was noted for its ham and egg teas, and frequented by visitors to the spas at Llandrindod Wells. The barns were later incorporated into the inn itself.

In 1956 the **Fforest** was bought by Tom and Win Lander who stayed there until the mid-1970s. Ten years ago it was bought at auction by Ken Lloyd, a farmer from New Radnor. He said:

> Being related in some way to Silver John, I was determined to buy the Forest if it ever came up for sale, ... I was selling sheep in Cirencester when I heard about the inn being auctioned in Cardiff so I put in a telephone bid and bought it.

The inn has since been run by tenant landlords. Recently refurbished, it now offers a restaurant and accommodation.

Travelling back towards New Radnor, the B4372 takes one to Kinnerton, where near the church gates is Church House in the grounds of which was once an inn known variously as the **Red Lion**, **Lion**, and the **Crown**. In 1841 the innkeeper of the **Lion** was Edward Harley, aged 40, who lived there with his wife Ann, also 40, and their four children. Edward Harley was still there in 1859 when the name had changed to the **Crown**. Local tradition has it that the inn was forced to close down, around the turn of the last century, following complaints from the vicar of drunkenness by some of the customers. The building was eventually demolished.

Tavern Trap used to be where Trappe House, Evenjobb, now stands

From Kinnerton a minor road leads to the B4357 and Evenjobb which at one time had two pubs, both on the outskirts of the village. The first one is just past the church, on the left-hand side of the B4357 going towards Knighton. Called **Tafarn Trawdd**, otherwise **Tavern Trap**, and later **Tavern Tap**, it was sited where Trappe House, with the date 1863, now stands. It comprised two cottages which were demolished to make way for the new property which still retains the old cellar. The name 'Trap' suggests that it welcomed travellers in the days of the pony and trap. A garage was formerly a coach house with a cobbled floor and the remains of a pig sty survive at the rear. Living there for 40 years until recently, Nigel Waters, now of Knighton, has in his possession an old paper relating to the property written by the owner, Thomas Edwards of Rowley, on 2 December, 1862. Mr. Edwards noted that the two cottages were bought in 1743 for £10 each by Isabella Duggan from two sisters, Mary and Ann Wedge, of Bath. The cottages were described as 'nearly down, and very badly out of repair, inconvenient and dirty'. The cottages were still standing, however, more than a hundred years later as an invoice states:

> Received of Mrs. Hart, the sum of £5, being a deposit in part payment of £300 for 2 cottages and gardens called Tavern Tap. Possession to be given and the remainder of the money paid, subject to the approval of Messrs Leman 51 Lincolns Inn Fields, at Lady day 1863.

It was signed by Mr. Edwards. Because the inn lay equidistant between Knighton and Kington, Mr. Walters surmises that it would have been a staging post for horses to be changed.

The second hostelry – the **Yew Tree Inn** – is now a private cottage sited further along the B4357 opposite Newcastle Court, and closed sometime in the 19th century. The inn was aptly named, there being an ancient yew tree still standing to one side of the building.

Once the Yew Tree Inn, Evenjobb

One mile north of Evenjobb on the B4357 is the hamlet of Beggar's Bush and Beggar's Bush Farm, a private house, which started life as a drovers' inn called the **Bush**, with plenty of ground around for animals to shelter. This is one of the earliest pub names, originating from the Roman custom of placing a bush of evergreen leaves outside their inns. It is also associated with King Charles I who, after his decisive defeat at Naseby in 1645, came to Radnorshire with the remnants of his army

Beggars Bush Inn, where Charles I may have spent the night

and is believed to have spent a night there. The king knew the area well having hunted many times in North Wood, stretching from the hamlet to Presteigne, granted to him by James I when he was Prince of Wales. Because the inn could serve only a frugal fare, Charles apparently referred to it as **Beggar's Bush**, a name retained by the hamlet. Still to be seen on the door to one of the bedrooms are three different locks and a metal stay on the inside. It is nice to conjecture that this was the room where the beleaguered king stayed. Another version of the name's origin is that Charles I stayed there while disguised as a beggar.

In the 1841 census Richard Ball, aged 75, was the innkeeper, living at **Beggar's Bush** with his daughter Margaret, 35, and her three children. The inn probably closed at the end of the last century – it is not mentioned in Kelly's *Directory* of 1895 – and became a private house, although it was also run as a guest house. For some years a serving hatch between two rooms still existed but the dividing wall was eventually knocked down to make one room. Although extensively altered and added to, the building still has numerous old beams inside and there is an enclosed recess possibly concealing an inglenook fireplace.

The Old Post Office, Whitton, once the Red Lion or Whitton Arms

Continuing northwards to Knighton on the B4357 Whitton is reached, where the Old Post Office once traded as the **Red Lion** and then, after 1913 as the **Whitton Arms**, closing soon afterwards. In 1895 the landlord was Walter Evans and in 1906 it was run by Herbert Jay, who was also described as a grocer. A special attraction for customers was a long room at the back which served as a shooting range. A shed attached to one side of the pub was the local undertaker's establishment. Then in 1920, no longer a pub and having suffered from two fires, it was bought from Nancy Grice by William Woozencroft who a year later re-opened it as a post office. Mr. Woozencroft also ran a small dairy and cattle farm, providing milk and vegetables to the local primary school. In 1963 it was taken over by his son, Christopher, who ran the farm and acted as postman, while his wife, Marjorie, conducted the post office.

They stopped trading in 1973, since when it has been a private house. The farm buildings have disappeared and the ground built on, and a new bungalow has replaced the old shed. Inside, the shooting range has been converted into a kitchen, pantry and toilet. To one side of the front door is the lounge which, when the building was in use as a pub, was two rooms with the bar and serving area behind. On the other side, the front room was used as another bar, before becoming the post office, with an area behind used as a beer cellar.

Returning southwards along the B4357 to the A44, one comes to the village of Walton and the **Crown Inn**, the first hostelry in Wales on the

An early celebration at the Crown Inn

ancient route from Herefordshire to the west coast. Originally the building, dating back to the 17th century, may have centred round the old stone area now used as the kitchen, and since expanded. A coaching inn, with stables and a blacksmith's at the rear, it was in the Nott family from the early 1800s to the 1870s, when it was sold to a brewery. However one of the Nott daughters married Richard Ingram and they ran the inn as tenants. It was then taken over by their daughter Ada who married Harold Hughes in 1907. At some point a petrol station was installed and in 1930 the **Crown** was sold by the Royal Well brewery to Alton Court brewery. Mr. and Mrs. Hughes ran the inn during the two world wars until Harold died in 1945, when it was run by Ada. In 1956 Percy and Olive Hughes became licensees. Percy was a keen supporter of the local hunt, but drew the line when a horse came through the front door with its rider demanding a drink for both of them. Then in 1979

*The Vale of Radnor Agricultural Association meeting outside
the Crown Inn at Walton on 15 December 1905*

Ray and Denise Hughes continued the family tradition, even buying back the inn from Whitbreads in 1988, but were forced to leave for health reasons in 1993. A keen footballer, Percy was capped 11 times as goalkeeper for the Welsh national youth team but ended his life in a wheel-chair. Tony Roberts, manager of Barclays Bank in Knighton, bought the Crown in 1993 and ran it for about 18 months before selling it to another Mr. Hughes who owned the Royal Oak in Gladestry. The inn has since had another owner who at the time of writing has put it on the market yet again.

A flight of stairs opposite the front door was removed with the space utilised as an off-sales area for some years. The two bars are on either side with a dining room at the rear, now the Nakon Thai restaurant and takeaway. The petrol station was removed some years ago and converted into a car park.

The first house on the left-hand side of the hill leading out of Walton on the A44 towards Kington used to be an old drovers' inn called the **Horse and Jockey**, and still retains the name. It was known to have traded in the 18th century, and probably earlier, with a bar and another living room, both with large fire-places, but by 1819 it had become a private dwelling. Divided into two cottages, it was later converted back into the one house with an extension built on the other side of the living room. In the 1970s the **Horse and Jockey** was renamed Hedgehog

This was once the Horse and Jockey which closed in the early 20th century but still retains its name

Cottage and utilised as a post office. But after lying empty for three years it was bought 12 years ago by the present owners who restored its original name. Interestingly the **Horse and Jockey** was mentioned in the Radnor *Red Book* of 1913.

There was also another inn in Walton, the **Black Alehouse**, named in the *Hereford Journal* of 1773, but its location is unknown.

CHAPTER TWELVE

The Upper Teme Valley

The unspoilt Upper Teme Valley is still largely dominated by sheep farming. The river Teme, which rises high in the hills above Felindre and flows through the valley to Knighton, represents the boundary line between Radnorshire and Shropshire. On the Welsh side of the river runs the B4355 road which later joins the A483 to Newtown. Along the Radnorshire stretch of the road are five villages which over the years have boasted a number of inns to provide refreshment for drovers, travellers and local communities. Today four remain, all of which open only during the evenings and at weekends.

Leaving Knighton on the B4355 one soon comes to a large, solitary, two-storey, stone building on the right-hand side still called the **Halfway House**, which in the 19th century used to be a fully licensed inn. Above the doorway is a stone engraved with 'TP 1848', presumably the date when it was built. The name is believed to have come about because it stood half way between Craven Arms and Newtown. After ceasing to trade, the inn was used as a farmhouse before becoming a private dwelling.

The first village encountered is Knucklas, just off the B4355 and in the parish of Heyope, an area with a fascinating history. According to Welsh tradition, King Ogrfan Gawr (the Giant) of Castell y Cnwclas (Knucklas Castle) had a daughter called Guinevere who married King Arthur in Knucklas. Then in the early 13th century the Iron Age fortress was replaced by a castle built by Ralph Mortimer in his quest to control the ancient Welsh kingdom of Maeliennydd. A small quadrangular stone building with circular angle towers and a barbican to the west, it was destroyed in 1262 by Llywelyn ap Gruffudd, the last official native Prince of Wales. However, it was soon afterwards re-taken by Edmund Mortimer, who also established a borough in Knucklas, one of the smallest in Wales and rather short-lived. By 1406 Knucklas was regarded as a lordship without a castle. Greater activity occurred in the 1860s when a 465-yard long viaduct, with distinctive castellated turrets, was constructed to carry the Central Wales line from

The Castle Inn at Knucklas

Llandrindod Wells to Knighton, 69 feet above the valley floor to the west of Knucklas. Navvies working on the viaduct no doubt slaked their thirst in hastily opened beer houses as well as the local inns.

While the castle ruins lie forlorn and grass-covered, the village pub, not surprisingly called the **Castle Inn**, is alive and well. Situated on an island between two roads at the approach to the village, it is believed to have been originally built in the 17th century, some say by Cromwell's soldiers, and whose past was linked with another inn, the **Ship and Castle**, which closed over 100 years ago. When it became an inn is not known, although the first mention of it seems to be in the 1851 census, when it was run by Benjamin Wall and his wife Sarah. Ten years later the innkeeper was Richard Preece and in 1871 it was Henry Evans, also described as a road surveyor, who lived there with his wife, Mary, two children and a domestic servant. Then in 1881 it was run by 69-year-old George Deakins, also a farmer of 80 acres, and his wife, Margaret, daughter of Samuel Webb, of the **Ship and Castle**. At the turn of the century another Deakins, Eliza, aged 26, was in charge, living there with her elderly mother and two young sons. And the **Castle** remained in the Deakins family until the early 1980s.

After staying closed for a few years, the inn was inherited by Mrs. Pat Hughes, related to the Deakins, who with her husband Ted refurbished the property before re-opening it. The two bars were turned into one open-plan area, and a new bar counter was placed in a central position at the rear of the room. The trap door behind the bar leading down into the cellar, which covers the whole length of the building and where the servant girls used to sleep, was closed up. Some of the original flagstones can be seen by the large fire-place, now containing a woodburner. To one side of the bar is a dining area and behind it is a utility room which at one time housed a post office when the local shop closed down. To the rear of the building the old stables have been converted into a function room and five en-suite letting rooms. The Hughes sold the **Castle** in the early 1990s, since when it has had three new owners.

Next door but one to the **Castle** is Upper House, from where a stone carving business is operated and which was once the **Ship and Castle**, with ship, in this case, being a corruption of sheep. Probably built in the 17th century, the inn may have been the birthplace of Vavasor Powel, the radical reformer, who was said to have been born in the

At one time the Ship and Castle

public house in Cnwclas, the son of an innkeeper and oatmeal dealer. After losing his father while a youth, Vavasor worked as an ostler at a Bishop's Castle inn, before going to university and later becoming famous as a reformist in the times of Cromwell. The name, **Ship and Castle**, first appears in the Minutes of Radnorshire General Quarter Sessions in 1823. In 1841 it was run by Samuel Webb, described as a builder/carpenter. It then appears that his daughter, Margaret, married George Deakins and together they ran the inn in 1871, when it was known as the Old Public, before moving to the **Castle**. The oldest part of the building is at the rear and is now used as a living room, still retaining an old fire-range. The front was added in the late 18th century with the kitchen replacing the original bar area.

The next village along the B4355 is Lloyney, with the **Lloyney Inn**, orig-inally constructed in the early 1800s, when it was called the **Builder's Arms**.

The Lloyney float for the procession in 1902

The Lloyney fox

This was in recognition of the fact that it was built by Henry Griffiths, known locally as 'The Builder', having also built several other buildings including the Methodist chapel. Next door to the inn was a malthouse and a blacksmith's shop, which at times were run by the landlord. At the turn of the last century the Greep family lived at the blacksmith's, with Mr. Greep also involved in the timber business. They kept a pet fox which one day got loose and whose scent was picked up by hounds from the Teme Valley Hunt. Chased by the dogs, the fox ran across Lloyney Rock and down the bank behind the shop, over the roof and dashed inside. Denied his prey, the Huntsman told the Greeps he would get the fox one day. And he did.

The Lloyney in 2006

In 1928 Bill Farmer, the blacksmith in Llanfair Waterdine, moved to Lloyney to become landlord of the **Builder's Arms** and also to run the blacksmith's shop. During the day he made wheels and shod horses, and in the evening became mine host. He stayed there until 1959. In the 1960s, when the **Builder's Arms** was owned by George Steiner, who also owned pubs in Knighton and Presteigne. The blacksmith's shop was demolished as part of a road widening scheme; the malthouse, which became a carpenter's shop, was incorporated into the inn; while the old stables, later used as a garage, were converted into a pool room. In the late 1980s or early '90s, the licensee changed the name to the **Lloyney Inn**. Michael Edwards, who previously worked in civil engineering, and his wife Gillian have been at the helm since 1996.

Just across the border in Shropshire is the village of Llanfair Waterdine, which was mentioned in the Domesday Book and was at one time in Wales. Over the years it has had close connections with Lloyney, not least because of a school and a pub which was open on Sundays. This was the **Red Lion**, believed to have been built in 1570, and now called the **Waterdine**. It is built on the lines of a traditional Welsh longhouse and the very name implies it was once Welsh – the red lion being the emblem of early Welsh rulers and adopted by many leading families. The building was originally also a farm with over

A Fully Licensed Property

known as

" The Red Lion Inn "

LLANVAIR WATERDINE,

together with

Enclosures of Fertile Pasture Land,

the whole having an area of about

16 a.   3 r.   6 p.

THE HOUSE

which is built of Stone, Plaster and Slate, contains :—Sitting Room, Bar, Bar Parlour, Smoke Room, Kitchen with sink and copper, Dairy, Cellar with Barrel shute, and Coal house.

ON THE FIRST FLOOR is a large well lighted Club Room and Four Bedrooms with Landing.

Good GARDEN (with E.C.)

THE BUILDINGS

Adjoining the House is a Coach-house and Fowl-house, and on the opposite side of the road is a Range of Stone, Timber and thatched Buildings, including 3-horse Stable, Barn with Bays, Cowshed (4 ties) with Loft over, 2 Pigsties. There is also a timber and slate Store Shed adjoining the Main Road.

SCHEDULE.

No. on Plan	Description			Area.	No. on Plan.	Description			Area.
1611	Garden	..	..	.243	1623	Pasture	..	..	1.879
1610	Do.	..	..	.204	1611a	Do.	..	..	.594
1601	Pasture	..	..	1.721	Pt. 1620	Red Lion Inn (Estd.)			.171
1602	Do.	..	..	2.082	Pt. 1182	Pasture	,,	..	.900
1603	Do.	..	..	1.167	Pt. 1181	Do.	,,	..	2.015
1604	Do.	..	..	2.106	Pt. 1166	Do.	,,	..	.366
1605	Pasture & Buildings			1.033	Pt. 1609	Garden	,,	..	.020
1183	Pasture	..	..	1.202					
1184	Do.	..	..	1.083			A.		16.786

The whole is in the occupation of Mrs. Evans on a yearly Ladyday tenancy, subject to six months' notice.

OUTGOINGS.—Tithe Rent Charge Apportionment £2 5s. 1d.
Land Tax 6/5.

This Lot is sold with the right of obtaining a supply of water as heretofore enjoyed from the tank in field No. 1166, part of Lot 12.

Sale of the Red Lion in 1919

20 acres of land and may have been used as a watering hole by drovers. At some point the **Red Lion** became part of the Llanfair Waterdine Estate, which also possessed Llanfair Hall, eight farms, and cottages, in all

extending to 1,880 acres. Tenants of the estate, including the **Red Lion** land-lords, were subject to an annual Lady Day tenancy, and on this day they all met at the inn to pay their dues. They were then treated to a grand dinner in the ballroom by the estate.

At the beginning of the 20th century the inn was run by Bill Evans and his wife. Bill was very versatile; he was also the village carpenter, school caretaker, relief postman, and sexton of St. Mary's Church responsible for grave digging and grass cutting. By 1919 it was run by Mrs. Evans who paid a tithe apportionment of £2 5s. 1d. and a land tax of 6s. 5d. That same year the Llanfair Waterdine estate, including the inn, was put up for sale at the Norton Arms Hotel, Knighton and was bought for £25,000 by Mr. T.S. Jones of Llanfair Hall on behalf of the tenants. How much Mrs. Evans paid back to Mr. Jones to become owner of the **Red Lion** is not known.

The sale notice described the **Red Lion**, built of stone, plaster and slate, as containing:

> a sitting room, bar, bar parlour, smoke room, kitchen, dairy, cellar with beer shute, and coal house. On first floor – a large well lighted club room and four bedrooms. Adjoining the house is a coach house and fowl house, and on the opposite side of the road is a range of stone, timber and thatched buildings including a 3 horse stable, barn with bays, cowshed (4 ties) with loft over and 2 pig sties. There is also a timber and slate store shed ... together with 16 acres of pasture land.

The local hunt at the Red Lion in the 1950s

229

The thatched barn was also used for dancing, becoming renowned for its Morris Dances with music provided by the fiddles of the Romany family, the Locks. Demolished in the late 1940s, its old timbers and beams were used to renovate the **Red Lion**. This probably included the incorporation of the coach house into the inn, the building of a lounge at the rear, conversion of the dairy into a kitchen, and partition of the clubroom into extra bedrooms.

Living in the village was John, later Lord Hunt, and it would be nice to think that he and other team members planned the assault of Mount Everest in front of the fire at the **Red Lion**. Whatever the case, the inn played its part in the village celebrations, including square-dancing, bonfire and fireworks, and a fly-past of aircraft, when Hunt led the successful ascent of Everest in 1953.

In the late 1960s the land opposite the inn was sold to a local farmer. In the 1990s Chris and Judy Stevenson were the owners, followed by Mick Richards, until it was taken over in 2000 by Ken and Isabel Adams, who moved there from the Oaks restaurant in Ludlow. An internationally renowned chef, Ken changed the inn's name to the **Waterdine** and transformed it into a high-class restaurant. The lounge bar has been kept the same but the smoking room, the oldest part, has been turned into a dining area. The whole building, once in traditional black-and-white, has been re-painted in other colours.

Back on the B4355 one comes to the hamlet of Duthlas, where at the far end on the right-hand side is a private house which was once the **Harp Inn**, a popular name for a Welsh pub. It traded as a beerhouse in the 19th century and also conducted a small grocery business. In 1899 it was sold for £200 to Mr. Thomas; later belonging to his son, Thomas, of Beguildy. The licensee

Earlier the Red Lion, the Waterdine in 2006

The Harp Inn which closed in 1911

was Margaret Brick. However, trade deteriorated and by the time its licence came up for renewal in 1911 it was very little used. The licensing authority heard that the **Harp** was inferior to neighbouring inns with poor accommodation and no stabling. The value of the property was put at £300 with a gross rateable value of £12 and a rent of the same amount.

Thomas Swift, a brewer from Newtown, said that from January to December, 1910, 29 barrels of Pale in cask and 93 doz. Bass & Guinness, equivalent to about two barrels, had been supplied. Miss Brick said gross income from the pub and grocery business was about £100 a year, of which £40 to £50 was derived from the inn. Renewal of the licence was refused and compensation was agreed at £112, of which £12 went to the licensee.

Before Beguildy is reached on the left-hand side is Bryndrinog Farm, on whose property during the 19th century was apparently an inn, known as the **Bryndrinog Arms**. It appears in the minutes of the General Quarter Sessions for the period between 1823 and 1829. Owned at one time by the Irish peer Lord Dunsany, the site also boasted a courthouse.

The village of Beguildy, which means a shepherd's dwelling, was once the centre of a prosperous sheep-rearing district. It is believed also to have been the birthplace of John Dee (1527-1608), who attained eminence in the service of Queen Elizabeth I as a soothsayer and 'conjuror of spirits'.

The roadside inn is the **Radnorshire Arms**, probably built in the 16th century and originally used by drovers who would eat, drink and sleep there. Interestingly, to one side are three Scotch pines, a known indicator to drovers that hospitality was to hand for both man and beast. Further along is Pound Farm, where once the cattle and sheep grazed overnight by the river. At the same end of the inn is a store which used to be a stables and slaughter house, with channels in the brick floor still discernible. Inside, several changes have taken place over the years. For instance, the pool room was once a barn with an extension added, while the dining room to the left of the front entrance was a private sitting room. A staircase to one side of the front door has been removed and in the lounge bar the fireplace has been restored after being

The Radnorshire Arms about 1870 with its thatched roof
which was replaced in the 1940s or '50s

The Teme Valley Hunt meeting at the Radnorshire Arms

The Radnorshire Arms in the snow in 2005
and in much better weather later in the year

twice bricked up. To the rear a door, now enclosed, once led to a restaurant which is now a lounge-cum-office. A new serving area was introduced in the 1980s when Frank Taylor was the landlord.

The most colourful landlord was Jack Martland, who owned the inn for about 25 years until the 1970s. A former officer in the Royal Air Force, he

*Above: Recent internal views
of the Radnorshire Arms*

Right: The inn sign

always sported a blazer with an RAF badge. However, it is alleged another mine host 'bought the pub, drank it dry and then sold it!' The present land-lord, Peter Thompson, runs an unusual annual charity event called a 'Spudaganza' in which some 150 buckets of seed potatoes are sold with the winner being the one who manages to grow the biggest potatoes. Also popular is the pub's fishing club with members travelling to Aberdovy to go sea fishing.

Along the lane leading to the parish church opposite the graveyard gate is Church Cottage, which at one time was an inn called the **Oxford Arms**. It was probably named after the Oxford Estate owned by the Earl of Oxford, related to the Harleys of Brampton Bryan. In 1841 the inn was run by Alexander Joseph, described as being 'old'; it probably closed down later that century. An oak chair, with elephant heads on the arms, now resident in the church, is said to have come from the **Oxford Arms**. But, intriguingly,

This building was once the Oxford Arms

The chair, now in the church, is said to have come from the Oxford Arms

carved on the chair are the words: 'The Anchor Inn, Craven Arms, Salop', a reference no doubt to the **Anchor Inn** in Anchor (see on).

The last village in Radnorshire on the B4355 is Felindre, where the **Wharf Inn**, a two-storey building constructed in the late 18th century, can be seen. According to the 1851 census the landlord was Thomas Williams, aged 33, who ran the inn with his wife, Mary, and a female servant. It was later taken over by Richard and Elizabeth Jones, from Towyn in Merionethshire, who

Date when the Spirits were received	No. of the Certificate	Christian and Surname of the Person or Name of the Firm from whom the Spirits were received	Of what Place	Gallons of Spirits received	Kind or Quality of the Spirits	Strength of the Spirits
4	2329338	Thos Swift & Co	Newtown	0 4	P S	12 up
23	2329356	Thos Swift & Co	Newtown	0 1	P S	22 up
				0 4	P S	12 y
				0 2	B B	12 y
				0 1	R	12 y
				0 1	X	22 y
Dec 22	2329393	Thos Swift & Co	Newtown	0 1	P S	22 up
Jan 13	2329031	Thomas Swift & Co	Newtown	0 6	P S	12
				8 2	B B	12
				0 2	X	22
				0 1	R	12
				0 5	P S	22
				0 1	F B	22
Feb 2	2329045	Thos Swift & Co	Newtown	0 4	P S	12 y
				0 2	B B	12 y
Mar 2	2329069	Thos Swift & Co	Newtown	0 1	R	12 y
19	2329091	Thos Swift & Co	Newtown	0 6	P S	12 y
				0 2	P S	
April 19	409500	Thos Swift & Co	Newtown	0 6	P S	12
				0 2	R	12 y
				0 2	B B	12
				0 2	X	22
				0 1	X	50
				0 2	P S	22
				0 2	F B	22
	409537	Thos Swift & Co	Newtown	0 2	P S	22

A page from the Wharf Inn stock book in 1914

also set up a corn and flour business above the stables. They had 15 children with the youngest being the only girl. One of the sons, Arthur, and his wife Frances, kept the inn at the turn of the century. Their eldest son, Jack, was born in the inn, and one of his earliest memories at the age of four, is described in his reminiscences:

The Wharf Inn in 2005

My father was harvesting hay in the Blacksmith Meadow. Several of us children were playing around the weir, which turned the water down to Vron Mill. When I fell in [the river], my father smacked me severely and sent me home with the others – minus shoes, to my great humiliation – for my mother to dry me out.

When he was old enough Jack went to Beguildy School, riding with his father who went with horse and cart to Knucklas station to collect loads of corn and flour. While at school he heard that the First World War was over.

Once a year the Felindre wakes were held at the Wharf with a coconut shy and other attractions. ... The two large bedrooms above the tap room were cleared for dancing to the music of the fiddles played by the Marpole family. ... Meredith Thomas and part of his family kept the stores next to the Wharf. In those days there were as many as seven or eight assistants in the shop and warehouse, and there were seven ladies and girls in the tailoring and outfitting department upstairs and a couple of tailors sitting cross-legged on the floor.

Mr. A.J. Smith became landlord in 1926 followed by three other licensees. During this period a front room was used as a grain depot by the Radnorshire Company, with a tailor's shop above. In 1941 Mr. R.E. Bousefield took over. He came down from London to avoid the bombing, having lost both his legs while serving in a Royal Navy ship during the First

World War. He walked around with the aid of a pair of sticks. From 1949 to 1966 the **Wharf** was run by Les Morris and his wife Mary who sold it to the Wrekin Brewery. During their tenure several alterations were carried out including the incorporation of a passage between the bar and serving area into the bar; the main staircase above the cellar was removed; and a room at the back was knocked down. An extension was added where teas were provided for the Felindre Football Club, who changed in the stables, and which later became the games room. Another sporting activity connected to the inn was the Felindre tug-of-war team which won 200 trophies and competed in various parts of the world up until the 1980s.

Arthur Brick, who was in the transport business, and Blodwyn were the next hosts, buying the **Wharf** off the brewery. During the tenure of Geoff and Carolyn Duthie from 1978 to 1987, they built the front porch and created a car park. In the late 1990s the owner was Chris Griffiths, who also ran an international sales business. In 2003 it was bought by Brian Thomas, whose mother, Clarice, runs the village shop and post office. He has re-invigorated the inn, constructing a new central counter serving both the original bar and a new lounge bar, which was previously a private sitting room. The old bar still retains its original fire-place, although another five have disappeared over the years. The upstairs is now used as flats.

Opposite the village shop was an old stone building called Bridge House which, according to local inhabitants, was originally an inn, probably trading in the 18th century. Its name is not known, although of course it may have been known as the Bridge Inn. Bridge House, together with two shops, one a cobbler's, was demolished in the 1950s. At the crossroads on the minor road leading to Llanbister stands Upper House Farm, on whose property once stood an even more ancient inn, the **Black Lion**, which probably operated in the 17th and 18th centuries. Whether the inn was sited where Upper House, which contains a large cellar, now stands or on some other part of the farm is not known.

Further along the B4355 a minor road to the right leads to the village of Anchor and the **Anchor Inn** which, although just across the border in Shropshire, would have been frequented by many a thirsty Welshman, particularly on a Sunday. Rather than being connected to the sea, the name may have originated from the old Dutch word anker, which was a measure for wine and brandy with a 10 gallon barrel being one anker. While the present building was constructed in the early 19th century, with Mr. Stedman as landlord, tradition has it that there was a much earlier inn on the site although there is no reference to one on early maps. For instance, in his booklet *The Old Kerry Street Fairs from Private Treaty to Public Auctions,* published in 1996, George Jones recalled that there was a famous old road from

Aberystwyth across the Kerry Hills to Bishop's Castle with a southern spur going to Knighton.

> This was also the highway for the English merchants – none more noto-rious perhaps than the elderly dealers in precious metals and jewellery. They descended on the Anchor Inn and commenced trading their often illegally smuggled goods, without certification from the authorities. ... It is interesting to note that when the Birmingham Assay office opened in 1773, they adopted the Anchor sign motif as the official mark of confor-mity, being mindful, no doubt, of the unlawful business being carried out at this famous old drovers and coaching inn on the borders. Back in medieval times the Anchor Inn was also the venue for a substantial trade in animal furs and hides ... .

Then again, L.T.C. Rolt, in his book *Landscape with Figures*, published in 1992, who stayed at the **Anchor** in 1951, wrote:

> It came into existence in the days when cattle in great number were exported from Wales to England 'on the hoof', for it stands upon what was once one of the great trunk roads between the two countries.

Mary Webb prominently features the **Anchor Inn**, which she calls the Mermaids's Rest, in her novel *Seven for a Secret*, written in 1922, but set in the late 19th century. One character remarks:

> Mermaid's Rest? Why, surely, that's the old public off the road from Weeping Cross [Knighton] to Mallard's Keep [Bishop's Castle]? I was past there once, I mind it well. I got a quart there. Queer, seafaring sort of a sign. Don't they call it the Naked Maiden? That's the inn for the fellows, no danger.

de Courcy-Parry with his hounds

And she refers to earlier times when the landlord and maids turned out to meet frequent coaches.

In the early 1930s the **Anchor** was bought by huntsman Charles de Courcy-Parry, who wrote for *Horse and Hound* magazine under the nom-de-plume 'Dalesman', after being refused a drink at the inn while out hunting. In his book *Here Lies My Story*, de Courcy-Parry explained that he and a friend were faced with a 16 mile hack home on a blistering hot day when they came across the **Anchor Inn** only to find that the

> door was closed and barred at one o'clock by order of the law, we were rather put about; so the door was kicked until the landlord was aroused from his slumber – not very well pleased, either. 'If you want a drink,' said he, 'you must buy the house.' Well, that did not present much diffi-culty, for money was no object. I had none with me, nor any left at home, but what did that matter. After further argument a cheque for £700 was pushed under the door and the house was ours. Two pints at £350 each – and well worth it, too.

Apparently de Courcy-Parry had been looking for somewhere up among the hills for a long time where he might take his hounds during summer, and

> where better than a pub? ... In those days our puppy show at the Anchor was quite an occasion. We took down our bedroom walls to make our upstairs into what had once been the rent-dinner room when Naylor's estate was in its erstwhile glory. Into this room, with the floor propped up on tree-trunks from below, we crowded all comers, and a bottle between every two. ... The experiment of kennelling our United hounds at the Anchor Inn during the summer months turned out to be a very wise one, for hounds do very well there and always have done.

The hunt at the Anchor in the 1960s

240

Charles de Courcy-Parry sold the **Anchor** during World War Two, but bought it back again in 1960 'since the brewery who owned it could see no more profit in it and wanted to sell it very badly'. Once again he went hunting, this time for hares, and stayed on there in his retirement until the late 1960s.

The landlady in the 1940s and '50s was Mrs Phoebe Moody, who looked after L.T.C. Rolt when he stayed there for a week with his intended second wife in 1951. He wrote:

> at the time of our visit it was equipped to withstand a long siege with ample covered stores of fuel, and a general store and grocery whose well-stocked shelves seemed primarily intended to meet the emergency needs of the inn itself rather than those of the few scattered farms in the vicinity.

Then in the early 1970s the licensee was Joanna Preece who ran the **Anchor** with her two sons, Simon and Michael, and it was during their tenure that the inn enjoyed its most successful period with the formation of a country and western club and appearances by the Taylor Sisters and Boxcar Willie. The club, with local guitar player Trevor Adams as entertainments manager and his wife as secretary, became so popular that a large functions room was built to feature stars such as Jasper Carrot, Bert Weedon, Max Boyce, Frank Ifield and Acker Bilk. Cabarets were held four times a week with coaches coming from far and wide. The Preeces left in 1979, other landlords came and went and the club gradually folded. Its glory days over, the inn closed and remained empty for four years before it was bought in 1996 in a dilapidated condition by the present owners, Mike and Alex Steedman. They have since managed to restore it, but the functions room remains derelict although it may, subject to planning permission, be converted into holiday homes.

With the entrance down steps, the original bar was off the B4368 to Clun road and built into

'Anchor Live' in 1976

241

An aerial view of the Anchor Inn

a bank, while the present one is two levels down in what used to be the stables with a games room added on. The shop is now a dining area, while the main entrance is through the games room with the building extending round three sides of a courtyard. There is a five-acre paddock on which sheep and cattle sales were held as well as on land on the other side of the Clun road. The **Anchor**, which has six letting rooms and provides food to order, hosts the Anchor Fox Club and the local hunt.

CHAPTER THIRTEEN

The Wye Valley
GLASBURY, BOUGHROOD, LLOWES, CLYRO, RHYDSPENCE & MICHAELCHURCH

At the southern tip of Radnorshire, on the A438 from Hereford to Brecon, lies Glasbury – a village on both sides of the Wye which has always been a crossing point of the river even before a bridge was built in the 18th century. Until 1844, the whole parish was in Radnorshire, but it then became divided with Breconshire and is now, of course, part of Powys. Of special interest is Maesllwch Castle, founded as a manor house in the 16th century by William Vaughan, whose estate covered most of the village and beyond. A new house was later built on the same site, whilst the third and present one with its striking castellations was constructed in the mid-19th century by Walter Wilkins, M.P. for Radnorshire. One of the servants was Mary Morgan, believed to have been the last woman to be publicly executed in Wales. According to Roy Palmer, Mary, a 16-year-old undercook, gave birth to a baby girl in secret in her room on 23 September 1804. 'Almost immediately she killed the baby with a knife. At the inquest two days later Mary was found responsible for the death'. Mary's trial was held in April 1805 at the Great Sessions in Presteigne, where she was found guilty. She was executed at Gallows Lane. In 1942, during the Second World War, the castle was used by the women's Land Army, a use that continued until 1951.

Over the years there have been at least eight hostelries in Glasbury, but today only two still remain open, the **Maesllwch Arms Hotel** and the **Harp**. Just along the B4350 there used to be a cluster of three inns with a driveway behind leading to Maesllwch Castle, whose name, meaning field by the pool, was given to the hotel. The original building probably dates from the 18th century, but over the years it has been considerably extended. According to the 1841 census, the landlord was Henry Ioliffe and in 1851 the innkeeper was Richard James, aged 36, who lived there with his wife, Jane. Also

*Artist's impression of the Maesllwch Arms Hotel, with old gates
leading to the castle and the Plough and Harrow Inn, now a private house*

staying there was a brewer and a 13-year-old house servant. James was still there in 1864 when the number of servants had increased to three. Owned by the Wintons, or de Wintons as they became known, the inn was run from the turn of the century until the early 1950s by Mrs. Fernie, as tenant. In 1931, the **Maesllwch Arms** had 'accommodation for 15 persons for one night or longer, a garage with room for two cars and stabling for two horses'. Managers were then put in before it was sold in the early 1960s. An upstairs assembly room used for functions and dances was converted into bedrooms; the rod room turned into the present reception area, and the original bar extended to form the dining room. Oak panels in the dining room and the present lounge bar came from the Castle during the Second World War as did the fireplace in the lounge bar.

About 15 years ago the then owners went bankrupt and the **Maesllwych Arms** closed with windows boarded up; apparently there was even talk of it being converted into an old people's home. However, under new owners it re-opened and a later owner, Ian Birch, built the stone extension to one side for additional bedrooms (there are now 16) and store rooms. There is also a public bar with pool table and a small meeting room. In 2005 it was bought by Enterprise Inns for about a million pounds.

Just below what used to be the main driveway to Maesllwych Castle and at the back of the hotel is a cottage that was once the **Plough and Harrow Inn**. Built in the early 18th century, it traded for well over a hundred years

The former Plough and Harrow behind the Maesllwych Hotel, Glasbury

and was mentioned in the General Quarter Sessions minutes between 1823 and 1829. In the 1841 census James Watkins, described as a carpenter, lived there with his wife, Ann, and three small children. At around this time, it ceased trading as an inn and was used as a convenient place to monitor the building materials being delivered for the construction of the new castle by the Winton family. In 1910 an office was attached to one side of the property. During the Second World War it was used by the local Home Guard as their base, and in 1945 Mary Lloyd and her husband moved into the tied cottage. Mr. Lloyd, then recently demobilised, worked on the estate for many years as a forester. Mrs. Lloyd, now a widow, still lives there.

On the other side of the B4350 road and opposite the **Maesllwch Arms Hotel** is Lamb House which used to be the **Lamb Inn**. Built of stone with a slate and tile roof, it has a ground floor about two feet below the outside ground level. The building, when the landlord was David Jones, appeared in a list of pubs of 1815 which entered into recognisances to 'keep and maintain good order and shall not suffer any disorder or unlawful games to be used'. In 1829 Edward Meredith was the innkeeper followed, in 1841, by Edward Evans, aged 30, who lived there with his wife, Mary, and two sons together with a house servant. Evans was still there in 1864.

At the beginning of the 20th century the inn was owned by the Hereford and Tredegar Brewery with, from 1921, Robert Fernie as licensee. Ten years later it came before the County Licensing Committee for renewal of its licence. At that time the property was described as consisting of a tap room, bar, kitchen, scullery, pantry, store room and cellar, (all the walls of which were said to be damp), together with three bedrooms, sitting room and club room (in which dances at one time were a popular feature). Outside was a barn, a three-stall stable, pigsty (in bad repair), two bucket closets in the garden and a concrete urinal. There was no garage or coachhouse. Mr. Fernie, whose wife was licensee of the **Maesllwch Arms**, told the committee that 'trade was very little, didn't average a barrel a week', and that 'profits were not sufficient to keep him'. The company said it had spent £465 on renewals and repairs and had built a new kitchen. Trade in 1928 was 91 barrels of beer (drawn by hand from the barrel) and 55 gallons of wines/spirits; in 1930 it was 53 barrels of beer and 38 gallons of wines/spirits. In the event renewal of the licence was refused and compensation of £787 including £78 to the tenant, was later awarded. With the closure of the **Lamb**, Mr. Fernie no doubt went to help his wife at the **Maesllwch Arms**! Even after becoming a private residence, the owner retained many of the pub features with even the bar counter staying *in situ*, until it was sold recently when changes were made.

The site of the old Swan Inn, Glasbury in early 2006. A new house is being built on the site

Nearby is The Green where there was yet another pub, the **Swan**, an inn name and sign since the 14th century. Originally two old cottages with a thatched roof, the inn was run in 1841 by Benjamin Williams. By 1861 he had been succeeded by his son, also called Benjamin, and described as a blacksmith, who ran it with his wife, Sarah. Benjamin Snr., now 80 years old, still lived there together with his grandson, also a blacksmith, and a young apprentice. Thomas Jones was at the helm in 1871. Sometime around the turn of the century, the **Swan** closed and became a private residence. In 1922, the old building was demolished and a new house built on the same site. Later it was occupied by the Clayton family including 18 children! In early 2006 the building was again raised to the ground and from a heap of rubble a new Swan is rising as a private house.

Glasbury's other pub which still remains open is the **Harp Inn**, situated just along the B4350 road to Hay on the Breconshire side of the Wye. The inn may have originated in the 17th century as a cider house and was later frequented by drovers who, before the bridge was built, forded the river at the shallowest point and then left their cattle to graze on the Grove, an area of common land set behind the pub and running down to the Wye. No doubt toasts were drunk there in 1832 when a sturgeon 7ft. 6ins. long – a record still unbeaten – was caught about a mile upstream. In 1851 the innkeeper was William Davies, aged 58, also described as a musician, who lived there with his wife, Anne, and three children, together with an agricultural labourer and a plasterer. This musical tradition continued with another landlord, blind Ukin, and his daughter, Molly, playing appropriately the harp. They entertained at various local events including feast day at nearby Llanigon, when a great deal of dancing went on.

The inn was originally one of three cottages, the internal walls of which were knocked down at the turn of the century to make one building. There are four floors including a basement which contains a private lounge, kitchen and two cellars, believed to be the oldest part. During the Second World War the **Harp** was run by Alice Price whilst her husband was away in the Army. In those days there was a tiny sitting room by the fireplace where the ladies gathered, and a Bottom Bar for Labour with a Top Bar for the Tories. An off-sales area was behind the original front door which is now a window. In the 1970s, when Mr. and Mrs. Potter were licensees, the inn was refurbished including the building of an extension for a games room and toilets and the fitting of false ceiling beams. A rear garden with pig sties to one side is now a car park. Then for about 20 years the inn was run by David and Linda White, who added the porch to the front door. Upstairs are 11 rooms, five of which used to be let out. Among local functions held at the **Harp** are the Glasbury Gardeners annual garden show and auction, a raffle with proceeds going

The Harp at the beginning of the 20th century with
railings, a wall and a shed, all of which have disappeared

247

*The Harp Inn in the early 21st century with the extension
on the right and a new front porch*

towards an annual Christmas party for pensioners, and monthly meetings of the Three Cocks Vintage Society.

Close to St. Peter's Church used to be the **Six Bells**, with a sign of either church or hand bells said to speak all languages, which is now demolished. In 1815 it was included in a Licensing Authority list, being one of a dozen Radnorshire inns that agreed to 'keep and maintain good order, and shall not suffer any disorder or unlawful games to be played'. At that time the landlord was John White. The inn was still trading in 1851 when it was run by William Honeyfield, aged 42, also described as a wool sorter. He lived there with his wife, Elizabeth, and three children.

Also mentioned in the 1815 list was the **Hammer and Trowel** (tools used by masons and bricklayers), with Ann Berry as licensee. It was still an inn at least up to 1829. Among other inns trading in the 19th century was the **Castle Inn,** which in 1851 had 48-year-old Edward Gwynne, who was also a master saddler, at the helm. He lived there with his wife and four children and also resident were a saddler apprentice, house servant, two timber surveyors, a horse-dealer and a charwoman. The **Fleece** and the **Masons Arms** were other pubs mentioned, but are otherwise unknown. In the 1950s Glasbury House was a country club until it was bought in 1964 by the London Borough of Redbridge and converted into a centre for outdoor education.

Continuing along the B4350 towards the A470 Builth Wells road, there is a minor road leading off to the right towards Painscastle. Along here is Ffynnon

Gynydd (St. Cynidr's Well), visited for centuries by pilgrims for the well water's spiritual salvation and physical benefit. According to the census of 1861 the village also boasted the **Well Inn**, catering for the pilgrims' earthly needs.

Another minor road off the B4350 leads to Ciltrwch, where at the furthest end is the delightfully named Slumber Cottage which

Slumber Cottage was once a cider house

used to be a cider house, possibly known as **Rogue's Head**. This 300-year-old building of stone and slate, originally consisted of one living room with an outside kitchen and a room above, but has now been extended. It was probably used by drovers *en route* from Wales to Herefordshire and closed sometime in the late 19th century, becoming a private residence.

Near the junction with the A470 from Builth Wells to Brecon, the B4350 passes through Boughrood, where stands the **Boat Inn**, by the bridge over the River Wye. Before the bridge was built in the 1830s, horses and cattle crossed

The Boat Inn at Boughrood

over the ford, often impassable due to flooding, while a ferry boat took passengers across. The inn was a convenient stopping place for refreshment, also enjoyed by boatmen who tied their boats alongside. The earliest reference to the **Boat** is in 1815, when it was one of the dozen Radnorshire pubs which agreed to keep order, In 1851 the landlord was David Jones, aged 53, also described as a mason, who lived there with his wife, Mary Ann, and six children. In the 1930s the licensee was Jane Lewis, nick-named Ghiah, who ran the pub for about 30 years. She also kept cattle and sheep on six acres of land opposite. In those days there was just a little bar with the main entrance facing the river and the usual outside toilets. Celebrations were no doubt held in the **Boat Inn** in 1934 when payment of tolls for using the bridge came to an end. Then in the 1960s the licence was taken over by Mrs. Lewis's grand-daughter, Mona Richards, who has remained there ever since. The entrance is now on the road side of the building with the old door converted into a window. A second bar has replaced a storage area, while a pool room is in the former living room.

On the other side of the bridge in the village of Llyswen is the **Bridge End Inn**, built in 1842 the same year that the toll bridge was opened and after which it takes its name. The bridge links the two villages and is part of the boundary between Radnorshire and Breconshire. Among changes over the years have been the building of two extensions to the rear of the pub, while the games room has been turned into a dining area. Gary and Shirley Evans were licensees for many years towards the end of the last century. The tradition of giving regular customers nicknames, such as Foxy, Shrimp, and Ferret, still continues.

Returning to Glasbury and travelling along the B4350 towards Hay-on-Wye, one comes to the **Hollybush Inn**, just across the border in Breconshire. Behind the pub is a camping and caravan park and woodland walks leading down to the Wye. Originally a traditional pub with two small bars, it was run from 1911 to 1937 by John and Mary Lewis, with Mr. Lewis also working on the railway until his eyesight failed, and then later for about 30 years by the Dobie family. A modern annex was later added at one end and a dining room to the side. Bought two years ago by a syndicate – The Light at the Hollybush – the inn has undergone further structural alterations with an internal wall knocked down to make one large bar, while the bar counter has been transferred from near the French windows to the front wall. In addition to providing meals and beverages, the **Hollybush** also offers spiritual courses based on the Celestial Prophecies.

Back to Glasbury and following the A438 towards Hereford one comes to the village of Llowes and the **Radnor Arms**, with its many-sided roofs. Believed to have been built in the 17th century, the inn may originally have been called the **Butcher's Arms**. At any rate, this was the name of a Llowes

The Radnor Arms in Llowes

pub in the 1815 list, when the publican was William Fryer. In 1851 the innkeeper was Thomas Pritchard, aged 53, also described as a gardener, who lived there with his wife and five children, together with a sawyer. One of his sons, William, seems to have taken over the licence for in 1891 a man of that name was summoned for permitting drunkenness at the inn. The *Brecon and Radnor Express* of 1 May 1891 reported that William Pritchard, of the **Radnor Arms**, allegedly supplied Thomas Evans, a bill porter from Hay, with drink whilst in a drunken state. Evans was subsequently found dead in a field, but the case against Pritchard was dismissed.

In the mid-20th century the inn was run by a landlady who brought beer up from the cellar in a jug, and who ran a farm on nearby land, since sold off. Sometime in the 1970s the low ceiling in the public bar was removed to make more of a feature of the room. To reinforce the upper walls and roof, iron girders had to be inserted in the wooden beams across the level of the old ceiling. Other changes have included the knocking down of the rear wall in the main bar to extend the room, and the construction of a new kitchen. The present owners, Tina and Brian Gorringe, who have been there for the past 24 years, have been running the inn more as a restaurant than a pub with dining in the old public bar as well as in the main bar, both served from the central bar counter.

According to the Revd. D. Stedman Davies in his *Radnorshire Inns*, there was also the **Dolybongham Inn,** described as being 'in the dingle', apparently on the lane leading to the Begwns. It probably closed in the 19th century and became a farmhouse.

The next village along the A438 is Clyro, where the Romans built a fort and the Normans a castle. However, it is far better known for a Victorian villa near the church now called Ashbrook House, where the Revd. Francis Kilvert lived for seven years from 1865 to 1872 when he was curate there and during which time he started to write his famous Diary.

Rather confusingly the village has two hotels both named Baskerville after Thomas Baskerville Mynors Baskerville, who owned a large estate in the village. One is the **Baskerville Arms Hotel**, formerly the **Swan**, and the other the **Baskerville Hall Hotel**, which used to be Clyro Court.

Coaches by arrangement; lorries any time!
A 1950s accident at the Baskerville Arms

The former was an old coaching inn and, as the **Swan** with Thomas Lilevale as innkeeper, was included in the 1815 good-order list. A popular national sport in those days was cock-fighting which in Clyro was probably held at the **Swan** or nearby. It is said that some cock owners even buried a prayer book

The Baskerville Arms Hotel in the 1950s

under the turf in the cockpit ring, believing that the other cocks would then refuse to fight.

The inn is mentioned again in 1842, this time as the **White Swan**, when two barristers, appointed to revise the List of Voters in the election of a Knight of the Shire, met there for the Hundred of Painscastle. In the 1851 census the inn, now called the **Baskerville Arms**, was run by Peter Chaloner, aged 56, also described as a farmer of 126 acres. He lived there with his wife, Arabella, and two grown-up children together with a land surveyor and two house servants.

However, in *Kilvert's Diary*, the inn was still called the **Swan**. He noted in 1870:

> A wild rainy night. They are holding Clyro Feast Ball at the Swan opposite. As I write I hear the scraping and squealing of the fiddle and the ceaseless heavy tramp of the dancers as they stamp the floor in a country dance [with people swarming round the door and steps of the Swan] laughing, talking loud, swearing and quarrelling in the quiet moonlight [and laying] by the roadside at night drunk, cursing, muttering, maundering, and vomiting. [In short, he witnessed] 'the World and the Flesh reeling about arm in arm.

The landlord at that time was probably William Price, who was certainly there in 1864 when Magistrates Courts were held in the dining room. Then, according to the hotel's Spirit Stock Book, John Evans was in charge from 1882 to 1891 followed by Sarah Evans, presumably his widow, until 1907, and Margaret Evans, who was at the helm from 1907 to 1935. In 1940 a half-year's rent was £23 10s., but in 1946 the Baskerville Estate was put up for sale and the hotel was bought by Harold Rowson, who stayed there until 1957. It was then bought by Roy Corner, who 10 years later sold it to Stanley Smith for £10,250. Mr. Smith was co-owner with Mrs. Audrey Orton and it was during their stay that numerous changes were made including the construction of a new restaurant which opened in 1979 at a cost of £40,000. A local newspaper, *The Express* of 12 July 1979, reported:

> Tables that can seat parties of up to eight people, set back in new alcoves, are a spectacular feature of the new development which was personally designed by the owner. ... Tastefully furnished throughout, this new extension, which has taken 12 months to complete, can accommodate up to 100 people. And apart from dining, the clientele will be provided with live entertainment every night of the week. An additional facility is a dance floor area with suitable music being provided by a regular D.J.

The new restaurant with alcoves in 1979

The Baskerville Arms in early 2006, with a hound on top of the porch

Mr. Smith, who employed 25 full and part time staff, installed a false ceiling in the main bar and also put up beams, which came from nearby Clifford Castle, and had been transported on the top of his Morris Minor. A keen worker for the Lions' charity, he organised annual walks from Hay-on-Wye to the hotel – an event supported by hundreds of people.

In July 1987 he sold the hotel to Alan and Charlotte Hudson, from Swanage, and Ian Hudson, of Pembridge for £65,000. They, in turn sold it on a year later to Peter and Pamela Harmsworth for £250,000. After two further owners, the hotel, which has 13 *en-suite* bedrooms, was bought by Lyn and Phil Strahan in 2003 for £340,000. Its present owners, Dave and June Slade, moved in at the end of 2005. A plot of land by the hotel and a large car park by the main road had earlier been sold for houses which have since been built. The stables were converted into garages, while the alcoves in the restaurant were removed. Recent improvements have included the replacement of curtains by wooden panels in a meeting room off the restaurant and the reinstatement of a games room.

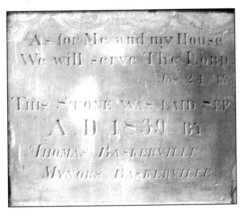

Above: Clyro Court foundation stone

Right: The roadside sign shows Sherlock Holmes

The **Baskerville Hall Hotel** was once Clyro Court, a 19th-century Jacobean-style house and part of the old Baskerville estate. It was built in 1839 by Thomas Baskerville Mynors Baskerville for his second wife, Elizabeth. A frequent visitor was Sir Arthur Conan Doyle, a family friend, who while staying there heard the legend of Black Vaughan, of Hergest Court, whose ghost accompanied by a demon dog terrorised Kington in the 15th century. The dog legend formed the basis of Conan Doyle's famous Sherlock Holmes story, *The Hound of the Baskervilles*, although he set it in

Above the front door of Baskerville Hall Hotel is the Baskerville coat of arms and those of Thomas's wife. Also a wolf's head with broken spear and five drops of blood

Devon at the request of the Baskervilles to 'ward off tourists'. Another visitor was the Revd. Francis Kilvert.

Thomas Mynors' eldest son, Walter Mynors, inherited the estate and in turn left it to his eldest son, Captain Ralph Hopton Baskerville, who died in France during the First World War. His sister, Dorothy, lived there until 1946 when she sold the estate to Radnorshire District Council with the property becoming a school. The hall and gymnasium were added in 1954. The introduction of comprehensive education and the requirement for children to go to school in their own county, forced the closure of the school as most of the pupils lived in Hay-on-Wye, which is in Breconshire.

In 1972 the Council sold Baskerville Hall to Thomas Knott who changed it into a hotel and health farm. The first-floor schoolrooms were converted into luxury suites, the swimming pool was added and the courtyard covered over to form a bar and dance floor. After several years of neglect the present owner, David Hodby,

The grand staircase at Baskerville Hall

The imposing frontage of the Baskerville Hall Hotel

took over in 1984 and undertook the extensive work of restoring the hall to its present state. Many modern features have been added such as solar panel water heating, a computer central management system, a complete new roof, and newly-equipped kitchens. A course for 4 x 4 vehicles has been built across the hillside. The Baskerville coat of arms and those of Thomas's wife are above the front door. The foundation stone with the inscription 'As for Me and My House We will Serve the Lord' is inside the entrance to the main bar.

At the northern end of Clyro is a minor road to Newchurch at the bottom of which is a three-storey building which was once the **New Inn**. In 1851 it was

The one-time New Inn

run by Edward Owens, aged 48, described as a Baptist minister, and his wife Margaret. Living there also were their five children and a 17-year-old female servant. Somewhat later a registry office wedding was held between Catherine Price of the **New Inn** and a young Painscastle blacksmith called Davis followed by a splendid reception. Kilvert wrote in 1871 of what he heard:

The wedding feast was at the New Inn which is now shut up as an inn and abolished. As I passed the house I heard music and dancing. They were dancing in an upper room, unfurnished, tramp, tramp, tramp, to the jingling of a concertina. The stamping was tremendous. I thought they would have brought the floor down.

On the approach to Rhydspence, just off the A438 on the right, is Cabalva House, a rambling old country residence which at one time was the **Cabalva Inn**. Rather than being just a drovers' inn, it is thought more likely to have been a coaching house, being situated about half-way between Hereford and Brecon. There were lodges on either side of the building, with the oldest part dating back to the 13th century, and extensive stables. The stables remain but one of the lodges has gone, while the house itself has been considerably extended. Cabalva means ferry or horse place – the river being fordable at this point.

After ceasing to trade in the early 19th century the building was bought by John Broadwood, founder of piano manufacturers, Broadwood and Sons, who took piano design from the old box piano to the grand piano, and introduced other technical innovations. Mr. Broadwood enlarged the property and turned it into a gentleman's residence. Cabalva House eventually became part of the Baskerville Estate, but was sold off at the turn of the last century and became a school during the Second World War. Then in 1946 it was bought by the Guest family who have remained there ever since.

The road continues to Rhydspence, on the border with Herefordshire, where drovers on the 'Black Ox Trail' from the Welsh mountains used the ford across the Wye to travel into England. Before doing so they would have availed themselves of the hospitality and shoeing service at the **Rhydspence Inn**, a handsome, timber-framed building which is still a landmark today. Built in the 14th century to provide sustenance for travellers and pilgrims from Abbey Cwmhir to Hereford Cathedral, it is just across the border in Herefordshire, the stream in the garden marking the division. The inn may have been built by the Vaughan family of Hergest to a 'hall house' design with two-storeys at one end and a large open barn area with a central open fire and a thatched roof. Later it became two stories throughout with a stone-tile roof and a handsome two-storey porch.

After the dissolution of the monasteries, it is likely that this ecclesiastical hostelry, when Thomas Watkins was the tenant in 1590, became the main assembly point for Welsh drovers before fording the Wye into Herefordshire. As well as the blacksmith's shop there was 140 acres of land split into farthing, half-penny and penny fields – the amount paid depending on the quality of the pasture. While the top drovers paid 6d. a night to sleep in the inn, hired hands slept with their charges in one of the fields, but they were

A painting of the Rhydspence Inn in 1891 by H.T. Timmins

supplied with cider, produced from the inn's horse-operated cider press. It is probable that from this time the inn gained its name, with 'Rhyd' meaning 'river crossing' and 'spence' possibly a corruption of 'pence'. One landlady is said to have bewitched drovers' cattle, rooting them to the spot, until all bills were paid.

In 1783 the owner was Buskin Shirley with William Colley as innkeeper, and the inn was included in the 1815 list of pubs when it was run by Abigail Morgan. A Ten Shilling Licence for the Purveying of Liquor was issued in 1830 to the proprietor, John Morris, and the owner, John Watkins. According to the 1851 census, 66-year-old James Whitcombe and his wife, Elizabeth, were in charge. Residing there that night were their daughter, two agricultural labourers, a journeyman tailor, and a retired grocer. The Revd. Francis Kilvert described the inn as bright with lights and gaiety. He also noted in his *Diary* for 8 July 1872 of the mischief caused by the previous day's flood.

> Pigs, sheep, calves swept away from meadow and cot and carried down the river with hundreds of tons of hay, timber, hurdles and, it is said, furniture. The roads swept bare to the very rock. ... Four inches of mud in the Rhydspence Inn on the Welsh side of the border ...

259

The Rhydspence Inn with its recent extension in 2006

In 1880 Sarah Ann Clark, the landlady and wife of Philip Clark, was murdered and her ghost is said to still haunt the inn. Wearing a pale blue dress with a high neck, she only appears when there are children staying and is said to be 'very friendly'.

The **Rhydspence** continued into the 1950s as an inn and farm, but then the land was sold off and the forge, which at first became a private living room, was converted into a bar. The present owners, Peter and Pam Glover, who took over 21 years ago, built a large extension to one side to provide space for a dining room, new kitchens and three more bedrooms, and have upgraded the whole property to turn it into a comfortable hotel and restaurant.

Rhydspence Cottage, adjoining a larger property, on the Welsh side of the stream, is thought to have been an old cider house, whose customers no doubt would have crossed over the border to the Rhydspence to take advantage of England's Sunday drinking laws.

A minor road which heads northwards across

Rhydspence Cottage, thought to have been an old cider house

Herefordshire leads to Michaelchurch-on-Arrow, which is in Radnorshire. Just outside the village, on what used to be an old drovers' road to Kington, were once two hostelries. The first, on the left-hand side, is the **Summer Pole**, now a private house, which traded in the 18th and 19th centuries. The inn, probably built in about 1750, was included in the 1815 list when the landlord

The one-time Summer Pole Inn

was Edward Smith. It also appeared in the Minutes of the General Quarter Sessions for the period 1823-29. The present owner believes that the name was originally **Summer Pool**, after a pond in the garden which becomes more of a pool in the summer. By 1841 the property, when it had some 50 acres of land, was listed as a farm and it continued in that capacity until about 35 years ago.

Originally the building was long and narrow with low ceilings, but has been considerably enlarged over the years. The front part retains original features such as the front door and flagstones in the kitchen.

Further along the road, on the left-hand side, is the **Red Lion,** now a private residence, but another former inn. A sale notice of 1906 noted that the inn had a blacksmith's shop, stable and buildings, in the occupation of Benjamin

Once the Red Lion, a drovers' inn

Howard at an annual rent of £16. The notice concluded:

> The Property adjoins the main road leading from Kington to Hay, and is suitable for carrying on a profitable trade, including a good blacksmith's business.

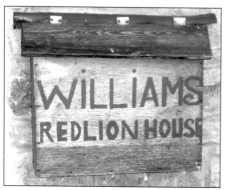

*Pubs may close, but often
the name lingers on*

However, the inn remained in the Howard family, for William, probably the son, was landlord until after the First World War, living there with his wife and large family of no fewer than 16 children. In 1922 the inn was bought by Joe Williams, a champion ploughman, and his wife, Aimee. But they did not renew the licence and the inn ceased trading.

The stone property, built in about 1770, has not changed very much over the years. Original swing doors open into a living room which used to be the main bar with, on the facing wall, an antique mirror which would have been behind the bar counter. To the right of the entrance is another living room, with a beamed ceiling, which was a second bar. Upstairs, however, rooms have been created on the large landing where dances and other functions were once held. Outside, the blacksmith's shop is now a store.

CHAPTER FOURTEEN

Radnor Forest & Upper Wye

GLADESTRY, GLASCWM, ABEREDW, ERWOOD & PAINSCASTLE

Leading off the A44 from Kington to Rhayader is the B4594 leading to Gladestry, a village which once boasted at least five inns – possibly eight including cider houses – of which only the **Royal Oak** survives. Built in the 18th century, this stone and slate two-storey building derived its name from Charles I, who in 1645 took shelter in Gladestry Court which was demolished by the pursuing Roundheads. The Court was later rebuilt and owned by Lord Ormathwaite who built up an estate of 4,344 acres including 47 farms (many in adjacent parishes) and other properties including the **Royal Oak**.

In 1900 the landlord was Peter Evans; in 1910 James Price was at the helm; and Pryce Vaughan, who was also the church clerk, was there from 1929 until just before the outbreak of the Second World War. During the war the inn was headquarters of the Gladestry Home Guard, who met twice a week in the cowhouse. On Sunday they would practise rifle shooting and, as the inn was not officially open, they would gather in a room at the back to have a beer. The landlord then was a Mr. Musk, who kept goats and supplied petrol.

In 1945, the Ormathwaite Estate was put up for sale and the **Royal Oak**, which was then vacant, was sold for £1,625 including six acres of land. It was bought by Mr. Hughes, of Stonehouse, who then sold it to Arthur Miles. In 1959, following a prolonged storm, part of the village was flooded including the inn. It was reported that trout were seen swimming in the bar! The local football team met at the **Royal Oak** and used the old stables as changing rooms. Mr. and Mrs. Joe Pattison, who first introduced the food side of the business, were in charge for several years until their retirement. The stables were later converted into a games room and are now used as a coffee shop. There are two bars, a dining area and three letting rooms.

The Royal Oak in 2006

*Two members of the Morris family (centre) outside the blacksmith's shop
at the former White Hart*

Near the gate leading to the parish church graveyard is a private house called the **White Hart** (the badge of Richard II), which used to be an old drovers' inn. In addition to providing refreshment and accommodation, the inn offered a blacksmith's shop and forge where the drovers could get their horses re-shod and new shoes for their cattle, which were quartered on a plot of adjoining land. An Elizabethan building, the inn is mentioned as the **Hart** in an advertisement in the *Hereford Journal* of 5 December 1776 for:

the sale of Clock and Watchmaker's tools at Gladestry, belonging to James Richards at his dwelling house known by the sign of the Hart. Also set of Blacksmith's tools belonging to John Bayliss jnr dec'd.

The one-time White Hart

Part of the Gladestry estate of James Watt, of steam engine fame, the **White Hart** is last mentioned as in inn in the Minutes of the General Quarter Sessions for the period 1823-29. In 1811 Watt left the inn and the Court of Gladestry to his agent, Mr. James Crummer, an Irishman of Kington and Howey Hall. The same year Crummer, aged 61, married the 28-year-old Esther Davies, and on his death in 1821 the properties passed to his widow, who was also a director of Kington Bank. On her death in 1858, Esther, being childless, left the **White Hart** to the Banks family, into which her brother had married.

As recently as the beginning of the 20th century, a well in a field at the back of the inn was used by the villagers for their general water supply. In 1864 the property was owned by Mr. Layton Morris – possessing excellent hand-writing, he was responsible for the collection and collation of local rates – and in 1930 by his son, Isaiah, who continued to operate the forge as well as being a butcher, available to kill the villagers' pigs. When the property was purchased by the present owner in 1979, it was in a derelict condition necessitating a new roof, new windows and general restoration. Inside there is an Elizabethan simmering hearth, at one time used to keep food warm. The kitchen was orig-inally built on the side of the house as a shop in the early 20th century. The old forge and bellows are still in the blacksmith's shop. Some of the land was previ-ously sold off and two houses have been built on the plot.

Among the other hostelries were the **New Inn,** mentioned in the *Hereford Journal* of 1806, and the **Red Lion**, referred to in the *Hereford Journal* of 1845, the location of both being unclear. Just outside the village, half-way up a hill leading to Offa's Dyke, is another old drovers' inn, the **Camp**, now a private house.

Further along the B4594 just before Hengoed is a cross-roads with the right turning going towards the hamlet of Colva, where there is Colva Farm, with 120 acres of land, next to the church which was once the **Sun**, an inn

265

used by drovers bringing sheep from West Wales to the markets in the Midlands right up to the early 20th century. The stone building is believed to be about 450 years old. 'They would stay at Colva for a few days to rest and graze the sheep', recalled one local inhabitant. 'My grandfather told of drunken nights and fights between the drovers. It sounded like the Wild West!' Thomas Davies was the innkeeper of the **Sun** from about 1840 to the 1870s. His great-grand-daughter reckoned that Tom never drank at his own pub, preferring to go instead to Glascwm, from where his daughter had to fetch him. Apparently cock-fighting took place upstairs, with contestants staying all night, and dances were also held. Not surprisingly Kilvert was a visitor in the early 1870s. In his Diary he wrote:

> Mrs. Phillips, the landlady of the Sun, was much frightened when I asked for her husband, uneasy and nervous lest I should have come to appre-hend him for having been in a row or doing something wrong. But when I said I wanted the words of an old song, she was greatly relieved and said at once 'Oh, I know who you are. You are the gentleman from Clyro'. I laughed and she began to smile. Mrs. Phillips took me into the parlour where I sat down; tore a leaf out of my pocket book and wrote with my address a request that Phillips would send the songs by post. Mrs. Phillips brought me a pint of excellent light bright beer, some hard sweet home-baked bread and some hard cheese, carrying the bread and cheese in her arms as she ran in with it, as I was in a hurry to push on.

The old Sun Inn at Colva in the early 20th century

Once the Sun Inn at Colva

Trevor Davies outside the former Drovers Arms which he has owned for the last 50 years

The longhouse style of the former Drovers Arms

The **Sun**, also possibly known as the Rising Sun, ceased trading about a hundred years ago. The parlour where Kilvert enjoyed his beer is now a living room, and the serving area has been enclosed apart from a small hatch behind which is a cellar. The former granary and peat store has been incorporated into the house and an extension added.

Continuing down this minor road one reaches the village of Glascwm, which was on one of the major drovers' routes along which the black cattle of Cardiganshire were driven into England. Because of this, the village had as many as four inns in the 18th and 19th centuries. One of the oldest was the centrally situated **Drovers Arms**, a Welsh longhouse style building of stone and tile, mentioned in the Minutes of the County General Sessions for the period 1823 to 1829. The inn had four rooms on the ground floor with four above and stables to one side. It was still a drovers' inn until 1913, although by that date the drovers who took food and shelter there would have been on comparatively short journeys. Now a private residence and painted white, its present owner, Trevor Davies, has lived there for the past 50 years. He recalls his father telling him that the inn used to be packed out at nights with men working on the local farms. A stone pit has recently been discovered in the back garden, but what it was used for is not known. The stable is now a woodshed.

The former Beavan Arms in Glascwm

Another pub was the **Beavan Arms**, which originally may have traded under a different name. It closed sometime between the two world wars, became a post office and is now a private house. The story goes that, at the turn of the century, Mr. Morris, of the Three Wells farm, used to buy barrels of beer from the pub and cart them up the hill to his small farm. On one occasion, a prank was paid on Mr. Morris with water being substituted for the beer! The last landlord of the **Beavan Arms** was a preacher, who kept chickens in the pub. This pub may well originally have been either the **Radnorshire Arms**, mentioned in the Minutes of the County General Sessions between 1823 and 1829, or the **Carpenters Arms**, referred to in the *Hereford Journal* during the 1850s.

Not far from the present Three Wells Farm and just outside the village on the road to Hengoed, there used to be another farm of the same name which was burnt down about a hundred years ago. It started life as the **Masons Arms**, mentioned in the *Hereford Journal* of the 1850s. Grassed over ruins and an old well are all that is left.

Until 1900, one annual event which must have attracted considerable extra custom for the inns was the Christmas Day football match between the men and boys of Glascwm and those of Bettws Disserth, near the A481. According to W.H. Howse, 'it was no ordinary football, for the two churches or their churchyards formed the goals and the battle was fought by teams of 40 or more a side over the four miles which divided the churches'.

Further on is Cregrina, where in Tudor times the last wolf in Wales is said to have been killed. Being on two drovers' routes it was an important centre for cattle shoeing and had an inn known as the **Black Lion**, which appeared

The former Black Lion Inn at Cregrina

in the Minutes of the County's General Quarter Sessions for the period 1823-1829. Until the middle of the 20th century there was a forge next to the **Black Lion** where the shoes, or cues, were made and fitted to animals. The inn closed in 1906. It is now called Middle House with a large gate to one side which must have led into the blacksmith's shop.

Nearby is Abderdw Hill over which cattle were driven on their way to Cregrina and on which was once a drovers' inn, or beerhouse, called the **Tafarn Mynydd** or **Tabor Wye**. Although there are no building remnants, there is a triangular piece of land which, owing to its fertile nature, is thought to have been where the cattle took shelter over a long period of time.

Not far from Cregrina travelling south is Rhulen which had a drovers' inn called the **Cross Keys**, mentioned in the Minutes of the County's General Quarter Sessions between 1823 and 1829. **Penrhiwlais**, another shoeing shop and drovers' inn, still exists in ruined form on Glan-edw Farm at Rhulen.

Passing through Llanbadarn-y-garreg one comes to Aberedw just before the road joins the B4567, where the **Seven Stars Inn** stands near the entrance gate to the churchyard. The story goes that a stranger to the church was told by a man standing there that 'the church tower is the highest in Wales'. The stranger responded: 'How is that, seeing it stands in a valley?' to which the man replied, 'Because it is higher than the Seven Stars'. The sign probably refers to the Pleiades in the constellation Taurus.

The village, described by the Revd. Francis Kilvert as 'Oh, Aberedw, Aberedw. Would God I might dwell and die by thee', boasted a Norman castle which in the 13th century came into the possession of Llyewelyn ab Gryffydd, the last native prince of Wales. Llyewelyn became an occasional resident during his efforts to unite the whole of Wales, but after being betrayed may have spent the night at a cave before meeting his death at nearby Cilmeri. Two of the many tales surrounding his last days involve the blacksmith – firstly that he betrayed Llywellyn for a bribe, and secondly that he helped the prince escape his pursuers by shoeing his horse with reversed shoes.

The Seven Stars Inn at Aberedw

The blacksmith's forge was later part of a row of cottages of considerable age next to the **Seven Stars**. In the late 19th century Mary Morris was landlady for some years and at the turn of the last century, the inn was probably owned by Willoughby Baskerville Mynors as part of the vast Baskerville estate. In the 20th century it was run for many years by Jane Lloyd whose husband, Richard, ran the forge and was the village's last blacksmith. He died in 1944, three months after Jane's death. The inn was bought in the 1940s by David Williams, the Builth brewer, with the Lloyd's daughter, Bertha, who was born in the pub, as tenant until her death in the late 1980s or early 1990s.

The **Seven Stars** was closed for a couple of years during which time anonymous poems were pinned on the front door bemoaning its fate. One such poem read:

> As you pass
> This house to church
> Please don't leave
> Us in the lurch
>
> Just say a word
> If you can
> So we can find
> A wealthy man

270

To buy this pub
And open up
So we can meet
And have a sup.

In 1995 it was bought by local builder Malcom Gartery and his wife, Sîan, who set about refurbishing the place. Originally the pub consisted of a hallway leading into a small bar with a living room and a games room where the dining room is now situated. The toilets were in the old forge. The bar was opened up with a new counter installed, a new dining room and kitchen completed and the forge converted into a second bar, later called the Llywellyn bar. Its original character was retained, however, with open stonework, flagstone floors and exposed beams. Their work was recognised in 1997 when the inn won the South and Mid Wales Pub of the Year award. Under new owners, the **Seven Stars** has won another award – the Radnorshire Pub of the Year competition run by the *County Times*, while around its walls hang framed copies of the anonymous poems.

Southwards eventually leads to Erwood, just across the Wye in Breconshire, where two pubs still survive. The village name is a corruption of the Welsh 'Y Rhyd', meaning the ford. The oldest pub is the **Wheelwright Arms**. Believed to have been built in the 16th century, it is of cottage-style with whitewashed walls of Welsh stone, and was frequented by drovers on their way to Painscastle and beyond. A mounting block for horse riders by the front door proclaims its pre-motor car history. Known as the 'top pub', the **Wheelwright**

The Wheelwright Arms at Erwood in 2006

housed an ammunition factory during the Second World War, and was the headquarters of the local Home Guard. In the 1950s it was run by Dai Symonds and then in the 1960s by his widow. After several other owners, the inn was closed for about four years until taken over, in derelict condition, nine years ago by the present owners, Glyn Price and his wife, Irene, daughter of Mrs. Symonds. During their refurbishment of the place, they converted the sitting room into a dining area. Previously the bar counter had been transferred from near the fireplace to a more central position, stairs by the front door were removed, and a restaurant built in a one-storey extension at the back.

The other open and 'bottom pub' is the **Erwood Inn**, a stone and slate building now painted in garish ochre and blue to 'make it stand out'. Originally called the **Three Hollies**, possibly after three trees on the road to Painscastle, and then the **Erwood Arms**, it was built in the 17th century and was an old drovers' inn. One traveller in the 19th century who found the inn to his liking was the writer Henry Mayhew who sought refuge there from his London creditors. While staying he wrote short stories which were to appear on 17 July 1841 in the first edition of *Punch*, which he co-founded and which went on to become one of nation's most popular magazines. In 1851 the inn, which also had a malthouse, was run by William Davies, aged 41, described as a victualler, who lived there with his wife, Anne, four daughters and two servants. Then there were two landladies: in 1861 May Edward, aged 41, who had four young children, and by 1871, Eleanor Morgans, described as a 67-year-old widow. The village was particularly lively on market days when farmers used to take their animals into the pub.

An early 20th-century photograph of the Erwood Inn

*An amusing sign about one of the illustrious hosts at the Erwood Inn
and the main inn sign (right)*

The **Erwood Arms** also had a part to play in a dramatic event involving a howitzer. According to *Hills and Sunny Pastures* compiled by the Erwood Women's Institute Working Group and published in 2000, Mrs. Lionel Trafford, daughter of Mr. and Mrs. John Vaughan, of the local manor, saw an advertisement in a national newspaper in 1920 regarding the sale of a light field Austrian howitzer. She decided to buy it to commemorate the end of the First World War and in memory of her brother, Sub-Lieutenant John Vaughan, who was killed in 1916. The artillery piece only got as far as Erwood station, however, when Mrs. Trafford died in one of the first motor accidents in Herefordshire. The gun remained in a field near to the toll house on the Radnorshire side of the bridge. But there was rivalry between the men of Erwood and Llandeilo Graban and the men of Erwood decided they wanted the gun. After making their plans in the **Erwood Arms**, they brought the gun back and parked it in the yard opposite the pub. Not to be outdone, the men of Llandeilo Graban re-took the howitzer and dragged it by horse across the bridge to Garth Farm. And they removed its wheels so it wouldn't be moved again and it stayed put for the next 80 years. However, it was renovated and in 2000 was pulled by shire horse to Twyn-y-Garth, its original destination, where it now proudly stands. Until the 1980s there used to be a tug-of-war across the river between Radnorshire and Brecon.

From 1936 to 1964, the **Erwood Inn** was owned by Ivor and Edith Jones, who ran it with help from their daughter, Verlie, when she was not driving the local bus. The inn then possessed a garage, brewhouse, and a coachhouse –

The Erwood Arms is one of the few pubs that still has a petrol pump in 2006

there is still a petrol pump. They were succeeded by Pryce and Arvona Lewis, who stayed for 30 years, retiring in 1996. Alongside a sign proclaiming that short stories written by Henry Mayhew at the **Erwood Inn** was the birth of *Punch*, the landlord placed another sign. This read: 'Pryce Lewis resided here in the mid-20th century. His works led to the founding of Alcoholics Anonymous'! After a brief interlude by another owner, the pub has been in the hands of Phillip Butcher and Jean Arthur for the last nine years.

In addition to the Mayhew and Pryce Lewis signs, a feature of the bar is a fireplace with a double flue and bread oven. Over the years it had been replaced by no fewer than four other fireplaces, then rendered over with an 8ft. long radiator placed in front of it. At one time the counter was by the front door with stairs next to the fireplace. The garage has been converted into a games room, and the malthouse is now a cottage.

Back along the A470 and turning right over the bridge onto the B4594 leading towards Painscastle, one comes to a driveway on the right leading to Glanyrafon House on the Wye, which used to be an old drovers' inn called the **Boat Inn**, more colloquially known as the **Cafn Twm Bach** after one of the landlords, Twm Bach (Little Tom). At this spot the river, although wide, had a smooth rocky bed across which the herdsmen drove their cattle on their way to Painscastle. If the river was high and in full flow, the landlord operated a ferry boat, a wooden box winched by chain, to take the cattle and sheep across. Tradition has it that in the late 18th or early 19th century Twm Bach and his son carried a herd of cattle over the river when it was flooded. Half way across, the cattle, terri-

The one-time Boat Inn

fied by the raging currents, rushed to one side of the boat which capsized. The two drovers in charge saved themselves by grabbing the animals' tails, but Twm Bach and his son were swept away and drowned in trying to rescue the boat. Probably re-built in the 1820s on the original site, the inn, part of the Vaughan estate, was run in 1851 by David Evans, aged 65, and his wife Sarah. Also living there was their son, Thomas, a miner, and a female servant. By 1861 an iron bridge had been built on the site of the present bridge, the ferry closed down and the droving trade petered out. However, the **Boat** continued and in the 20th century was run for some years by the Bevans before it was taken over by the Mitchells and then finally closed in the mid-1960s. The building was bought by Lord Swansea, modernised and altered to become a gentleman's residence with a new name. Alterations included the addition of a porch, changing the entrance, moving the staircase and converting two large upstairs rooms which opened onto a landing into bedrooms, and a rear extension. The car park was transformed into a lawn leading down to the river. The house was sold in the 1980s, when it was used for a couple of years as a guest house for fishermen, but was sold on and is now a private residence again.

Further along the A470 is a left-hand turning to Llanstephan, where in the 19th century there was an inn called **Ty-yn-y-cwm**. In 1851 the licensees were David and Elizabeth Jones, and also living there was a mason, his wife and two children. There was another inn in the village – the **Plough** – one of the commonest pub names, which was mentioned in the Radnor Red Book of 1913.

Heading back towards Builth Wells, the B4594 is reached again and just off it, to the left, is Llandeilo Graban, where there used to be a pub called **Church House** with John Pugh as landlord in 1815. The inn was also mentioned in the minutes of the County's General Quarter Sessions for the period 1823-29. Houses of that name originally lodged masons and artisans who helped build church towers and belfries. Later they became communal houses, and were used for those celebrations that the Puritans did not want to be held in church. **Church House**, a Jacobean building, was situated opposite the main gate to the churchyard, but was demolished early in the 20th century to be replaced with two barns. There was also another inn called the **Black Swan**. It is mentioned in 1863 and was on the other side of the church-yard by the cross-roads. The Black Swan first appeared as a tavern sign in the 16th century and may have been a reference to the landlord as being a bit of a rare bird. All that remains of the building today are grass covered stones and bricks, but the outline of the site is still recognisable.

The next village along the B4594 is Llanbedr, where in 1815 there was a pub called the **White Hart**, a name stemming from Richard II's heraldic symbol and also a generic term for a tavern.

Further along the B4594 is Painscastle, named after a motte and bailey castle built by the Norman baron, Paine Fitzjohn, in the 12th century and later enlarged under the Mortimers. The castle was defended for many months against a Welsh army led by Rhys ab Grufydd by Maud de St. Valerie, whose husband, William de Broase, was known as the Ogre of Abergavenny. For taunting King John about the murder of Prince Arthur, Maude was locked up in Windsor Castle where, with her eldest son, she was starved to death.

A 1950s view of the Maesllwch Arms at Painscastle

The Maesllwch Arms in 1959

Below the castle Paine Fitzjohn also built a village, which became a market centre, but was to later flourish more as a shoeing station for drovers. It boasted six inns which, with their associated enclosures, offered hospitality for both man and beast.

The first pub the drovers came to was the **Maesllwch Arms**, which served as both inn and smithy, a common doubling of functions. Opposite was a field where the animals were put to graze at halfpenny per head per night. It was later re-named the **Black Ox**, to avoid confusion with the Glasbury hotel of the same name, and is now the **Roast Ox**, for reasons which will become apparent. Probably dating back to the 17th century and built of Welsh stone, the inn was run in 1851 by Charles Bowen, aged 35, who was also the blacksmith, and his wife, Elizabeth. In the 1860s, it was visited by the Revd. Francis Kilvert, who records that he had a meeting with the local Mayor in the front porch, with its built-in Victorian seats. From the 1920s to the 1950s, George Morgan and his family ran the business. An extant photograph shows George by a ciderpress outside the inn. Then, in the late

The new sign for the former Maesllwch Arms

277

The Roast Ox in 2006

1950s, the first fire occurred during a particularly bad winter; apparently the fire engines could not get through to the village, and the building was severely damaged. The landlord, a Mr. Dixon, had the first floor taken off and replaced with a new one covered by a bitumen flat roof. Rubble left was used to form the car park. The pub re-opened and continued to trade under new owners with the name changed in the 1980s to the **Black Ox**, after the predominantly black Welsh cattle which had passed through the village.

The second fire broke out 14 years ago when the building was totally gutted, with only the retaining walls left. In 1994/95 the ruin was bought by Nigel Burnett, who put in train the reconstruction work which started in 1999 and finished in 2005, including one year out due to the foot-and-mouth disease and another six months lost after flooding. Although the inn has been almost entirely rebuilt, it has been brought back to what it might have been like in drover days. It is being run by the British Outdoor Professionals Assocation, which furthers the interests of people involved professionally in outdoor activities, with the Wales Tourist Board having given a grant towards the rebuilding. The inn holds two to five day courses organised by BOPA, while it also looks after participants in Trail Riding tours run by the next door farm.

The inn, now called the **Roast Ox**, is entered through the original front porch, to which has been added a second one with two windows with leaded lights and a door with stained glass. The now open-plan bar is a mix of natural materials with exposed stone walls, flagstone floors and ceiling beams, under which are 24 corbel stones – copies of medieval ones.

Numerous oil lamps are another feature. A new bar counter is centrally positioned, whilst the top of a 16 ft. deep well, which had been enclosed with a staircase built over it, has been restored. The old blacksmith's forge is now a dining area and a new extension has been built at the back with facilities for conferences; there are nine letting rooms. The man responsible for overseeing the building work was Chris Charters, general secretary of BOPA, who ran the Eagle Hotel in New Radnor for five years.

Then there was the **Castle**, mentioned in 1807; the **Radnor Arms**, where in 1851 Thomas and Margaret Lloyd were the innkeepers; the **White Hall,** mentioned in 1823; and the **Red Lion**. Interestingly, its innkeeper in 1851 was Thomas Sheen, who was also the local castrator. Living there too was his wife Mary, their four children and a 53-year-old pauper. The inn was still trading in 1913.

Two other drovers' inns were on the nearby Clyro Hill – the **Coldbrook** and the **Black Ox** (Yr Eidion Du), both mentioned in 1823. Kilvert spent many hours trying to locate the sites in 1870. According to the Clyro Tithe Map the former was located close to the present Whitehall Cottage, and although there is no reference to the **Black Ox**, its name is still part of local tradition. The drovers continued from Painscastle to Rhydspence and thence into England.

Not far from Clyro Hill on the B4594 is Rhosgoch, where once was the **Rhosgoch Inn**, mentioned in a list of pubs dated 1815 with Jacob Powell as the innkeeper. The inn comprised a kitchen, parlour, bar, back kitchen and pantry, with five bedrooms, while outside there was a two-stall stable, cowhouse and barn, a smith's shop, and a pen house. In 1921 the then landlord, William Gore, left the premises which were then occupied by the owner, Thomas Davies. He did not apply for the full licence to be transferred and although the renewal

The one-time Rosgoch Inn still has a nostalgic sign

279

came up before the County Licensing Committee the following year, the matter was not proceeded with and the **Rhosgoch Inn** remained shut to customers. Another hostelry, the **Plough Inn**, also existed but probably closed towards the end of the 18th century.

The one-time Royal Oak

After passing through Dolleycanney, the next village on the B4594, one arrives at Newchurch, which straddles the cross-roads. In the village is a farm called The Oak which used to be the **Royal Oak**, a substantial, white-washed, stone house with a slated roof. In the early 20th century it also included a carpenter's shop, a grocery business, and the local post office. The inn itself had an entrance hall, parlour, kitchen and bar cellar, together with four bedrooms and a box room. There was stabling for four horses and several outbuildings with 4½ acres and a kitchen garden. Trade was not very good, however, and from 1919 to 1924 only between 20 and 30 barrels of beer was sold in a year, plus three to four dozen bottles of ale and one to two bottles of spirits a week. During 12 police visits there had been only eight customers and as a result, when the licensee/owner, John Thomas, applied to have his licence renewed in 1924, the application was turned down. By way of compensation, he was awarded £100.

CHAPTER FIFTEEN

Mid-Radnorshire

CROSSGATES, LLANBADARN & BLEDDFA

One of the few pubs to have been built by the publican for himself is the **Builders** at Crossgates. Situated on the A483 from Llandrindod Wells to Newtown where it is met by the A44 from Rhayader to Kington, it was later known as the **Llanbadarn Hotel**. It was built in 1847 by John Wilding, a local builder and contractor, who had already constructed the church school and school house at Crossgates.

Wilding remained as landlord for 22 years and it was here that the first five of his eight children were born. Trade prospered not only from local custom but from workers on the Central Wales railway line which was laid between 1858 and 1868 from Knighton to Llandovery via Penybont and Llandrindod Wells. The workmen enjoyed spending their evenings drinking, singing and dancing, with the Wildings – a musical family – obligingly providing the accompaniment. In 1869, Wilding decided to take up a new challenge and left the **Builders Arms** for an established coaching inn, the Severn Arms at Penybont. However, he retained ownership and put in tenants to run the Crossgates' business. Soon after the death of Mrs. Wilding in 1891 (Mr. Wilding had already died in 1885), the inn was sold and the proceeds divided between the Wilding children.

At the beginning of the 20th century, William Houghton was the landlord and at some point the name was changed to the **Llanbadarn Hotel**, after the name of the parish, when it advertised 'good accommodation and fishing' – the latter in the nearby Ithon. The hotel was later bought by David Williams, a brewer from Builth, who let it to John Williams, presumably a member of the same family. John, together with his son, ran the business from the late 1940s to the early 1960s. He also operated a butcher's shop at the rear with hams hanging in the bar. The shop was later used as changing rooms for the local football team and is now a workshop. A dining hall, which could seat over a hundred, was used for dances and functions. The hotel was run for

Top: The Builders when it was known as the Llanbadarn Hotel

Bottom: The Builders Arms when Edmund Lloyd was licensee

Top: Hams hanging in the bar of the Builders Arms

Bottom: Possibly landlord and family in front of the Builders Arms

The Builders in 2005

about 20 years by Tom, who was also a jobbing builder, and Linda Musker and in 1992 it was bought by Ron and Yvonne McKay, the present licensees, who changed the name back to the **Builders**. Today, the pub has a bar and games room on one side of the front door with a dining area on the other side. There are three letting bedrooms and a holiday cottage which has replaced the functions room.

This private house at Crossgates used to be the Hernog Inn over 100 years ago

Opposite the petrol-filling station at Crossgates is an old stone building, now a private residence set in its own gardens, which was once the **Hernog Inn** and included a blacksmith's forge. Probably built in the early 1800s, it was run for many years by John Phillips, who was both innkeeper and blacksmith. He was

284

there in 1841, at the time of the first census; then aged 40 with a wife, Margaret, aged 35, two sons John, 15, and William, 7, and two daughters Mary, 14, and Ann, 2. There was also a 15-year-old female servant. He was still there 20 years later with his wife and one son, William, by then an agricultural labourer. His daughter, Ann, lived in the next door cottage together with the houskeeper. In 1892 there is a reference to 'a sale of blacksmith's tools at Hernog House'. It would appear that Mr. Phillips had died and that the inn had ceased trading. At some point the building was considerably enlarged at the rear.

Today, the house has been modernised although there are a few reminders of its licensed days. Wooden window seats in what used to be the main bar and another living room remain together with an inglenook in the latter, while an iron bar across the inside of the front door is thought to be original. The beer cellar, however, has been blocked off with concrete, and a rear entrance to the cellar sealed. The old forge has long been demolished.

Set back off the A44 road leading towards Rhayader, on the right-hand side, is the imposing black and white **Greenway Manor Country House**, which used to be a hotel. It was built about a hundred years ago as a manor house called **Glanclywdog**, named after the local river, on a

Greenway Manor Country House, a former hotel

large estate including several farms. Later it was turned into a hotel to benefit from the growing popularity of Llandrindod Wells as a spa town. Built of brick with a mock Tudor black-and-white facing, the hotel had 14 bedrooms with a function/dining room and lounge. Towards the end of the last century, an extension was built on the rear of the property with a cottage behind that. When the building was bought four years ago the new owner divided it into two and sold off the front half, re-named **Greenway Manor**, together with a caravan park. Today the Manor offers bed and breakfast and has a bridal suite, caravan facilities and fishing in the river at the bottom of the sloping 5-acre gardens.

On the other side of the A44, also set back off the road, is the **Park Motel**, formerly the **Rhos** or **Ross Inn**, and nick-named the Rag and Louse. The building probably dates back to about 1790. In the census of 1841,

Formerly the Rhos or Ross Inn, then a farm and now the Park Motel

The Park Motel, with its new reception area

The Clewedog Arms was in the middle of the row with a shop on one side and a coach house on the other. It closed in 1910

Richard Morgan, aged 40, was the publican and lived there with his wife, Sarah, their four children, and a servant Mary Roberts, aged 15. Also staying there on the census night were a shoe maker, two masons, a carpenter, an agricultural labourer and a hawker. At some point in the last century it ceased trading as a pub and became a farm. Then about 20 years ago it was turned into the **Park Motel** with a reception area added to the front of the building and an extension with a flat roof added at the rear. The original bar, still retaining an inglenook fireplace although now enclosed, is now a lounge leading into the restaurant. The motel, which has seven self-contained motel units, is set in three acres of land. There is also a small pool, patio and conservatory.

Further along the A44 is a small cluster of houses on the left-hand side including a terrace of three houses which once consisted of a shop, an ale house called the **Clewedog Arms**, and a coach house. The pub was closed in 1910 by the Radnorshire County Licensed Committee who declared that 'the number of licensed houses in the district is excessive', and that 'the licence is not required to meet the wants of the district'. The owner, Nathan Weale, had told the committee that the annual value of the inn was £10. He received £50 as compensation, some of which went to the landlord, John Bebb.

There used to be a connecting door between the pub and the coach house, at the corner of which is still the stable, complete with mangers and stone floor. Iron railings adorned the front of the pub and there were latticed windows. The room where the beer was kept has since been converted into a bathroom. The upstair walls are still lath and plaster, but the downstair flag-stones have been covered and the black-leaded ranges disposed of. The shop sold sweets and tobacco. About 50 years ago the terrace was bought by Thomas Mills and further modernisation carried out including the installation of water and electricity. They are now three separate houses.

Continuing towards Rhayader one comes to the village of Gwystre where stands the roadside **Gwystre Inn**, dating back to the late 19th century. Belonging to the pub were three fields on the opposite side of the road which were used by farmers taking cattle from the Rhayader area to the market in Penybont. The fields were the main reason why it was bought in the early

An old sign is still on the wall of the inn

287

The Gwystre Inn in the 1940s

1920s by Tom Jones, of nearby Lower Talcoed Farm. He leased the inn to Jonathan Edwards, who kept the Royal Oak at Pencelli near Brecon and who, in 1926, passed the tenancy on to his son-in-law, Mr. Evans. The latter, with his wife Gwenllian, known as Madam Gwen, ran the **Gwystre** until 1947, eventually buying the establishment. They had four children, including Glyn, born in the pub in 1927, who, with his wife Daphne, wrote *Reminiscences of the Gwystre.* In these notes he recalled:

> There was an old drover, Archie Brooks, who used the pub as a stop-off point, before cattle were transported by lorries. The old drover would come from Rhayader in the late spring, when there was enough grass for the cattle to graze on the way, heading with his charges for R.P. Hamer's cattle market in Penybont. Once the cattle were bedded down for the night, he'd come to the pub and order a pint of beer, bread and cheese. He took a red-hot poker and thrust it into his beer. Before he fed himself, he fed his border collie, Turk.
>
> The pub did very well before the war. They had a CTC sign and cyclists came en route from the Midlands to the coast. One couple cycled from Birmingham on a tandem every holiday for 14 years before they got married ... The pub could sleep 15 people for bed and breakfast and for that they charged 4s. Breakfast was always ham and eggs – their own eggs and harm carved from the local hams hanging from hooks in the middle bar. These hams were treated with Bulmers cider and a bar of salt ground fine; after this they were hung to cure, with hessian at the bottom

so they didn't drip on customers. ... In the war, there were 15,000 troops stationed at Penybont Common, living under canvas. Some soldiers used to run in their gym gear up to the pub, down a few pints and then run back to base ... The pub only opened Friday, Saturday and Monday from 11.30 to 2.00 and from 5.30 to 10 as they couldn't get the beer.

Glyn's father used to send him down to the cellar with two big jugs to fill – one mild, the other bitter. There were 66 glasses and all were used. The Evanses were a musical family: Madam Gwen sang and played the piano and Glyn sang. Glyn also recalled that the pub used to have a shop, open from 9 to 5, which supplied most of the provisions for the rural community around.

At Christmas time, Pickfords sent a pantechnicon up from Cardiff and they used the **Gwystre** as a headquarters and collecting point for poultry. Farmers brought birds in by pony and trap which were weighed on a pair of scales in the shop.

The Rhayader Hunt with Mr. Collard as Master met at the **Gwystre** with most people following the hounds on foot.

A lorry full of hounds would arrive, then the Master would hammer on the door for a stirrup cup before the Hunt was up. One day chickens in the back yard were rudely disturbed by a streak of tawny brown and then by yelping hounds following their quarry.

The pub was also the headquarters of the local Home Guard who were driven around by Albert Oakley in his lorry which fuelled up at the pump outside the shop window. One day the Home Guard performed an exercise requiring them to be German paratroopers attacking the **Gwystre**. The exercise started seriously, but ended in stifled laughter in the bushes as the 'enemy' surrounded the pub. Glyn's father was a corporal in the Home Guard and the sergeant was Bert Smout, whose wife worked in the pub.

On one occasion, an English gentleman was at the bar. Bert approached him and asked if the gentleman would buy him a pint if he stood on his head. Bert took off his cap – he was bald – laid the cap on the stone-flagged floor and stood straight as a rod on his head. He got his pint.

The pub had two darts teams and rings, skittles, shove ha'penny and tip-it were also played. Goalposts were kept at the back for the local football team who played in the field opposite.

After the match, the mud-covered players would strip off and the great tin bath in the kitchen would become the team bath. The other offices were equally primitive. The privy was out at the back - it had a pail under a big wooden seat. Drinking water came from a nearby spring. Glyn's job was to take two empty water pails on a yoke and fill them up whenever drinking water was needed.

The Gwystre Inn in 2006

Water for other purposes was pumped by hand from the Camlo brook at the rear of the inn. The brook used to, and still does, flood the inn, with beer barrels floating in the cellar.

The police came out on a circular tour every evening from Llandrindod Wells, Glyn recollected:

> to make sure that the licensing laws were being adhered to, probably knowing full well that they weren't but being secret sympathisers. One friendly police constable rang up at about 9.55 and say 'the police car will be starting off any minute now', which gave those with full pints time to nip out the back with them and hide in the shrubs and bushes behind. The policeman would come, look around at the empties on the bar and wish the company a good evening. Once he had gone, honour satisfied, the recalcitrants would emerge from the bushes and continue where they'd left off. Many an evening they sang until 11.30 or later.

The petrol pump has long since gone and the shop has been converted into a dining room, and it is hoped to turn the old stable into two-storey living accommodation. Internally, the **Gwystre** has seen many changes particularly after Danny and Pamela Sherwood took it over in 1986. A wall with an archway in the main bar was demolished and the former sitting and front rooms have been turned into another dining area and lounge with new windows. In 2003 the pub was sold and at the time of writing it has been sold again.

Further westwards along the A44 is the village of Nantmel where, between the chapel and the church, is a private house which was once the

The former Seven Stars Inn in 2005. It probably ceased trading over 60 years ago, but the house is still named in both Welsh and English

Seven Stars Inn. The name probably derives from the Pleiades showing, according to classical myth, the seven daughters of Atlas, but it was also a religious symbol denoting the seven stars in the crown of the Virgin Mary. Tradition has it that the church tower is the highest in Wales. Why? Because it is higher than the **Seven Stars**! The present stone building dates from about the end of the 18th century, but may well have replaced an older establishment which burnt down. A clue to this lies in the timber-framed cow shed which includes charred timbers that may have come from the original inn.

A twin loo in the old privy at the Seven Stars

An old shoe, believed to have brought good luck to the Seven Stars

Being on the main drovers' route from Aberystwyth to Kington, the **Seven Stars** most probably started life as a drovers' inn, but was also a small farm. The 1841 census indicates that John Jones, aged 60, was the innkeeper, and he lived there with his wife, Elizabeth, aged 55, and their three children. Also residing there were two agricultural labourers and three lodgers. The inn, however, was owned by a wealthy landowner, Edward Middleton Evans. Ten years later Thomas Greenhouse, described only as a farmer, lived there with his wife and four children. Among those also staying there on census night was a daughter of Lord Howard, a dressmaker and two servants. In 1861 the publican was Thomas Edwards, described as a farmer with 26 acres. From 1871 to 1881 the innkeeper/farmer was John Addis, while in 1891 Mary Hughes, aged 78, who was described as widow/publican, lived there with her daughter, Sarah, 46, who acted as barmaid.

Trade must have increased when the pipeline from Rhayader to Birmingham was being built at the rear of the inn towards the end of the 19th century, providing refreshment for numerous thirsty workers. The **Severn Stars** probably ceased trading sometime before the Second World War when the last landlord decided to close it down. It was then used by a carpenter/wheelwright who owned a saw-mill opposite until the new road was constructed in the 1970s. Since then it has been a private house.

Taking the B4518 from Rhayader towards Llanidloes, the village of St. Harmon is reached where the **Sun Inn**, known as **Y Dafarn** until 1837, is situated near the church and the old railway station. In 1878 the Revd. Francis Kilvert attended a wedding there. In his diary, he wrote:

> Friday, 26th April. To St. Harmon's by 9.10 train to marry David Powell and Maggie Joes of Tylare. Mrs. Jones of the Gates had made a triumphal arch of moss over the Churchyard gate and flowers were strewn in the bride's path. Maggie was surprised and delighted to see and be married by her old friend. Fog signals were laid on the line and the wedding party issued from the Church just as the noon train came down with the banging of crackers and guns and a great crowd at the station crossing gates. The wedding party and guests went to the Sun where I joined them for a minute to drink a glass of wine to the health of the bride and bridegroom.

Price Worthing took over the **Sun** in 1902 after being landlord of the Welsh Harp, in Rhayader, which had closed down. By 1904 David Williams, who ran a brewery in Builth, had become the owner and the **Sun** was run by tenants. The landlords appear to have combined the business with farming, as attached to the inn was a 14-acre farm. In 1946 the land-lord/farmer was Mr. H.P. Worthing. Later Bill and Heulwen ran the inn, which soon became known as the **Jam Jar** – apparently glasses were in short supply and customers literally drank out of jam jars! Cattle were

The Sun Inn, St. Harmons, at the beginning of the 20th century

housed in a cowshed next to the small bar, while on the other side of the bar was the landlord's living room. The inn was taken over in the 1970s by Haydon Gough, a local builder, who instigated some radical changes. Most of the farmland at the rear was used to construct bungalows as part of a housing estate called Sunnyhill, while internally the **Sun** was transformed. The cowshed was demolished and an extension was built in its place which became the dining room – known as the Cowshed. The pub's inner side walls were knocked down – one next to the dining room and the other dividing the bar and private room which then became part of the main bar. A further area was turned into a pool and games room. In 2000 the landlord was Andrew Cook who offered the pool room for use by the local post office, which was threatened with closure. However, the offer was not taken up and the post office closed. Mr. Cook then used the room to house his pet falcons.

The **Sun** was closed as an inn for two years until, in 2002, it was taken over by Phillip and Wendy Evans, local farmers, to provide the village with a focal point. They gutted the upstairs to provide five letting rooms and a flat, installed central heating and refurbished the whole bar area. The local football club re-opened and now use the inn as its headquarters while the Afonwy Hunt from Rhayader met there on New Year's Day until 2004, the last year of hunting with dogs.

An old photograph of the Sun, looking from the side

A traditional scene outside the Sun Inn some 30 years ago

The Sun Inn in 2005

Travelling westwards on the minor road to the junction with the A470 road and then northwards, one comes to the hamlet of Dolhelfa where there used to be an inn called the **Severn Arms**. In 1861 the licensees were Thomas Hughes and his wife Ann, who previously ran the Hill Gate Inn near Rhayader. Mr. Hughes also looked after an 80-acre farm.

Back on the B4518 from St. Harmon, the next village is Pant y dwr where the **Mid Wales Inn** is situated on a hill top with views all around. It was orig-

inally part of a terrace of three buildings at least a hundred years old. In 1926 the land-lord was Robert Sharp, who was also the village station-master. The station used to be situated in a valley to the rear of the inn, but it closed in the 1960s and the track was then taken up.

An early photograph of the Mid Wales Inn with a shop on the left and a private house on the right

The Mid Wales Inn at Pant y dwr

The painted bar counter in the Mid Wales Inn

In the 1970s, Noah Udin, from London, purchased the whole terrace and extended the inn to include the shop and the house. The shop is now the dining room and part of the house has been turned into another bar area, which has a long counter made from a plastic mould and circular windows, made from old cartwheels. He also raised the roof, which is now fibre glass, closed one of the front doors and turned a stable at the rear of the property into a games room. In the original bar is another unusual counter, made of hardboard and wood, painted with rural scenes. Today there are five letting rooms and a beer garden at the rear. The busiest day of the year for the inn is the Pant y dwr show with sheep dog trials as the main event.

A little further on is Nantgwyn where a farmhouse at the northern end of the village was once the **Eisteddle Arms**, which probably means sitting place (*eistedd*: to sit or to seat). It probably started life as a drovers' inn and then catered for the needs of the local community with a shop selling sweets and tobacco. It was also a farm with nearly 70 acres of land. The last licensees

Now a farm, this was once the Eisteddle Arms, Nantgwyn

were Mr. and Mrs. John Ingram, who were there from at least 1926 until the 1940s. Tramps were apparently made welcome, three or four at a time, who were allowed to sleep in the barn. Mr. Ingram was well known for his drench cure for sick horses. On Mr. Ingram's death in 1944, his widow closed the pub but kept the shop open until her death a year later after which the shop closed.

Living there in 2006 is John Woosnam, aged 92, who as a 16 year-old worked on the farm, and whose son runs the farm which has been extended to about 150 acres. In 1985 they had the brick building rendered and new windows put in. The bar used to be at the far end, now the lounge, and beer barrels were kept under the staircase.

On a minor road, midway between St. Harmon and Llanbister, is the remote village of Abbeycwmhir (the abbey of the long valley), where once an imposing Cistercian abbey flourished. This is the burial place of the celebrated Welsh prince, Llywelyn ap Gruffudd (d. 1282). Founded in 1176, the abbey was first damaged by Owen Glyndwr in 1401 and finally surrendered in 1537. The site passed to the Fowler family and was then battered by Roundhead cannon in 1644 during the Civil War. Today, only the foundations remain, but the village pub, the **Happy Union**, one of the oldest buildings in the village, continues to trade. The age of this grade two listed building is not certain; it may have been a drover's pub as the old route from Aberystwyth to Kington passes through the village. It is constructed of stone and bricks, believed to have been hand-made in the local brickyard, with locally-crafted cast-iron windows. Originally it was built at two different levels with two roofs and a valley in-between but sometime in the early 1900s these were replaced with a hip roof.

The unusual name is said to refer to the union in 1536 between Wales and England. The inn sign, recently re-painted by a local artist, depicts a jolly man on a goat holding a pot of ale in one hand and a plate of cheese and bread in the other and wearing a tall hat decorated with leeks. Why is he riding a goat?

An early photograph of the Happy Union

One, rather malicious, theory is that the goat represents an Englishman!

In the 1841 census the publican was Evan Williams, aged 50, who lived there with his wife, Mary, 45, and their two chil-dren. Also living there was a 15-year-old servant girl and two 20 year-old painters. Twenty years later the innkeeper was William Price, aged

An 1893 wedding group photograph displayed at the Happy Union

43, described also as a grocer. He lived there with his wife, Ann, 41, and chil-dren James, 11, William, 8, Mary, 6, Edward, 3, and Lloyd, 2 (all described as scholars). Also in residence were two female house-servants.

Surprisingly for such a remote place, Abbeycwmhir boasted a cricket team in 1869 under the leadership of the local squire, Mr. G.H. Philips. No doubt, after the matches, thirsts were quenched at the **Happy Union**. The inn was the focal point of other village activities as, for instance, in 1874 when Mr. Philips celebrated the birth of a son and heir.

The Happy Union before the whitewash was removed

A procession was formed, headed by a band, followed by gaily dressed wagons containing two magnificent beasts, after which came the whole of the tenantry on horseback. The beasts were cut up and distributed among the workpeople, the menfolk dined at the local inn, and tea was provided for the labourers' wives and children in the schoolroom. There were fireworks and balloon ascents in the evening and dancing and conviviality continued to a very late hour.

By 1926 the landlord was George Bevan and in 1939 it was taken over by John Thomas Jones – it has remained in the Jones family ownership ever since. John Thomas bought the pub when it was put up for sale by the local squire, who owned most of the village buildings. As well as being innkeeper, the industrious Mr. Jones ran the next door tailor's shop, and later sold groceries. He also sold his wares from a van travelling round to the neighbouring farms. Above the shop he arranged for dances and boxing matches to be held. On his death in 1963 the **Happy Union** was run for a couple of years by his widow, Margaret, before their son, David, took over the inn and continued to run the grocery business and mobile shop. A favourite family memory is of David, watching the first landing on the moon in 1969 on the kitchen TV, when a calf climbed up the bank, which covers one side of the ground-floor cellar, and four legs crashed through the kitchen roof! An

The Happy Union in 2006, cleared of the whitewash

earlier, more welcome, visit was made by Donald Campbell, who held the land and water-speed records.

Changes that have been made to the inn include the demolition of an internal wall to extend the bar area into the family dining room and the re-positioning of the bar counter. A warehouse to the front of the tailor's shop was turned into a grocer's and post office, while the old shop was converted into a holiday cottage. When David died in the 1990s his widow ran the inn for a while before their son, another John Thomas, took over in 1995. In recent years John has been restoring the inn to its original state. Externally, the whitewash that covered the walls has been sand-blasted off, while inside the plaster has been removed to reveal the old stone and brick walls. Ceiling beams have been exposed as has an inglenook fireplace, while the ancient red tiles remain *in situ* on the bar floor. A photograph in the bar dated 1893 shows a group of villagers who attended the wedding of the vicar's daughter; a hundred years later the **Happy Union** arranged a similar group photograph followed by a barbecue celebration. In addition to running the pub, shop and post office, John also looks after 200 acres of farmland and operates a twice daily school bus to Crossgates. During the season, tourists visit the ruins of the abbey and later join the regulars for a drink at the **Happy Union**.

From Abbeycymhir the road goes on to join the A483, and heading north from the junction towards Newtown the first village encountered, just off the main road, is Llanddewi Ystradenny, where stands the former **Walsh Arms**, previously known as the **Llandewy Inn**. The front part of the building is about 200 years old with a side wing added about 70 years later, increasing the number of bedrooms to twelve. At one time there was also extensive stabling and a farm. In 1841 the publican was 50-year-old Susannah Griffiths

who lived there with one female and one male servant. Also staying there at the time of the census were a curate with a 10-year-old servant, a drover, and a man of independent means who had a male servant. Twenty years later the innkeeper was John Ellis, aged 30, who was also a farmer. At the turn of the 19th century the inn, now owned by the wealthy landowning Walsh family, was re-named the **Walsh Arms**, complete with family crest on the front. In 1946 the Walsh estate was sold off including the **Walsh Arms**, which then became a free house. In ten years the inn saw no fewer than the same number of landlords, until

On the front of the Walsh Arms is the coat of arms of the Walsh family

The Walsh Arms, Llanddewi Ystradenny, which closed eight years ago

The old Red Lion at Llanbister, now a
private house with an extension on the right

18 years ago when it was bought by Chris Jones. He ran it for 10 years with some success but 8 years ago, with business dwindling, he decided to close it down, although he still lives there. Denied a local, the villagers put a bar in the village hall which now serves drinks at the weekends.

The next village is Llanbister, now just off the main road, where close to the church and opposite the shop is a house called the Poplars which was once the **Red Lion Inn**. In the 1841 census the publican was John Davies, aged 75, who lived there with his wife, Anne, aged 70, and daughter Mary, a 25-year-old seamstress. Also staying there were five soldiers, possibly going on or coming off duty in connection with the Rebecca Riots.

The Lion Hotel in Llanbister

In 1861 it was run by Thomas Watson, aged 55, who was also a farmer, and lived there with his wife, Mary, aged 50, their 7-year-old daughter Ann and a female servant. Later the inn was run by the Lewis family who owned land stretching down to the Ithon river. They decided to build a hotel near the main road to capitalise on the increasing popularity of Llandrindod Wells as a spa town and the **Red Lion** ceased trading as a pub. Today, it is a private residence with an extension housing a picture-framing business and gallery.

The new hotel, called the **Lion**, overlooking the Ithon river, opened in about 1878 and was run by the Lewises. It was described as 'an excellent house of call' and was ideal for 'ladies and gentlemen wishing to pursue fishing, walking and other countryside activities'. When Mr. and Mrs. Lewis died in the early 20th century, the hotel was left to their daughter, but as a single woman she could not hold a licence. So in 1913 it became the **Ithondale** private hotel with Ada Kinsey as the tenant, but still owned by Miss Lewis. The latter had a daughter who married a Mr. Poacock sometime after the Second World War – the hotel being used as a private house. In 1981 it was bought by Peter and Ann Johnson who first introduced a craft shop, then a restaurant and eventually it became in more general demand as a drinking establishment. The present owners, Ray and Janet Thomas, took it over in 1993 and returned it to its original use as a commercial hotel. One of the first things they did was to arrange a new sign – the rampant golden lion on a red field, once used in the coat of arms by the local ruling family, the King of Maelienydd. Today, the hotel has two letting rooms upstairs and three more in a converted barn. The dining room is on one side of the central staircase and a bar and games room on the other.

The Lion Inn signs are based on the coat of arms of the King of Maelienydd

Two miles from Llanbister on the B4356 road to Llangunllo is the Pound House which, in the 19th century, was the **Pound Ale House**. It was on an old drovers' route from Rhayader to Knighton and the name probably derived from a field being available for the men to leave their cattle overnight while taking sustenance at the alehouse. It may already have stopped trading by 1841 as the census of that year states that a 49-year-old farmer, Sarah Morris, lived there with her three children, In the 1860s John Morris, presumably Sarah's son, lived there, running a blacksmith's shop, grocery and general store. The house had a thatched roof and instead of a fireplace had a stove with a pipe leading out. It was apparently due to this arrangement that the house caught fire and burnt down. A new house was built in the 1870s and for many years operated as a small farm.

Further along the road, just before the hamlet of Crug, is an old farmhouse, now deserted, which was once the **Dafern**, an old drovers' inn. Yet another pub in the Llanbister area was the **Cross Keys**, mentioned in the minutes of the General Quarter Sessions for Radnorshire in the early 1800s but not thereafter.

Just before reaching the small hill-farming village of Llanbadarn Fynydd, along a lane on the right-hand side is Brook Cottage, a building with a large verandah that used to be the **Radnorshire Arms**, an old drovers' inn. In the 1841 census, Edward Farmer and his wife Mary were both listed as farmers rather than publicans. There is no reference to the inn in the 1861 census so it

Brook Cottage, Llanbadarn Fynydd, was once the Radnorshire Arms – an inn that closed about 150 years ago

must be assumed that by then it had ceased to trade. Originally built of stone, the property has since been re-faced with brick and slate and a verandah fitted both sides of the front porch, behind which used to be the main bar. It is now lying empty but is to be completely refurbished.

Near the church, on what was once the main road, is a private house with the name **Rose and Crown** on the glass front door. Possibly of medieval origin, this ancient inn may have been the successor of the church house

The glass front door
of the one time
Rose and Crown

where the churchwardens brewed beer and baked bread for the village feast and other events. The sign indicates loyalty to the monarch and to England. It became a coaching house and the venue for cattle markets until the arrival of the **New Inn**. In the early 19th century the inn was run by Walter and Mary Evans, but by 1841, following the death of both sons and Walter, their daughter Adeliza, aged 23, became the publican. In 1852 Adeliza married John Hughes and together they were innkeepers until John's death in 1885. She remained at the **Rose and Crown** until her death 10 years later. In 1892 Mrs. Adeliza Savage, Adeliza Hughes's daughter, collected £10 for the parish church roof restoration fund. Mrs. Savage was apparently also of a musical disposition, joining well-known local inhabitants at a musical soirée in the **New Inn** two years later.

The inn was owned by 14-year-old Price Savage, of Clun, who let it out at a rent of £25 to Albert Powell, of Newtown Brewery. He in turn sub-let the property for £21. By 1930 the sub-lessee and licensee was John Gough, who also worked on the construction of the new road through the village. When the licence was renewed by the county licensing authority, it was stated that part of the property, stone-built with a slate roof, was old and dilapidated. The rooms were small and low – entrance hall, dining room (with moveable wooden partition), bar, tap room, living room, back kitchen and cellar, plus four bedrooms and a storeroom. There was also a wash house, coal house, pigsty, two stables with loft over, coach house and a small earth closet in the garden. There was no properly constructed urinal. During 1929 the police made 35 visits finding only a total of 63 people, while in 1930 in 17 visits there were only 18 people. Profits were said to be small, with no spirits sold for 12 months and only 20 barrels of beer supplied in the same period. While the licence was renewed, the writing was on the wall and two years later, when it was run by Mr. Powell's mother, its renewal was refused. Compensation paid was £375, including £25 to the tenant, not even enough to pay off Mr. Savage's £500 mortgage on the premises.

The property was empty for many years and, when purchased in the early 1970s, was in such a bad state of repair that most of it had to be pulled down. However, the two end and back walls were retained and most of the roof; the

The Rose and Crown with the new extension on the left

beams in the kitchen and dining room are also original. An extension was built on the side nearest the church. Also present is an old stone barn with a baking oven and a nearby potato store.

On the A483, set in four acres of land, stands the **New Inn**, a late 18th- or early 19th-century roadside hostelry built on the site of an earlier inn, whose name is not known. Being on the main Chester to Cardiff route, it was a coaching house of some importance with extensive stabling. Cattle and sheep markets, which were transferred from the **Rose and Crown,** became an increasingly popular feature. For some years in the 1830s the inn was run by Mr. Philips later to be succeeded by his widow, Elianor. The 1841 census shows that, now aged 45, she lived there with her two sons William and Edward together with two servants. Also staying there at the time were two clerics – Revs. Evan Powell and John Lewis. In 1861 the innkeeper was John Lloyd also described as a farmer, who was married to Mary and had five sons and one daughter.

From the 1890s to the 1930s the landlord was Thomas Williams, who had 'Welcome to the New Inn' depicted in snowdrops on the front lawn. A description in the 1890s read: 'The New Inn, only in comparison with the much older Rose and Crown, is a comfortable hostelry with a reputation for good food'. In 1894 Mr. E.G.B. Watts, of The Woodlands, entertained 50 farmers and friends at the inn and 'a fine meal was set before the party by mine host Mr. Williams'. Another 'pleasant' evening was spent there the same year when Mr. and Mrs. Watts, Colonel Echalaz, and Mrs. Savage, of the **Rose and Crown**, were amongst those who 'gave musical items'.

The New Inn from the side in 1923

A letter just signed as 'Visitor' in the *Radnorshire Standard* of 31 August 1898, contained the following:

> Here at the New Inn is every accommodation for man and beast, and one of those comfortable hostelries which, I imagine, many a poor worked out soul, sick of the hurly burly of town and its worries is in search of at this moment. The place is unique – peace and contentment is breathed over all, and the old-world garden containing some fine ornamental timber and a wilderness of fruit trees, is a spot to go and see. Here the brain wearied can 'refresh' without fear of disturbance by brass band, nigger minstrels or barrel organ. He can recline literally *sub tegmine fagi* and relieve the monotony by an occasional walk, fly rod in hand, to entice the witty trout from the pretty reaches of the river. Residents and visitors at Newtown (13 miles distant), have already discovered the charms of this sylvan retreat, and I strongly recommend it to those at Llandrindod, only a mile further distant, from which place I reached it last week with most pleasurable results.

In 1939 Ernie Jones, the local blacksmith (as were his six brothers and father), bought the **New Inn**, which was not far from his forge. Local auctions were held at the inn with two yards for cattle to one side of the stables and a field for sheep at the rear. Often a ring was formed across the main road to auction off the livestock, and at the biggest sale of the year the inn's takings for the day reached £100. A shop, located by the side door, kept the villagers supplied with general provisions. As often happened in rural areas, rents from neighbouring farms were collected in the bar. During the war the stables were full of horses used by woodsmen to drag out logs from the nearby woods. Later, Mr. Jones gave some of his land for the building of the first village hall, necessitating the cutting down of one of the three Wellingtonia trees. Electricity for the inn originally came from a dam and

The New Inn at Llanbadarn Fynydd in 2005

water-wheel constructed by Mr. Jones at the waterfall to the rear of the property. In about 1949 Mr. Jones sold the inn, but bought it back again in time to open for Christmas – it was well known for its food, especially farm eggs and home-cured ham.

After Mr. Jones left for the second time in the 1960s, internal changes were made to the inn. A bar at the side, which used to have a serving hatch for drinks, was incorporated into a new dining area built as an extension at the rear, while the front bar became the main drinking area. Another extension on the other side provided more dining space. Outside, the stables have disappeared, the cattle yards have been turned into a car park, and an old barn is no longer L-shaped, having lost one section when the road was widened. The present owner, Stephen Armstrong, has been there since 1999.

To the west of Llanbadarn Fynydd is Red Lion Hill named after an isolated farmhouse that was once an old drovers' inn called the **Red Lion**. Nearby is David's Well, which was renowned in the 19th century for its medicinal properties and attracted large crowds from miles around especially on a Sunday evening. Even mangy dogs were bathed in the water – 'strongly impregnated with sulphur' and 'extremely efficacious in all cutaneous and scorbutic afflictions'. A small village grew at nearby New Well, but 30 or 40 years ago most of the cottages were bull-dozed down. Yet another old drovers' inn, **Cwmaur**, long since used as a private residence, is situated on a lane running eastwards from the village going towards the B4355.

Returning to Crossgates and then taking the A44 road towards Kington, one comes to Penybont where the **Severn Arms Hotel**, variously known as the **New Inn**, the **Golden Fleece** and the **Fleece**, is a prominent landmark. The **New Inn** was built near the bridge in about 1755, probably replacing an even older pub, by wealthy John Price, owner of the local shop, who also built the first Penybont Hall. He probably ran the inn himself until 1770, but the following year a tenant took over with an announcement in the *Hereford Journal* of 13 June 1771:

> John Jones begs leave to acquaint the public that he has taken the New Inn at Penybont and fitted it up in a genteel and commodious manner for the reception of those Ladies and Gentlemen who will please to honour him with their company, having laid in a fresh assortment of neat Wines, Brandy, Rum etc, together with fine rich Cordials, where he hopes for the favour of those Ladies and Gentlemen travelling that road ... An assiduous endeavour to please will entirely regulate the conduct of, Ladies and Gentlemen, Your most Humble Servant, John Jones.

The advertisement added: 'A main of cocks to fight at the above Place. To fight 21 in the main. And to weigh on Wednesday 3 July and fight the following day'. He did not last very long, for the following year the *Hereford Journal* recorded that John Jones, proprietor of the Penybont Inn, was among those who were to be 'confined in the County Goal in Presteigne as an insolvent debtor'. John Price placed an advertisement in the same paper: 'To be lett, ... a good Inn, lately rebuilt and furnished in an elegant manner, fit for the accommodation of gentlemen, and has hitherto been well accustomed ...' Mindful of what happened with Jones, Mr. Price added: 'No person need apply unless his character and circumstances will bear a strict enquiry'.

Later the inn was re-named the **Golden Fleece** as an advertisement in the *Hereford Journal* of 1783 bore that name when announcing the sale of a tenement. It was usually referred to after this as the **Fleece**. Soon after Price's death in 1798 the landlord was David Davies. By 1807 accommodation had been increased and extra stables built to meet the demand, the inn having become a staging post with mail arriving by coach three days a week and horses changed for the next stage of the journey, either to Rhayader or New Radnor. The landlord also acted as postmaster. In about 1814 the name of the inn was changed to the **Severn Arms**, following the marriage of Price's only surviving daughter, Mary, to John Cheesment Severn, the local squire, who now owned the property. A guide published in 1825 states: 'on the left side of the road stands the Severn Arms and Post Office, a superior looking tenement where the coaches change horses. It is kept by Mr. [William] Parton'. He died in 1832.

Later the inn was rebuilt on its present site, the *Cambrian Travellers' Guide* of 1840 reporting: 'a very large and commodious new inn is nearly completed in the Elizabeth style called the Severn Arms Hotel'. At the helm in 1841 was William Stephens, aged 45, with his wife Alethea assisted by no fewer than five male and four female servants. In the same year an annual Card and Dancing Assembly, known as the Penybont Ball, was instituted at the hotel. Another popular event was Penybont Fair, attracting 10,000 people to the village twice a year. An account of the Fair in 1857 states: 'The leading inn was extended to twice its size by a curtain tent extended outside and filled to excess with drinkers ... to get anything to eat there at such a time was quite out of the question, the drinkables bringing so much more profit to mine host than the edibles ...'. Weekly cattle markets and Hiring Fairs were also held at the inn.

In 1869 John Wilding, his wife and family took over, leaving the **Builders Arms** at Crossgates, which they owned, in the hands of tenants. As well as

running an increasingly busy hotel, staging post, and post office, they were tenants of the size-able Cwmtrallwm farm near the new railway station, and had to look after the meadows across the river Ithon where the Agricultural Show and annual Horse Races were held. They quickly built up a reputation, with a succession of summer

Coaches at the Severn Arms, Penybont

The local hunt outside the Severn Arms Hotel

guests coming to enjoy the fishing and shooting. Even special tableware was made with the letter 'W' in a shield surmounted by a winged lion device. The hotel also had its own gardens and an orchard, and a variety of carriages were kept in the livery stables for the convenience of visitors.

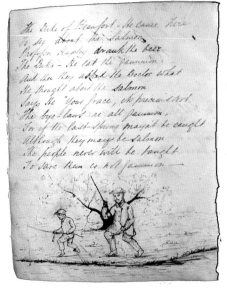

Entries in the visitors' book for 1881:

Left: Duke of Beaufort
Above: Sarah Bernhardt

A Visitor Book from 1879 to 1894 contains numerous comments about the **Severn Arms**, many enhanced with poems and pen and ink drawings. In 1879 Ellis Jones of London wrote 'very much pleased with all the attention ...'; Mr. Critchley of Bristol stated 'Gloriously provided for – all dyspeptic for a week after excessive eating but then the viands were so nice couldn't help it'; while 'Colonel Hawkings stayed here over a fortnight – very comfortable. (Stayed here another fortnight.)'. The Duke of Beaufort and friends stayed in 1881, leaving a poem which began:

> The Duke of Beaufort – He came here,
> To see about the salmon,
> Professor Hardy drank the beer,
> The Duke – he eat the gammon.

The same year the celebrated actress, Sarah Bernhardt, 'travelling incog. in gentleman's attire', wrote the following:

> I love to stray from busy haunts of men
> To woo wild nature mid wood, grove & glen
> And thus in seeking Cambria's fresh charms
> A happy fate led me to Severn Arms
>
> Oh how I love the charming sweet hotel
> And the Welch rabbit that they cook so well
> Ah' would that I could dwell for ever here
> Mid sylvian scenes, Welch rabbit & good beer.

Another visitor in 1881 was Walter Severn, who wrote:

> I have much pleasure in presenting Miss Wilding with this phot[o] from my picture of 'Our Boys', and only wish they were here. I am interested in seeing the 'Severn Arms' Inn, which, if only distantly approaching 'The Hall' in comfort, must be the very best inn to be found in all the world.

No date or name was given to a drawing of a wagonette, followed by the lines:

> How on fishing all intent
> In Wilding's wagonette, we went
> Facing a snow storms' loving charms
> And driving for the Severn Arms

The second verse of a poem left by three people from the Isle of Wight in 1885 went:

> Of excellent food we cannot complain
> The various viands we now try to name:
> Ducks, chickens & lamb
> Fresh eggs & good ham
> And bilberry tarts were truly 'real jam'.

That year saw the death of John Wilding on the very day he bought Coleman's Hotel (renamed the Bridge Hotel and now the Metropole) in Llandrindod Wells. A diary entry by his son, also John, noted:

> I got the transfer of Coleman's Hotel and paid Vaughan Thomas [the owner] the deposit of £110 and paid Coleman £33 8s for the furniture. Father much worse this evening, sinking fast. He died very quietly at a quarter to seven o'clock. He had his senses to the last.

Mrs. Wilding remained at the **Severn Arms** with her other son, James, and daughters Margaret and Catherine, while John Jnr, brother William and sisters Elizabeth and Annie moved to the Bridge Hotel.

Business continued as usual at the **Severn Arms** and in 1887 C.W. Sherborn and Harry Smith, of London, left a fishing drawing in the Visitor Book with the words 'The pleasure of fishing is going after them' and 'Here a month. Very comfortable – well satisfied with everything'. In the 1880s and '90s members of cycling clubs from Birmingham and Manchester stayed as did cyclists from Jesus College, Cambridge. In 1890 two gentlemen 'Were made very comfortable for 12 days. Fishing considering the cold weather very fair. Killed 200 trout. If the number of rods was more limited this stream would be a good one'.

When William Wilding married in 1891 he and his wife, Mary, took over the hotel from Mrs. Wilding who died later that year. But in 1895 they left,

The Severn Arms in 1916, featuring Edwin Jones

having failed to get Mr. Percy Severn to reduce the rent from £130 per half year, plus a tithe charge of nearly £8.

In about 1900 the Iron Room, so named because of its corrugated iron roof, was added to one side of the hotel to provide more space for social events, and later a garage and petrol pumps were introduced. In 1920 William

Collard, previously at the Royal Oak in Rhayader, first became the landlord and then, in 1926, the owner when the inn came up for sale. Mr. Collard was a well-known sports personality owning race horses (importing some from the U.S.A.), winning greyhound coursing trophies, and refereeing top boxing matches, including one involving the legendary Tommy Farr. He restarted the annual Penybont races in the early 1920s on land at the rear owned by the hotel, and introduced trotting. After Mr. Collard left in 1945 to take over the Lion Royal in Rhayader, Fred and Bessie Brown were in charge until 1970; from 1983 to 1999 Geoff and Tess Lloyd were the licensees after which it was bought by a Cardiff consortium. Today, the hotel offers 10 bedrooms, a restaurant and bar. Outside is a beer garden and over six miles of private fishing. The Iron Room was demolished in the 1990s and replaced by a community hall; the petrol pumps have gone and the stables are now used as workshops. The

The Severn Arms sign

250th anniversary of the **Severn Arms** was celebrated in September 2005.

The next village heading towards New Radnor on the A44 is Llandegly, once a spa with sulphurous and chalybeate springs, which then boasted two pubs and possibly a third. The main one was the **Burton Arms**, a coaching inn originally known as **Llandegly Inn**, and now a private residence called Burton House. The property was bought in 1772 by Edward Burton, who soon gave it his own name. A visitor in 1804

The Severn Arms Hotel in 2005

The former Burton Arms at Llandegly
was a coaching house in the 19th century

complained 'that the accom-modations of the little inn are insufficient to admit of his lengthening his visit'. But according to the *Handbook to the Breconshire and Radnorshire Mineral Springs* by John Pryse in 1854, 'the Burton Arms and boarding house is the only house [in] which a respectable visitor can find accommodation. It is a large and commodious house; the charges are similar to those at Llandrindod'.

One visitor died at the inn in 1830, a circumstance recorded on a stone fixed to the outside of the church.

> Near this spot are deposited the remains of Reverend Benjamin Scott M.A., Vicar of Bideford and Priors-Salford in the County of Warwick, who died at the Inn in this place on his way to the coast.

Another, more cheerful, reference to the **Burton Arms** was in 1837 when Thomas Turner, on his way from Gloucester to Aberystwyth, stopped at Llandegly and remarked:

> We found at this secluded spot a comfortable and very neat inn, which was chiefly occupied by a party of ladies, who were sojourning here for the benefit of the waters.

To capitalise on the popularity of the springs, reputed to treat, among other ailments, St. Tecla's disease or the falling sickness, the inn had a sunken bath installed in a downstairs room with adjoining rooms for other treatments and changing. Opposite the inn were extensive stables and a path which led to the springs where Well House was built, probably by the inn's landlord. In the 1841 census James Griffiths, aged 40, was the innkeeper and lived there with his wife, Maria, 35, and three female and two male servants. In 1853 it is recorded in the last surviving parish rate book for Llandegley church that the inn made a payment of 8s. 9d. In the 1870s and '80s the **Burton Arms** was run by the Hughes family, but by 1891 Charles Norton, aged 31, was in charge with his wife, Annie, and three daughters. They must have been unsucessful for by 1919 the inn had ceased trading and was then referred to as Burton House.

Continuing on the A44 towards Kington, on the left-hand side just outside Llandegly is a typical Welsh longhouse called Larch Grove, once the

The Drovers' Arms, Llandegly, in the 1880s

Drovers' Arms, where drovers and poor travellers found refreshment and accommodation. At one end are two stables with cobbled floors and at the other an old cow shed. Until recently rooms above were used as bedrooms. To the side of the cow shed, still with cow ties, there used to be a blacksmith's shop. The roof may originally have been thatched as there is evidence that it has been slightly raised. At the rear of the property is a field still called Welshmen's Field, which was probably used by the drovers to secure their cattle while they took shelter at the inn.

Larch Grove farmhouse used to be the Drovers' Arms

In the census of 1841 the **Drovers' Arms** was occupied by William Powell, aged 60, who was described as a blacksmith, as was his son, John, aged 20. It was probably his wife, Mary, who ran the pub. The parish rate book for 1853 shows that the inn made a payment of 1s. The Abberley family were running the inn in the 1870s and for a short time it may have been called the **Larch Grove Inn**, but by 1882 it appears to have ceased trading and was then known simply as Larch Grove.

According to a list of pubs compiled by W.H. Howse, there was another inn in Llandegley in 1816 called the **Fox and Hounds**.

Returning to Penybont, the A488 road towards Knighton passes through a community known either as Llanfihangel Rhydithon or the more modern name of Dolau. Over the years the village has been 'refreshed' by half-a-dozen pubs, all of which have disappeared. Perhaps the best known was the

The owners of Fronwen Garage live in this house, formerly the Old Hall Inn

Old Hall Inn, now a private house called Fronwen, occupied by the owners of Fronwen Garage, about a mile east of the village. It was built in 1836 by the Middleton family, wealthy landowners who lived in nearby Old Hall, for the express purpose of being a fully-licensed house. A blacksmith's was at one side of the building and stables to the rear. In 1841 the inn was run by Morgan and Mary Jones after which the licensee for many years was Thomas Griffiths, a stonemason by trade, who brewed his own beer and retired about 1890. One of the season's highlights would have been the driving of cattle from nearby farms to the **Old Hall Inn**, where they were quartered overnight before going on to Dolau station for entrainment. A newly-slaughtered pig was roasted and jugs of beer consumed. The licence was abandoned voluntarily in the 1920s, some say because the Middletons could no longer stand the drunken habits of the inn's staff! Since then the establishment has continued to support the local farming community, firstly as a lorry garage and filling station, then for the last 20 years as four-wheel-drive specialists. While the house has been transformed, many of its traditional features have been retained. The licence for the **Old Hall Inn** may initially have been transferred in 1836 from a much older pub, known as the **Lane**, a quarter-of-a-mile distant on the old main road.

Next to the church a minor road leads onto the hills, where a recently-built house called Upper Penrhw stands on the site of an old drovers' inn, known as the **Radnor Arms**. It probably closed in the 19th century and was used as a small farmhouse before becoming derelict.

On the other side of the A488, going towards Penybont, is a road leading to Dolau station, opposite which is Dolau House Farm, which was once an inn, possibly known as the **Railway**. It was built in 1867 soon after the station was opened on the line connecting Knighton and Llandrindod Wells. The inn ceased trading in about 1885 when the owner, Thomas Watkins, a farmer and devout Quaker, decided to live there and it has been a farmhouse ever since.

Once an old inn, possibly called the Railway, opposite Dolau railway station

On a minor road leading back to the A488 opposite the Old Hall Inn, is a row of cottages where at No. 2 was once the **King's Head**, which may have opened in the 1860s when the railway was being constructed; it sold beer and cider. On the A488 is a house called **Tynyberth** which is mentioned by the same name as being a pub in the Minutes of the General Quarter Sessions for the period 1823 to 1829. It later became a post office.

The cottage on the left was once the King's Head

Further along the A488 towards Knighton is the village of Bleddfa in which stands the **Hundred House Inn**, so called because it is where the Hundred Court of Justice (roughly

Top: Villagers outside the Greyhound when the film
Second Best was being shot
Bottom: The Greyhound in 2005

there as tenants. About 50 years ago Mr. Bryant, who owned the pub, apparently came to an untimely death. While riding his donkey, he fell off and drowned in the gutter. For the last 40 years Bill Matheson, now aged 92, has been the owner. Since 1996 one of the pub's front rooms has been run as a community shop.

One of the highlights in recent years was in 1993 when scenes for the film *Second Best* were shot in the village with the **Greyhound** as one of the backdrops. The film, produced by Warner Brothers, starred William Hurt and Jane Horrocks with many villagers taking part as extras. A group photograph in the bar records the occasion.

CHAPTER SIXTEEN

Newbridge, Disserth, Howey, Llanelwedd & Hundred House

About halfway between Rhayader and Builth Wells on the A470 lies Newbridge, a crossing place on the Wye as far back as Roman times and a place that grew in importance as a stopping-off point on the drovers' route between Tregaron and the English cattle markets. Several fairs were held there every year which attracted even more trade. Not surprisingly, numerous public houses opened – as many as 13 in the 19th century – to cater for thirsty travellers. So many indeed that one house was even bought for the express purpose of doing away with its licence, and by 1890 the number had

Ye Olde Horse Fair at Newbridge, which was transferred to a yard next to the New Inn in the 1930s

decreased to five, at least one of the others being turned into a Temperance hotel. The horse fairs continued until after the Second World War, while the livestock market moved in the late 1930s to a permanent yard next to the **New Inn**, before closing in 1959. The number of shops had increased to more than 20, but these too gradually closed leaving only one or two today.

However, two public houses remain open. One is the **New Inn**, an imposing building on the junction of the road from Llandrindod Wells and the A470. A 16th-century stone building and one of the oldest in Newbridge, the inn originally started life as two cottages within a row of cottages and farm

The New Inn in the 1950s

The cabin bar at the New Inn in the 1960s

326

The New Inn in the 1960s

A statue of a drover stands proudly in front of the New Inn

The New Inn in 2006

buildings. It is said that farmers travelling to Rhayader would entrust local children to drive their cattle about half-a-mile while they enjoyed a meal at the **New Inn**. Then, suitably refreshed, the farmer would 'catch up with the children and pay them one penny for their trouble'. Over the years the inn has been considerably extended with the building of a new lounge at the back which is now the dining room, the stables being converted into a pool room. A large functions room, with garages underneath, was also added together with new kitchens. The original bar is now the small Cabin Bar off the reception area which was the dining room. There is also a main bar and bars in both the dining and functions room. There were originally 10 bedrooms, now reduced to seven, but all with *en-suite* facilities. A car park now covers the old livestock market.

Licensees in the 1960s to the end of the 1980s were Nigel and Norma Parkinson, famed for their roast duck and fresh salmon specialities, with literally thousands of ducks ending up on the dining table. During their tenure several politicians, including Gordon Brown and Norman Tebbitt, and various show-biz stars, stayed at the hotel. It is presently run by Dave and Debbie Lang, who also own the Garth Mill in Garth, which is a pub, bed and breakfast establishment and a farmers' market shop.

The other pub still open is the **Golden Lion**, situated on the A470 in the Rhadader direction. Built in the 19th century, the inn was run in 1881 by Edward Dale, aged 26, also described as a carpenter, and his wife, Elizabeth. For many years it was a favourite eating place renowned for its 2s. 6d. meal known locally as the Goose Dinner. In 1946 the **Golden Lion** had Percy Lewis as tenant and was owned by brewers, David Williams of Builth. It possessed a stable, outbuildings and some land. The inn has been run for the last two years by Nigel and Norma Parkinson, who were in charge of the New

328

The Golden Lion in 2006

Inn for 25 years. They have changed it back into a traditional two-bar pub, popular with the local footbal team, but they no longer serve food.

Further along the road next to the carpet shop is an old, empty building which was formerly the **Red Lion**, mentioned in the minutes of the General Quarter Sessions for the period 1823-1829. It was also called the **Old Lion**, probably re-named after the Golden Lion was built. It has long been a private dwelling. There was also the Old Lion brewhouse, which has been knocked down.

About 60 yards further along the road, but on the opposite side, houses are being constructed on the site where once stood the **Sun Inn**, also known as **Brynhaul**. It was a beerhouse with Mr. C. James as the licensed retailer of beer, porter and cider. In the 19th century it was regarded as a safe house for

Once the Old Red Lion in 2006.

rioters, both during the Rebecca Riots of 1843-44 against unfair tolls on farm produce, and later against the Fishery Laws with salmon poachers adopting the same name and disguise. In the 1881 census Sarah Powell, aged 55, was the innkeeper, and lived there with her three daughters and two sons.

In 1913 the **Sun** came before the County Licensing Committee for renewal of its licence. Thomas Williams was the licensee, and the owner being Thomas Worthington of the Drovers' Arms, Builth. The stone-built premises, with a yearly rent of £16, consisted of 'a fairly wide entrance passage, dining room, tap room, small serving bar, also a small living room, with five bedrooms, very low'. There was also a cellar and a yard, but no stable. There were three other inns nearby. Thomas Worthington said he purchased the premises in May 1912 for £410; the tenant being under verbal agreement to obtain all draft beer and mineral waters from him. He had supplied in a year 54 barrels of beer and 106 dozen mineral waters. The licensee said trade was fair, with an average yet steady business. Renewal of the licence was refused, but £375 compensation was allowed including £30 for the tenant. After the inn ceased trading, it became a private house before being demolished in the 1970s for road improvements. A petrol filling station was then erected, but this has in turn been demolished to make way for new housing.

One of the inns popular with drovers was the **Mid Wales**, now a private house, at the start of the B4358 road to Beulah. A substantial building, it provided overnight accommation as well as beer and food for the drovers, while their animals grazed on land between the inn and the River Wye.

The Mid Wales Inn in the 1930s with Ros Thomas, wife of the landlord, Alfred

The Mid Wales Inn is now a private house

With the advent of the railway and the building of the station at the back, it was referred to as the **Railway Inn** and catered for rail workers and passengers.

Apparently the last landlady used to insist on taking the workers' pay packets and taking money for the evening's drinks before handing the pay packets back just before they went home. The inn was inherited by two sisters who disapproved of drinking and let the licence lapse with the inn ceasing to trade at the end of the 1940s. It became a private residence, then a private art gallery, and today has reverted to being a residence.

The Bridgend, a former pub now a cottage, taken in the 1970s before the old bridge was taken down and rebuilt

Another old pub was the **Bridgend**, now a private house, on a lane leading back into town just before the bridge over the Wye, while the **Saddlers Arms**, on another back lane, was demolished when the railway passed through in 1863. It was unoccupied in 1851.

Just outside the village on the A470 road to Rhayader is a house called Merry Hall set back off the road on the left. Apparently in the early 19th century it was a drinking den, known locally as **Merry Hell**, but closed in the 1850s.

Opposite the New Inn is Arosfa House, which used to be the **Bell Inn**, while further along the road towards Builth Wells on the left-hand side is

a private house still bearing the name Crown Temperance and Commercial Hotel, which was once the **Crown Inn**. Built in about 1870, the inn consisted of a lounge and public bar, parlour, kitchen and five bedrooms which were let out. Probably the first innkeeper was Evan Meredith, who is mentioned in 1877, followed by David Meredith, who sold the property to brewer, David Williams.

Now divided into two houses, the former Bell Inn

In 1911 it was sold on to George Jones, who turned it into a Temperance Hotel. Then in 1920 he sold it for £350 to two spinsters, Anne and Jessie Powell, who continued to run it until the 1960s. The hotel was bought for £1,450 in 1970 by Reginald Tyler, farmer, who modernised the building, which 10 years later regained its licence and traded as a restaurant. However, the new venture did not prove to be a success and the owners eventually went bankrupt.

The Crown Inn is in the row on the left in this 1890s photograph

Now a private house, the former Crown Inn, Newbridge

The hotel eventually became derelict and was bought in 1998 by Paul Allam, of Allam Antiques, who has refurbished the building. His antiques business is not far away, set back off the road, near which used to be the **Wyvern Inn**, which closed at the end of the 19th century. Used as a joinery for some years, the building was demolished in 1974.

Further along the road is Oak cottage which was formerly the **Royal Oak**, mentioned as an inn in 1905. It is said that the inn was bought by Cara Venables, sister of Lady Katherine Minna Venables of Llysdinam Hall, just to do away with its licence. Apparently she found that beer was being taken into a shed at the back where customers were playing cards. Still owned by the Venables family, it is now a private dwelling.

A marriage arch for Mr. and Mrs. Llewellyn in 1893 outside the Royal Oak

The one-time Royal Oak Inn

At one time the Pontarithon Inn

Just over the bridge, on the road leading towards Builth, is a private house which used to be an old coaching inn called the **Pontarithon**, It closed in 1855, with the last landlord being Evan Meredith.

Another two pubs were the **Wheelwrights** and the **Lamb**. The latter is mentioned in the 1851 census, but both have since been demolished.

Travelling towards Builth Wells along the A470 there is a turning on the right to Builth Road, just off the main road, where lies the **Cambrian Arms**, which started life as a railway refreshment room known as the **Refresher**. Part of a long building, also including waiting rooms

The Cambrian Arms when it was a refreshment room on the station platform

and ticket office, it was originally built in about the 1870s soon after the construction of a small gauge line from Brecon to Newbridge and on to Aberystwyth. A water lift, one of only three in the country, connected it to the top line from Shrewsbury to Swansea, which is still operating. Rows of terraced houses were specially built to accommodate some 150 railway staff based in the village. In the early days the **Refresher** was well known for its picnic meals packed for passengers on the top line. After the line fell to Dr. Beeching's axe in 1964, the **Refresher** remained empty for several years before it was bought by Arthur Miles in the 1970s and transformed into the **Cambrian Arms**. According to the present tenant, Angela Mason, who has run it for the last 10 years with her husband, Michael, who is also a quarry-worker, 'Mr. Miles wanted the pub for the village and both the rent and beer had to be reasonable'. The main bar and counter is still very much as it used to be, but an interior wall has been knocked down and what used to be a waiting room is now part of the bar. Up until his death, Mr. Miles and his wife used to live in the converted ticket office. The pub was passed on to his son, Leigh, who is still the owner. At the road end of the inn is a

The Cambrian Arms in 2006

defunct post office and shop that is now used as a store room. The post office closed five years ago and the shop two years later.

Returning to Newbridge and taking the B4358 road towards Llandrindod Wells, there is a minor road that leads to the hamlet of Disserth. Here, opposite the church, is a private house, whose owners now run the Disserth Place caravan and camping park. The house was originally an inn, known simply as the **Disserth**, which was frequented by drovers on their journey to England. The date 1786 has been carved on a timber at the back of the house, but the front may be even older. In the middle of the house are two 2 ft. thick walls. The parlour-type bar with a slate-topped serving counter is now the kitchen.

It was still called the **Disserth** public house in 1823, but in later years was referred to as the **New Inn** before closing in 1897. It then became a farmhouse, with some 50 acres of land. However it retained a memory of its earlier life, having a cider press until the late 1940s. In 1955 it was bought by Dennis Jones, who

This was the New Inn at Disserth in the 19th century

turned it into a caravan park. In 1985 the property was re-licensed with the barn containing small bars on two floors, usually open on Friday and Saturday although there is a seven-day licence. The park now has 23 holiday homes and 25 touring pitches.

According to W.H. Howse, there was also the **Fox** public house near Trewern Farm on the Builth road, mentioned in the Minute Book of Justices of Turnpike Roads in 1796. The mention in the Disserth vestry book – 'John Jones, late of the **Fox**, deceased, Oct. 1797' – may indicate an end to this pub. Two other inns also mentioned were the **Royal Oak** and the **Woolpack,** the latter in 1838.

Once the Crossways Inn

From Disserth the road reaches a T-junction joining the A483 Builth Wells to Llandrindod Wells road where, right opposite, is a private dwelling called **Crossways**, which used to be an inn of the same name. The inn was run by James Meredith in the 1850s and '60s and probably closed in the 1920s.

Heading towards Llandrindod Wells, the A483 by-passes the village of Howey which, two hundred years ago, was a thriving community at a time when Llandrindod was its undistinguished neighbour. It had two inns, one on each side of what used to be the main road. These old pubs catered for the needs of drovers, other travellers and the local community – one being the **Drovers Arms** and the other the **Bridge End**. Both still operate today; the former in the guise of a Thai restaurant, and the latter now known as the **Laughing Dog**.

An old photograph of Howey showing the former Bridge End Inn and the Drovers Arms

The **Bridge End** has been licensed since 1872, but the building dates back to about 1750 when it was originally a private dwelling. It consisted of a parlour, tap room, back kitchen, beer cellar, lumber room and bar cellar together with three bedrooms and a clubroom. There was a stable with four stalls, and a blacksmith's shop. In 1920 its licence came up for renewal before the County Licensing Committee, where the police sought to prove that the village did not need two public houses. However, after a petition

*An early 20th-century photograph of the Bridge End Inn
showing the old blacksmith's shop*

*Tanner Jones (centre) being installed as Howey dock-master
at the Bridge End Inn*

was presented by local farmers, ex-servicemen and residents, the licence was renewed. In 1946 the **Bridge End** was owned by David Williams of Builth with Penry Stanley Jones as tenant and landlord for many years. On his death it was run by his daughter, Dorothy, for a while until, in 1977, it was bought by Dereck and Joyce Holder. During their tenure until 1988 they converted the old smithy and stables into a dining room/lounge and pool room. They also turned the original cellar into a small lounge and built a new one.

Stan Jones, Landlord of the Bridge End in 1946

A regular customer was Stan Jones, Jnr., who was probably born in the pub and known by his nickname Tanner, said to have derived from the sixpence, or tanner, he earned acting as a golf caddy. Although only a small brook flows through the village, the **Bridge End** was sometimes referred to jokingly as **Howey Dock** and Tanner was installed as its dock-master. An old photo-graph shows him in cermonial garb with staff (a pitch fork wrapped in tin foil) and a bowl of water on which float paper boats. Until his death in the 1990s, Tanner was the only person allowed to wind the pub's wall-clock, which was originally installed by his father, and has only been moved once since.

Opening of the new lounge at the Bridge End in about 1979 with member of staff, Joan, presenting a bouquet of flowers to landlady Joyce Holden (right) flanked by Tanner Jones and landlord Derek Holden

The **Bridge End** was run for a time by a consortium, but in 2001 it was bought by Paula Shepherd and Sean King who closed it for several months while refurbishment work took place. In an effort to change the inn's whole image, they decided to change its name as well, to the **Laughing Dog**. This

Once the Bridge End – now the Laughing Dog

came about because they had owned a pub in Cambridge called Walk the Dog and owned a German Shepherd named Lysander.

Ghost stories associated with the pub include a Victorian lady, dressed in black and white, who appears from the old blacksmith's shop area; an old gent in the toilet area; creaking chairs as if someone had sat in them, and a bradawl behind the bar which suddenly flew across the counter swerving to land near the lounge. A large stone is still outside at the front, where customers dismounted from their horses.

Opposite was the **Drovers Arms**, built later than the **Bridge End** but possessing a 13th-century cellar. It was badly damaged during a fire in the 1890s and re-built with a stylish red-brick Victorian façade. The adjoining cottages have disappeared, but the old stables have been converted into other cottages. The inn originally owned land at the rear which included a car park. This has been sold off and developed for housing.

There used to be two bars with a raised platform in one for dining, and a serving hatch for off-sales. Apparently a haunt for local poachers at one time, the inn displayed a poem in one of the bars commemorating their activities. Two years ago, the present owners refurbished the building and transformed it into the elegant **Drovers Thai Restaurant** with oriental decor and furnishings, including a parrot, and live background piano music. The bar counter is still centralised to serve both rooms.

The friendly rivalry between the two pubs in the past usually took the form of competitions with teams from both taking part. These included an

The Drovers Arms is now a Thai Restaurant

annual tug-of-war over the brook with the losing team ending up in the water, pancake tossing, and egg-and-spoon races.

Just before arriving at Builth Wells along the A483 is Llanelwedd, just on the Radnorshire side of the River Wye. It is home to the Royal Welsh Showground and, in 1993, was host to the National Eisteddfod. The village also used to be a busy light industrial area, with a goods and coal yard, waggon repair shop, bus depot, creamery, saw mill and quarry until the railway closed in the 1960s.

Up until the mid-19th century, however, it had more a reputation for cock-fighting. Where the vicarage stands by the church was once the **Carpenters Arms**, described as a commodious inn, which for one week each year was packed with sportsmen who came to witness the cockfighting championship of the three counties, Herefordshire, Breconshire and Radnorshire. The cockpit, measuring 33 ft. in diameter, was situated about 200 yards north-east of the church just above the old turnpike gate. Roger Williams, in 1937, described similar proceedings elsewhere:

For the combat the natural spurs of the birds were removed and replaced with silver or steel spurs called gaffles. By the Welsh rules, 32 birds were cast into the pit and sixteen pairs began to fight. The defeated birds were successively removed until the two triumphant cocks remained. From tiers of seats around this spot people watched the final pair in deadly combat. In those days Welsh people were very superstitious, and many of them would not allow the birds to enter the ring until the pit had been sprinkled with salt, which they believed would break the spell of any exercise of witch-craft and make the fight a fair one.

The old vicarage was formerly the Carpenters Arms, Llanelwedd

Some of the leading farmers in the Llanelwedd neighbourhood were breeders of a noted strain of game birds and devotees of this pastime. Cock-fighting was outlawed following Parliamentary Acts of 1835 and 1849, but continued clandestinely until the 20th century. The Llanelwedd pit was still in a good state of preservation up to the 1950s, when it was filled in and is now waste land. After the fighting ended each day, there was invariably a dinner at the **Carpenters Arms**, with many toasts and songs the order of the evening. With the banning of the sport, the inn's popularity declined and it ceased trading in the 1860s to become converted into the vicarage. It is now empty but has been sold.

Another early house was the **Groe House Inn**, opposite the Llanelwedd Arms Hotel, named in the *Hereford Journal* from 1770 to about 1860. For many years it was kept by a member of the Rushbach family. But both the 'old public' and family have long since disappeared.

The sole surviving licensed premises today is the **Llanelwedd Arms Hotel**, near the bridge over the Wye and at the junction of the Llandrindod and Rhayader roads. It was built in the 17th century, but only licensed in 1860. In 1873 there was a dispute between its landlady, Mrs. Price, and the local vicar, the Revd. G. Sharpe. This was not over any unruliness or rowdiness on the part of the inn; Revd. Sharpe brought an action against Mrs. Price for damage done to a fence alleged to have been in his occupation.

The turkey fair outside the Llanelwedd Arms Hotel in 1905

Apparently the Revd. Sharpe rented land adjoining the Prices, and he had pulled down an old fence and replaced it with wire. Benjamin Price, son of the defendant, saw that the new fence had been put up 'a foot or two' on his land, and he pulled it down. It was decided to let the respective counsels arbitrate the matter.

The hotel, owned by the Llanelwedd Hall Estate, consisted of entrance hall, a smoke room with folding doors leading into the commercial room, a large dining room, front bar, second bar (with separate entrance), private room, large kitchen and back kitchen. There were also eight bedrooms on the first floor, a sitting room, a bathroom with W.C. and a lavatory basin, and servants' W.C., with another two bedrooms and three attic rooms on the second floor. In the basement were two cellars. Outbuildings included two stables with 20 stalls and two loose boxes, two coach-houses, pig-cots and sheep pens. In 1922 the Estate was put up for auction including the

The Llanelwedd Arms Hotel in the 1920 sale details

343

Llanelwedd Arms, several other properties and 412 acres. The hotel had been let to David Williams, the Builth brewer, for 21 years at an annual rent of £76. During the term of the lease, Williams, his friends and visitors had the right to fish for trout in the River Wye adjoining Groe Field. However, it was not until 1924 that Lieutenant Colonel Herbert Howell of Llanelwedd Hall, and other members of the Howell family, finally sold the hotel to David Williams together with Groe Farm, for £2, 916 13s. 4d.

On one side of the hotel used to be two wrought iron gates opening onto a coach house and stables with a field beyond where the horses were kept. When the 'age of the railway' was at its height, the hotel was very much a watering hole for rail workers, coming from the station yards and the waggon yard at the rear. Until the formation of Powys, the pubs in Builth Wells, being in Breconshire, closed half-an-hour earlier than the Llanelwedd Arms and customers used to 'gallop' across the bridge to reach the inn before closing time. Apparently, sometimes they were even met on the bridge by the landlord with a tray of pints! Flooding occurred regularly, especially in 1947 when flood water went over the hotel's window-sills and there was three to four feet of water inside.

Many structural alterations were carried out in the post-war years by Keith and Christine Price, who stayed there until the early 1970s. Then in 1974 the hotel was bought for £41,000 by Ferdinand and Gloria Miele, who had a large picture of themselves, dressed like Fred Astaire and Ginger Rogers, to welcome customers. After other owners, the hotel went into receivership in 1987 and lay empty for a while until it was bought for

The Llanelwedd Arms Hotel in 2006

£85,000 by Robert and Christine Southcott. During their time, they altered the bar, changed the layout of the dining room and closed the back entrance. They had the cellars, which used to flood, concreted over, and made the bedrooms *en-suite*. The Southcotts stayed until 1993 and leased it out for a further four years before selling; they now live in a house they built on hotel land at the rear. For the last three years, the hotel has been run by two sisters, Kathleen Williams and Eileen Hackett.

From Llanelwedd the A481 cuts across to New Radnor and on Beili Bychan Common, about two miles before reaching Hundred House, there used to be the **Tynrheol Inn**, also known as the **Drovers Arms**, which although described on its sign as a Cider House, sold mainly beer. In the *Radnorshire Transactions* there is an account of the **Tynrheol** by Capt. E. Aubrey Thomas, of Cefndyrys, based on information given to him by his farm bailiff, who had been brought up at the inn from boyhood and lived there until his marriage in 1901.

> It was a small thatched house with only one door, a kitchen, a small store room for beer and two bedrooms. ... The windows could only be opened with difficulty, if at all. There was no bar. ... The last licensee was William Price, a roadman, who kept the house for some 40 years till his death about 1905, though he had given up the licence in 1902, and it was not renewed after that date. A considerable business was done with farmers and labourers from the Hundred House district going to and returning from Builth on foot or with carts. It was a popular place of call for travelling gipsy vans, those selling nails, chains and farm tools, etc, called Nailers, also sportsmen shooting in the district made it their customary headquarters for lunch. The beer was bought from Williams (Celsau's) brewery in Builth and their regular supply of beer was two 36 gallon barrels per month. Mrs. Price took particular care that the barrels should be well settled before they were tapped. So Tynreheol beer had a very good local reputation. She used to keep her clock ten minutes fast to ensure that all customers turned out before closing time at 10, and never allowed any drunkenness on the premises. Beer in those days was 6d. per quart and a very favourite winter drink was Hot Beer, warmed up in a special vessel over the fire and flavoured with ginger and sugar.

In the parish of Llansantffraed-in-Elfael – the village being just off the A481 – there used to be two other ancient inns, the **Cock** and the **Star**, both of which appeared in the Minutes of the General Quarter Sessions for the period 1823-29.

The next village is Hundred House where the **Hundred House Inn** still thrives. Both are named after the Hundred Court, or Moot, which tried trespassers, small debtors and other minor offenders, and was held at a building which is now the vicarage, a few yards back on the road to Builth

The Hundred House Inn in 2006

Wells. It was originally a Calvinistic Chapel built in the late 1770s, but was used by the justices before they were transferred to Builth Wells in 1884. The congregation moved to Hope Chapel in about 1861 and there may have been an in-between period when the Court was held at the inn. At any rate, the justices no doubt adjourned to the inn after their deliberations. The inn was included in the 1823 list of licensed houses and has remained open ever since. It was used by drovers until the development of the railways made cattle droving obsolete.

In 1946 the **Hundred House**, with stables, other outbuildings and one acre of land, was owned by David Williams of Builth, and was in the occupation of Herbert Price as tenant. Since then the stables have been converted into a pool room, suitably adorned with rosettes and trophies won by the present landlord, Roger Philip, for breeding and showing Welsh cobs not only in this country but on the Continent. The lounge and restaurant on the other side were added later.

The following anonymous poem hangs in the main bar:

> A Hundred House sheep dog named Sally
> Has an owner who's inclined to dally
> In the Inn at the bar;
> It's as well it's not far
> To go home to the farm in the valley.

Bibliography

GENERAL WORKS
The Drovers' Roads of Wales, Shirley Toulson, 1977
Roads & Trackways of Wales, Richard Moore-Colyer, 2001
Welsh Cattle Drovers, Richard Moore-Colyer, 2002
Powys in Buildings of Wales Series, Richard Haslam, 1992
An Artist Rediscovered (Thomas Jones) edited by Ann Sumner & Greg Smith, 2003

THE COUNTY
Radnorshire, A Historical Guide, Donald Gregory, 1994
History of Radnorshire, Revd. Jonathan Williams 1859
Radnorshire from Civil War to Restoration, Keith Parker, 2000
History of Radnorshire, W.H Howse, 1949
Pictorial Radnorshire of Bygone Days, Cherry Leversedge, 1989
Folklore of Radnorshire, Roy Palmer, 2001
The Archive Photographs Series – Radnorshire, compiled by Powys County
      Record Office, 1997

TOWNS AND VILLAGES
Aspects of Aberedw, Alan Charters
A Pictorial History of Builth Wells, Malcolm Morrison, 1989
Disserth, W.H. Howse, 1952
Hills & Sunny Pastures – Life in Erwood, Erwood Women's Institute
Notes on Glascwm, W.H. Howse
Knighton, Mary Cadwallader, 1996
Knighton & District, W.M. Hatfield, 1947
Alice's Knighton, 1916–1925
Voices of Llandrindod Wells, compiled by Joel Williams, 2000
Llandrindod Wells in Old Postcards, Olivia Harris, 1985
Llanfair Waterdine – A Parish Remembered, Brenda Davies & Jocelyn Williams, 1988
Twentieth Century Llanyre, June Mackintosh
Newbridge-on-Wye, F.M. Slater
Pennybont – A Village History, Geraint Hughes, 2004
A History of Presteigne, Keith Parker
Impressions of Presteigne, Sarah Laws & Clare Purcell, 1997
Pictorial Presteigne of Bygone Days, Cherry Leversedge, 1988
Presteigne Past & Present, W.H. Howse, 1945

Church & Parish of Old Radnor, W.H. Howse
Early Photographs of Radnor, W.H. McKaig
Radnor Old & New, W.H. Howse

INNS AND TAVERNS
Radnorshire Inns, W.H. Howse, 1950
Radnorshire Inns, Revd. D. Stedman Davies, *c.*1941
Hidden Inns of Wales, edited by Barbara Vesey, 2000
Beer and Britannia, Peter Haydon, 2001
Welsh Pub Names, Myrddin ap Dafydd, 1991
A Dictonary of Pub Names, Leslie Dunkling & Gordon Wright, 1987
Pubs in Powys, R.J. Gibbs, 1980
Pub Walks in Powys, Les Lumsden & Chris Rushton
The Pubs of Leominster, Kington & north-west Herefordhire, R. Shoesmith & R. Barrett, 2000
Bridging A Century, 1872-1972 – The Story of the Metropole Hotel, Llandrindod Wells, R.C.B. Oliver
The Old-Fashioned Inn, G.E. Body, 1930s.
Seven Arms Hotel, Penybont, Geraint Hughes, 2005
Here Lies My Story, C.N. de Courcy-Parry, 1964
Landscape With Figures, L.T.C. Rolt, 1992
The Forest Inn, H.L.V. Fletcher
Seven for a Secret, Mary Webb, 1922
Reminisences of the Gwystre, Glyn & Daphne Evans
Ty Mair (The Hundred House, Bleddfa), Mary Busek, 1989

JOURNALS AND NEWSPAPERS ETC.
Brecon & Radnor Express
Hereford Journal
Hereford Times
Radnorshire Standard
Wellington Journal
Pigot's Commercial Directory
Kelly's Directory
Universal British Directory
Radnorshire Society Transactions
Knighton Town Forum Newsletter
Knighton Offical Guide
Knighton 1965, W.I. Jubilee Scrapbook
Knighton 1800-1950, Rotary Club of Knighton & District
Llandrindod Wells Official Guides
Making the Most of Rhayader, Charles Kightley, 1997

Index

In the following index all pub names, old and new, are indexed – where there have been name changes they are cross-referenced and shown in brackets. 'Inn' is not normally used in the title (apart from where an ommission would sound wrong). To avoid confusion the parish or village is shown for country inns; in Presteigne, Knighton, Llandrindod Wells and Rhayader the street name is included. Page numbers in bold type indicate the main and informative entries for that inn; italics refer to illustrations.

Also from Logaston Press

The Celtic Christian Sites of the central and southern Marches
by Sarah & John Zaluckyj

This book is the result of many hours poring over maps in the hunt for indications of early Christian sites along the central and southern Welsh border and delving into various tomes, including pre-Norman charters and various Lives of the saints. Then, armed with a gospel of information, the authors set off with missionary zeal to hunt out, visit, crawl over, observe, and note down aspects of all the sites and then collate the host of information that is presented here.

Introductory chapters detail the arrival of Christianity in Britain and give some background to its early nature and style. The pervading philosophy behind what became the Celtic brand of Christianity is discussed: the early house monasteries of wealthy sons, the development of isolated monastic communities, the role of bishops and abbots, the nature of Christian teaching, ending with biographical details of the most important saints who had contact with the area covered. In amongst this, the nature of a 'llan' is described, as are the features often considered to indicate early Christian sites – holy wells, yew trees, circular and/or raised churchyard enclosures, and the Christianisation of pagan sites, often denoted by barrows or again marked by yews.

This sets the scene for looking at the 168 sites covered in the gazetteer, 21 in Montgomeryshire, 28 in Radnorshire, 42 in Breconshire, 30 in Herefordshire (that part which was the kingdom of Erging) and 47 in Gwent. Each site is described along with the early features that can still be discerned. The site's early history, where known, is given, along with details of the early saint to whom the church still is, or once was, dedicated.

Sarah & John Zaluckyj are bookdealers living near the Welsh border who have also written: *Mercia – the Anglo-Saxon kingdom of central England*, also published by Logaston Press.

Paperback, 448 pages with some 250 photographs. Price £12.95
ISBN 1 904396 57 7 (978 1 904396 57 4)

Henfryn
by George F. Lewis

In the late 1930s George's family moved to Henfryn, a farm near Abbey-cwm-hir in Radnorshire. This book tells of life in the late 1930s and during the 1940s on a hill farm—the war years, with farmers being in reserved occupations; the local home guard; of quotas and all the usual characters that fill the countryside.

George F. Lewis is the author of *Haber Nant Llan Nerch Freit*. He farmed for many years around Abbey-cwm-hir, Llanbister and Llandewi in Radnorshire, and now lives near Hereford.

Paperback, 144 pages with 40 black and white photographs and plans. Price £7.95
ISBN: 1 873827 08 3 (978 1 873827 08 6)

Early Photographs of Radnor
photographs by W.H. McKaig, text by Laurence Smith

The essence of this book is a collection of McKaig's photographs along the English/Welsh border in Radnorshire, along with a brief introduction to McKaig and the making of photographic postcards in the early 1900s.

William McKaig probably picked up his interest in photography from his father, Leonard, New Radnor's schoolmaster, who used his camera, at least in part, to produce postcards for local sale. William was born in 1885. He left New Radnor's school in about 1900 and set up a cycle repair workshop to cater for the fast growing numbers of tourists who liked to cycle out to the country from places like Birmingham. A close friend of Alfred Watkins, inventor of the first exposure meter, he died only a few weeks after Watkins in 1935.

Paperback, 96 pages with 80 black and white photographs, Price £9.95
ISBN: 1 904396 18 6 (978 1 904396 18 5)

358